The Folies Bergère

By the same author

The
Folies Bergère

Charles Castle

Methuen . London

First published 1982
© 1982 Charles Castle
Printed in Great Britain for
Methuen London Ltd
11 New Fetter Lane, London EC4P 4EE
Filmset in Monophoto Bembo by
Northumberland Press Ltd, Gateshead
Printed in Great Britain by
William Clowes (Beccles) Ltd,
Beccles and London

British Library Cataloguing in Publication Data

Castle, Charles
   The Folies Bergère.
   1. Folies Bergère—History   2. Music-halls
   (Variety-theaters, cabarets, etc.)—France—
   Paris—History
   I. Title
   792.7'0944'36   PN1968.F/

   ISBN 0–413–49470–5

710 019329 -9

Contents

Illustrations

To
Stanley Hall

Acknowledgements

This book could not have been written without the constructive advice of some of my close friends. First, I extend my gratitude to Stanley Hall, who visited Paris with me regularly and helped in the research and final selection of material. Alec Shanks, the brilliant designer, was instrumental not only in providing some of the exquisite original designs that appear here, but also, as he was one of the top designers at the Folies Bergère during the early thirties, his invaluable recollections. Those, too, of Erté, who contributed to the success of the Folies Bergère between 1917 and 1932, are more than appreciated, together with his affectionate memoirs of the present owner, Madame Hélène Martini. His sixty-five-year affiliation to the Folies Bergère has been of incalculable value. For the reproductions of Erté's sketches and designs I am indebted to Sevenarts Ltd, London. The reminiscences, too, of Sir Anton Dolin about the many great artists of the period have made my plight so much more absorbing, and the invaluable help of Miss Bluebell has made it complete.

Others who have lent their recollections include Lord Delfont, Robert Nesbitt, Billy Milton, Arthur Rowe, Bernard Hall, Donn Arden – and Michel Gyarmathy, whose close artistic association with the Folies Bergère over the past fifty years has added to the book's authentication. Aside from the acknowledgements in the bibliography at the back of the book and the list of illustrations, I am indebted to the many English and French newspapers and magazines for quotes or references to their articles, notably to Eric Shorter and the *Daily Telegraph* for the piece on chorus-girls. Anthony Farmer, the designer and producer of some of the most lavish productions, was kind enough to allow me to use two of his Gyarmathy sketches, and other special mentions are reserved for the Lasson Gallery, London, who kindly allowed me to reproduce the painting of La Belle Otero, and the Courtauld Institute for the use of the classic Manet painting, 'Bar at the Folies Bergère'.

I owe an enormous debt of gratitude to Secker & Warburg, the publishers of Colette's *My Apprenticeships* (translated by Helen Beauclerk) and *Music-Hall Sidelights* (translated by Anne-Marie Callimachi), as well as to Farrar, Straus & Giroux, New York, for their own interests in those works together with their permission to reproduce an extract from Colette's *Les Vrilles de la Vigne*, first published by *La Vie Parisienne* in 1908. The extract from Charles Chaplin's *My Autobiography* is reprinted with permission of The Bodley Head.

Methuen's senior editor Ann Mansbridge has been particularly constructive and patient, and without her most able assistant Liz Hornby, the lay-out designer Geoff Chatterton and the art department (for the design of the cover), the book would not have emerged as splendidly as it has.

To them I give special thanks.

Foreword

The Folies Bergère in Paris was sixty-three years old when I first crossed the threshold of its stage entrance. I am therefore very pleased to be writing this introduction, although many others have known this fabulous theatre longer than I.

When I was just beginning my career in the dance world, the Folies Bergère was known all over the world, and to perform there was considered by all artists a sacrosanct goal to achieve. As American artists at that time strove to appear at the Palace in New York City, so most European artists deemed the Folies Bergère the zenith of entertainment establishments.

It is thus understandable that although my career has taken Bluebell Girls to the greatest entertainment rooms in the world, I have always guarded a special soft spot in my heart for the Folies. It was there that the first Bluebell group was born, and there also that I first saw my name in lights on the marquee.

How difficult it is to explain the feeling of pride one has upon achieving what one has for such a long time longed for. Having come from a very poor family, I never imagined that my destiny would carry me so far. My first professional engagement paid me the most exciting sum of two pounds weekly. Out of this, I was able to send thirty shillings to Mary Murphy, who was responsible at that time for my upbringing. My room and board being furnished, I found the other ten shillings completely adequate for my needs.

There is one other special reason why the Folies Bergère will always have a special place in my memories. It was there that I met the orchestra leader, Marcel Leibovici, whom I eventually married, and with whom I raised three fine boys and a delightful daughter.

Time has passed rapidly, but with very little effort I can close my eyes and remember the members of that orchestra giving Marcel a ribbing about his romance with me and calling me *'Bluebell, jolies cuisses'*, which, roughly translated, means 'Nice legs, Bluebell'.

Writing this here in Paris, I feel fortunate to have been part of two internationally known associations, the Cabaret Lido, where the Bluebell Girls have been starring for the past thirty-five years, and the renowned landmark of this book – The Folies Bergère.

Miss Bluebell
Paris, July 1982

1
The Palace of Pleasure

The Folies Bergère was the first music-hall to be
opened in Paris. Destined to become one of the major
tourist attractions of France, it is now second only
to the Eiffel Tower as an essential sight for visitors
who travel to the capital from the four corners of
the world.

It was built on the lines of London's Alhambra
theatre and comprised a sumptuous foyer with stair-
cases that swept up to the dress circle and swinging
doors in the foyer that led to the stalls which were
reached by passing through the 'promenade' where
the notorious Parisian 'ladies of the town' plied their
trade at the turn of the century.

But to trace the theatre's early beginnings we go
back to the thirteenth century. The site of the famous
music-hall began its life as a monastery which was
situated in a field beside a stream called la Grange-
Batelière. Digging among the foundations of the
theatre one day, Paul Derval, the Folies Bergère's
proprietor and director during the first half of the
present century, came upon the remains of a flight of
steps that led down to a little ruined fountain with
a bench beside it where the monks sat on mild days,
meditating – no doubt comforted by bottles of wine.
Later the monastery disappeared, having bequeathed
its land to the kindly Hospice des Quinze-Vingts, the
famous hospital for the blind founded by St Louis
in 1260. The property was used as a sanctuary. Its
grounds became a garden where under the shade of
the trees Parisians drank and sang and joined in local

entertainments. In later years the garden made way for the site of a mattress shop called Les Colonnes d'Hercule, and in 1867 the 'album of the theatres' announced that the new building next door to the Colonnes d'Hercule was to be an establishment for 'spectaculars' which was to be called The Folies Trévise.

'The term *folies* does not come, as one would imagine, from the ambiance created by the locals who used the gardens as a cover-up for their nocturnal assignations,' as a journal of the day explained, 'but from the Latin, *foliae*. The French translation *feuilles* (leaves) is interpreted as the house that stands hidden beneath the leaves.' The term *folies* had developed into an expression used for many years to describe a 'field' where clandestine lovers spent their romantic evenings. Later, the word came to

denote the public place where eighteenth-century Parisians danced, drank and watched small-scale entertainments in the open air. But the Folies Trévise almost did not open at all because of litigation brought by the Duc de Trévise.

The name Folies Trévise had originally been decided upon for the new music-hall as it was situated on the corners of the rues Richer and Trévise. But the Duke felt that this sort of establishment was bound to bring his honourable name into disrepute and brought out an injunction restraining the owners from using the name Trévise. He succeeded.

The opening being imminent, Monsieur Boislève, the director, had already started to contract artists; a new name was to be found immediately and Bergère was chosen – the name of the rue Bergère situated a few streets away which in turn owed its appellation to the master dyer, Jacques Bergier, who had worked for years on the site. 'It is true that one goes to the rue Richer to find next door to the mattress shop Les Colonnes d'Hercule a new *salle de spectacle*,' the 'album of the theatres' announced. 'The entrepreneurs are already at work. This new establishment, which will open its doors at the end of January, is going to inaugurate a new kind of spectacle composed of different elements; lyrical *opérettes-fantaisies*, pantomimes, music entertainments, acrobatic acts, etc. The inauguration of this theatre ought not to be *éloignée* because the director, M. Boislève, has already signed up several acts who will first appear from the beginning of March.'

From the Madeleine to the Bastille, traversed by the celebrated autobus of the same name, the great boulevards were the true 'centres' of Paris. The literary cafés, the newspapers, the Opéra, the *opéra-comique*, the theatres, the *cafés-concerts* were concentrated in this very small area. And so it was here on the unfashionable rue Richer next door to a bedding store that the Folies Bergère opened its doors on 2

May 1869. It seemed a propitious time to open a
theatre: Louis-Napoleon's Second Empire was at its
brilliant apogee, and the founders of the theatre fore-
saw a great financial success. But the 'album of
the theatres' was circumspect:

> The opening is to take place on 2 May 1869. As
> the Colonnes d'Hercule had the speciality of the
> *literie* one will call the new establishment *le Café
> du Sommier élastique*. The run of the show will not
> be very popular with the audience because it will
> be closed during the month of August, re-open
> during September and close again 1 March 1870,
> then passing into the hands of M. Durecu who
> will re-open it on 21 December with vaudeville
> and close 31 March 1871.

Performances were to be given seven times a week
at 7.30 p.m. The price of a seat, three francs, included
refreshments.

Its success, as prophesied, was far from immediate,
but for other reasons. Although the acts consisted of
operettas, ballets, songs and one-act sketches, the time
was not ripe for entertainments of this sort as the
patrons were accustomed to the established *cafés-
chantants*. There were more than 200 *cafés-chantants* in
Paris during this period and more than 10,000 songs
were sung there a year. These small theatres played
a social role; here the petty bourgeoisie and pro-
letariat could go to forget their misery and relieve
their emotions. The public shouted, whistled, wept
and laughed and joined in the choruses of the songs.
When a dancer appeared on stage it would be to the
shouts of: 'Knickers off! Higher! Let's have a look!'
Some artists, unnerved by the racket, would run
back into the wings, tears in their eyes.

Pleasing the customers in the cheapest seats was the
most difficult thing to do, and this applied to Britain
as well, where music-hall first began. But it was
particularly true of the 'neighbourhood' *cafés-concerts*
and halls strung out along the northern section of

Paris from Montmartre to the Place de la Bastille. Plusher theatres such as the Folies Bergère, the Moulin Rouge, the Olympia and the Casino de Paris, which opened later, catered (like the Champs Elysées *caf' conc's*) for an audience that was cosmopolitan or international. But the artists at these local houses were playing to a crowd drawn essentially from the poorer citizens in their own district. And, money being scarce, they wanted good value when they spent it.

The jokes therefore had to be at the right level. Allusions must be topical, preferably local, and not too highbrow or literary. Songs and sketches must be geared to tastes and the morals of the audience. Above all, the performers had to make themselves heard, and heard clearly in the *poulailler*, the upper gallery at the back of the house.

When an act displeased the *poulailler* (that was the one time that French music-hall and American bur-lesque found themselves on common ground), the field of raucous laughter, ironic applause, the catcall and jeering whistle, scabrous repartee between actor and audience, and empty bottles rolling down the aisles, took possession of the house.

French morals, especially locally, were not always as free as the 'Naughty Nineties' image of 'Gay Paree' would suggest. Colette was later unwise enough to play a sketch at the Moulin Rouge with her lesbian lover, the Marquise, the latter dressed as a man, play-ing the role of a painter infatuated with his model. The intrusion of life into art scandalized the audience, who witnessed the passionate kiss between the two women on stage. Whistling, booing and shouting broke out; the curtain had to be rung down as coins, cushions and even opera glasses were hurled at the stage. A similar scandal raged around the dancer Cléo de Mérode when the sculptor Falguière exhibited a statue of her completely nude. Public outrage sub-sided only when Falguière explained that Mlle de Mérode had posed just for the head, the rest being that of a studio model. Needless to say, Mlle de

Mérode's career hardly suffered from the resultant publicity.

The Paris music-hall derives from the *cafés-concert*, just as the English music-hall evolved from pub entertainments. French music-hall owes its origins to the great British tradition and as time went on, some of the top British music-hall stars influenced the shape of things to come on the French music-hall stage.

Short plays were put on in *cafés-concerts*, conjurors and acrobats would show their paces and a small orchestra accompany singers and dancers. No entrance fee was charged but the public was requested to sit down and order refreshments straight away; coffee, cocoa, an ice cream or a glass of beer was sufficient. Before the turn of the century, the prices of these refreshments depended on the seating chosen. In the most expensive seats a glass of beer would cost 1 franc 50 centimes but in the cheaper seats a cup of coffee could be ordered for only 50 centimes.

But disaster now struck on a more violent scale with the siege of Paris. On 1 September 1870 came the defeat of Sedan. The Chamber of Deputies was invaded; the Republic proclaimed. Within one *année terrible*, as Victor Hugo called it, the Commune had risen and fallen; the centre of Paris was in ruins. So apart from a few weeks of gaiety, the Folies Bergère's use for that second season was as a political meeting-place, a centre for political rallies, often addressed by Rochefort and Michelet, two of the finest orators of the period.

At last, in November 1871 at the conclusion of war, Léon Sari, the former secretary to Alexandre Dumas who had come from the Théâtre des Délassements Comiques, the famous music-hall of the Boulevard du Crimée, took over the management of the Folies Bergère.

'M. Sari brings the Délassements Comiques to the Folies Bergère!' the *Album des Théâtres* heralded. 'He has completely changed the theatre and put in a promenade, soon to make the Folies Bergère a popular venue.'

Sari changed the style of the establishment entirely and remodelled the auditorium, which had become a theatre of rioters, and above all he arranged a promenade behind the back seats of the stalls, an open space where one could stroll with a drink among a number of the ladies whose virtue was more obvious than real. It was to remain a feature of the Folies for many years, and was always to arouse the passions of reformers: 'The most notorious "ladies" of the district frequent it assiduously and it enjoys thereby the questionable privilege of attracting the hordes of foreigners sojourning in the capital,' complained one frustrated journalist.

The Folies Bergère, 1890. The notorious 'ladies of the town' propositioning clients.

Sari transformed and beautified the establishment completely. It was vast and very well decorated with a semi-circular balcony which protruded over the stalls. Where the foyer stands nowadays once stood an open garden which offered amusements and attractions. Léon Sari organized entertainments of a circus sort – a woman with two heads, a spectacular juggler, a 'prodigious magician who swallows live snakes, tears open his stomach and pulls out rosaries and pears which he presents to the ladies'. He also provided dancing-girls, of course – a *corps* which provided for the ordinary middle-class man a spectacle halfway between the parade of ballet-girls presented for the aristocracy at the Opéra and the openly outrageous ladies of the dancing-halls.

The first director to ensure the success of the Folies Bergère, Sari learnt the importance of advertising. Aside from the posters executed for the many numbers he presented (among them were the singer Anna Judic, countless ballets, the *Travaux de Voltige* ballet and the Hanlon-Lees pantomimes), he had several stock posters created for his establishment. Most of them depicted the interior of the Folies Bergère after his enlargement of the premises in 1875 and were designed by Lévy or Chéret. Performances took place every evening at 8.00 p.m. Three francs was the price for reserved tickets and two francs for all non-reserved seats. The first rows were always reserved for regular patrons; aside from providing the closest and best view in the house, they were the most comfortable leather armchairs to be found in any theatre. There was also a large box reserved for the members of the *Cercle de l'Epatant*, very much in style at the time. The entertainment included pantomimes, operettas, ballets and demonstrations on the flying trapeze or the slack rope, the greatest exponent of which, years later, was to be Barbette.

Although the Folies Bergère has never been a circus, it was, nonetheless, a show-case for many circus acts, especially before the turn of the century,

when Sari hired Rosinsky, a circus manager who had worked for and learned much from P. T. Barnum, to book acts for his music-hall.

The Folies Bergère began attracting artists from as far afield as the USA and in 1877 Miss Leona Dare, an American – and obviously proud to be one – was engaged to appear there. Not only did she slide down

a rope brandishing two American flags, but she had a stage costume made representing the colours of her country: 'stars' on her abdomen and 'stripes' on her thighs. She performed thus every night. Her real name was Adeline Stuart and she belonged to a family of acrobats; her brother, a one-legged gymnast, was also immensely successful in Europe. Miss Dare appeared all over Europe for considerable fees (2,000 francs monthly from the Franconi Circus, for instance). She became famous for her steel jaw: she would come down from the top of the dome of the theatre suspended from a bar. Married to an Australian banker, Leona Dare obtained a divorce in order to return to the circus and to live out her last years with a modest employee of the Australian railroads.

The Hanlon-Lees were the first to introduce a new, typically Anglo-Saxon genre, the pantomime, when they first appeared in Paris in 1867 in a production entitled 'The Village Priest'. But it was in 1878 that the five brothers Hanlon together with August (a former juggler they met in 1865 in Chicago) encountered their first success at the Folies Bergère with a scene borrowed from the Minstrels, the famous Do-Mi, Sol-Do. Engaged for one month for a fee of 9,000 francs, they proved so successful and popular with their audience that they were signed after the first performance for 15,000 francs a month and performed for the next successive thirteen months. An unexpected witness, the great writer Emile Zola, described their act: 'Then suddenly it starts, a hail of slaps and kicks mixed with music scraped on fiddles that stretch unexpectedly, guitars that take off like pistols, whole accordions whisper languorous notes and chairs are hurtled from the wings at the musicians who fall over; aerial trains pass by spewing rockets on the actors' dishevelled wigs.'

Vaudeville sketches, playlets, musical numbers in great variety, ballets, eccentric dances, acrobats and balancing performers, tightrope walkers, magicians and sleight-of-hand artists, trained animal acts, elaborate choral numbers, spectacular and mechanical effects on a vast scale, operettas and musical comedies attracted Parisians and tourists alike. For other patrons, intrigue and affairs of love in the promenades and the refreshment rooms of the Folies Bergère were the chief attractions.

The critic J. K. Huysmans gave a vivid account of the Folies Bergère as it was in 1879:

> It is ugly and it is superb, it is of an outrageous yet exquisite taste; it is incomplete like something which would really be beautiful. The garden with its upper galleries, its arcades cut out like coarse wooden lace, with its full diamond and its hollow trefoil, tinted in red and gold ochre, the garnet-red and tawny striped ceiling made of cloth with ornamental tufts and tassels, its imitation *Louvois* fountains with three women back-to-back between two enormous imitation bronze saucers, planted in the midst of green tufts, its walks covered with tables, rattan couches, chairs and counters staffed with fiercely rouged women, resembles at the same time the rush of the rue Montesquieu and an Algerian or Turkish bazaar.
>
> Alhambra-Poret, Duval-Moorish with, in addition, a vague odour of old suburban outdoor saloons, embellished with Oriental colonnades and mirrors, this theatre, with a playhouse whose faded red and dirty gold clashes with the spanking new luxury of the sham garden, is the only place in Paris which reeks as exquisitely of the make-up of paid love and the bark of the wearied corruptions.

In 1879, posters announced that '*Le théâtre des Folies Bergère restera ouvert tout l'été*' (the theatre of the Folies Bergère will remain open all summer). This was worth advertising since at the time the 'theatre season' did not last through the summer. Most houses

ANNÉE 1879
LE THÉÂTRE DES
FOLIES-BERGÈRE
RESTERA OUVERT
TOUT L'ÉTÉ

Imp. JULES CHÉRET & Cⁱᵉ 18, R. BRUNEL. PARIS.

closed because the audiences left for the spas and beach resorts.

At the end of 1880 Sari, on some inexplicable impulse, decided to change the style of the theatre and to devote it to *concert de grand musique*. He removed the ladies of the chorus and replaced them with a choir which sang classical music. He went so far as to sack his entire staff, considering them unsuitable for his future cultural plans. 'On 28 April 1881 rehearsals started with the orchestra of the *Concert de Paris* at the Folies Bergère,' reported a French journal, 'all under the patronage of a committee consisting of Gounod, Massenet, Saint-Saëns, Delibes, Joncières and Guiraud. The evening of the inauguration takes place in May.' But this proved to be a complete fiasco and after a month the theatre reverted to its original policy. Time, too, was running out for Sari. An inveterate gambler, he had already lost his fortune and four years later the Folies Bergère faced bankruptcy. Sari died soon after. The building still belonged to the Hospice des Quinze-Vingts and they now leased it to Monsieur and Madame Allemand, the most capable and respected proprietors of La Scala music-hall in Paris. They continued in the tradition of music-hall and on 30 November 1886 presented the first revue to be seen at the Folies Bergère, *Place aux Jeunes* (Make way for the Young). They had tempted the great Aristide Bruant away from his cabaret to star at the Folies in the forerunner of Paris's first *revue à grand spectacle* a year later.

Aristide Bruant had been compère at the Chat Noir, where he nightly released his hatred of the bourgeoisie in public. He had made a speciality of coarse Paris slang and simply tore his cultivated audience to shreds, just as the American Lenny Bruce was to do in the 1970s. The audience lapped it up. No doubt Bruant's appearance enhanced his reputation. He dressed in eccentric and striking clothes for the period: a black velvet coat with glittering metal buttons, a Breton waistcoat, scarlet shirt with scarlet neckerchief, corduroy trousers and knee-high Russian boots. Out of doors. Aristide Bruant appeared in a wide black cloak, a red woollen scarf thrown carelessly over one shoulder and a broad-rimmed felt hat, and he would carry a hefty, gnarled cane. This is how Toulouse-Lautrec portrayed him in one of his most evocative posters, with a sarcastic smile playing his lips. Steinlen, the Swiss poster designer, was one of Bruant's closest friends; together, arm in arm, they could be seen prowling the streets of Paris.

In the same year Edouard Marchand, who had married the Allemands' niece, took over the direction of the Folies Bergère. He turned it into a 'temple of variety'. A capable man with imagination, he spent considerable time travelling Europe and America looking for new attractions which proved to be particularly popular with his audiences. The influence and ideals he brought to bear on this famous house were to prove as inspiring and innovative as those of his predecessor Sari and his successor Paul Derval.

In the 1889 production, *Plaisirs de Paris*, Camille Débans described the Folies Bergère as

> a theatre which is not a theatre, a promenade where you may sit down, a spectacle which you are not obliged to watch – with two thousand men all smoking, drinking and joking and seven or eight hundred women all laughing, drinking and smoking, and offering themselves as happily as you could wish.... An overture, a polka is played ... and then you can watch in succession an India-rubber man, English lady singers, a crazy cyclist, seven acrobats, three clowns, a juggler ...

The first-night audience was of course familiar with the king of the *chansonniers*. They were used to his acid commentaries, they knew the broad, sardonic features and the leonine hair, the quizzical eyes beneath their thick brows. But they had never before seen him in so splendid a setting. They revelled in his caustic humour, rocked with laughter at his quirky use of underworld slang; they gasped at the trapezists, marvelled at the acrobats, cheered the dancers; and they reserved a specially warm burst of applause for the wry fatalism of Anna Judic, the star of Offenbach's *La Créole* as long ago as 1876 but singing now for the first time on a music-hall stage. The show, in short, was a smash hit.

Among the first-nighters who cheered loudest was a tall, thin medical student, Gabriel Tapie de Celeyran, son of a grand family in the south-west, and his cousin – a thick-lipped, bearded cripple with abnormally short legs who bore the noble name of Henri de Toulouse-Lautrec. At that time only twenty-two years old, Lautrec had recently arrived in Paris to continue his studies as a painter. He was still dazzled by the gaiety and vigour and exuberance of life in the capital, the teeming café society, the intensity of artists' theorizing in studio and garret, and the lubricious opportunities of the Montmartre bawdy houses. His eyes, normally wary behind a lorgnette, were bright that evening with excitement. He had forgotten the aggressive demeanour behind which he normally hid his self-consciousness and distress in the joy of watching these brilliant performers at work.

Prior to 1890, jugglers, acrobats, clowns and animal-tamers performed in music-halls until, step-by-step, the halls showed only revues and singing acts. Before that, they always had circus attractions on their programmes and the Folies Bergère, the greatest and the most beautiful of these establishments, presented the richest variety. This made it necessary to build a real menagerie behind the stage (which, however, was unable to house more than one category of large animal at a time). In 1877 part of the entrance had to be razed to let Delmonico's lion cage on stage. A short time after, things were so organized that elephants could regularly appear on stage. Describing the music-hall during this period, Louis-Léon Martin wrote: 'The entire world is at your disposal: Hawaii with its nostalgic guitars, the Orient and its disquieting equilibrists and jugglers, America with its eccentrics, its girls and dancers, India with its snake-charmers and magi, and more. The limits of the possible have naturally receded.' In fact, this thought applied perfectly to the Folies Bergère; during one evening, attractions from the four corners of the world were presented, including, between the acts, the Oriental Garden and the Gypsy band and, as a main feature, such astonishing spectacles as a real Zulu dance company.

The snake-charmers, male and female, have always been India's export to the music-halls of the world. Such was the case with Nala Damajanti who appeared at the Folies Bergère in 1890 performing with snakes entwined around her dusky body.

Freak shows flourished as part of the circuses and fairs of their time. In imitation of Barnum's side-shows, the exhibition of monsters – dwarfs, giants, bearded women and other marvels – criss-crossed the world and appeared under the big tops as well as on the stage of the Folies Bergère. Barnum himself presented a man-dog who appeared at the Folies with his progeny under the listing 'The Dogman and His Son'. The stage of the Folies Bergère has seen all kinds of animal acts, from the most classic (seals, horses, dogs) to the most bizarre (Douroff and his rats, Adby and his parrots, the six Spanish bulls, etc.). At a time when English boxing was the rage, a spectacular number, the Kangaroo Boxer, had its hour of glory. The Folies presented a fight of three two-minute rounds between a kangaroo and his trainer. The animal, which used its gloved front paws (and occasionally its hind paws) usually got the better of his opponent who, in any case, was hesitant to hit his precious beast for fear of losing his livelihood.

Target-shooting, using both pistol and carbine, had become very popular towards the end of the nineteenth century, many of its stars coming from America. The first Americans to come to France in the 1870s were Charley Austin and 'The Evil Spirit of the Plains', William (Doc) Carver; the Folies Bergère witnessed their feats of marksmanship. It was, of course, Buffalo Bill and his Wild West which reached the height of popularity during this period in Paris. Ira Paine, also an American, billed at the Folies as *'Le Célèbre Tireur Américain'* (The Famous American Marksman), performed many valorous feats, including the 'William Tell trick', shooting an orange from his wife's head while his back was turned, using a mirror. He died young, of indigestion, in a café right near the Folies Bergère where he had gone to drink an ice-cold beer.

Since the beginning of time, feats of strength have attracted and fascinated the crowds; at fairs and among circus acts, these exercises have always been numerous and much appreciated. Aside from the regular appearance of wrestlers, the Folies Bergère, like all establishments of this type, welcomed many strong men; Sampson, the chain breaker or 'Jack de Fer' – Iron Jack. To excite the imagination of the public, advertisements in the form of posters – being more or less realistic – presented ever more surprising and spectacular exploits: the strong man of Batacilan showed himself carrying on his back a small boat filled with people; the Hercules of the *Concert des Porcherons* dangling from a trapeze, lifted a jockey and his horse. It was this type of feat that Iron Jack carried out. He appeared, his powerful muscles taut, dressed in a tight-fitting jersey, shiny medals on his chest, in the process of lifting a horse. The posterist drew the horse disproportionately small, thus not only putting Jack 'front and centre' but making his feat believable.

Captain Constentenus belonged to the gallery of freaks to which the public was very partial at the end of the nineteenth century. A leaflet which was handed out on the Boulevards to announce the arrival of this new attraction at the Folies Bergère reads:

32

Captain Constentenus, tattooed Greek Prince. Born in the province of Albania (Turkey), in 1836. After the most fabulous adventures, during which he seduced the Shah of Persia's daughter, he got stranded in Kashgar and took up service with Chief Yakoob-Beg. There he was accused of having incited the miners to revolt, and the prince let him choose a torture among the following: hunger, impalement, the stake, being cut to pieces or tattooed. He chose to be tattooed, unaware of the tortures which were in store; the work took two months and the chief wanted him to survive as a living witness of his might, his body covered with 2 million pricks and 325 animal figures. Two other patients who underwent the same treatment at the same time died during the operation. Sold to the Turks as a slave, he was bought back by a generous American who gave him his unconditional freedom. It was then that Barnum showed him so successfully in both Americas.

At the price of the greatest sacrifice, the management of the Folies Bergère snatched him away from Barnum, for the duration of the World's Fair.

Acrobats, jugglers, clowns, elephants, trained dogs, and dancing girls filled the stage. The surprising thing is that if not all these acts appeared at the same time, one could see them all in one evening: in the smoke, the brouhaha of the conversations, from the hall to the promenade, from the promenade to the garden, from the garden to the galleries, something was going on everywhere in this gigantic palace of pleasure.

At the end of the nineteenth century, before it gave way to boxing, wrestling remained one of the public's favourite entertainments. Like many other houses, the Folies Bergère regularly presented this 'sport'. Skimming through the programmes we see them return regularly; in 1892 it was the great fights with Tom Cannon, an English giant who made all the French champions bite the dust. One of them started a small scandal when he claimed that he had been paid to 'lie down'. Then these contests were organized and became 'the golden belt' in 1902 and, beginning with 1905, 'the world championship of wrestling'. If we are to believe Jacques-Charles's testimony, the fights were all fixed; the results were arranged in advance so that there would always be a Frenchman in the finals!

Another of Marchand's great innovations at the Folies Bergère was the introduction of the chorus-girl, the first of whom was Lona Barrison, the eldest of the Barrison Sisters who were the first 'girls' to perform on a French stage. It seems that she occasion-

ally also appeared alone as an equestrienne. Particularly seductive, her leg bare to the top, her waist
tight-laced, a deep plunging neckline, a whip in one
hand, a cigarette in the other (the Barrison Sisters,
as an additional provocation, always had themselves
portrayed smoking), she appears radiant and smiling,
wearing a monocle (in imitation of Emilienne
d'Alençon). The eyes of the horse in the advertisement for her act tell us a great deal about the pleasure
it gets from the presence of this beautiful rider on
its back. We can only imagine the glances of the
regular patrons in the first rows of the stalls.

The second half of the show at the Folies was
opened by the five Barrison Sisters. They were not,
of course, sisters – but they were all of the same height
and build, each wore identical make-up and they all
performed in similar strawberry-blond wigs. Lona,

the eldest, married to Fleron, their impresario, Sophia, Inger, Olga and Gertrude helped to make the 1890s the finest days of the Folies Bergère. To a public for whom the dance so far had meant the languors of Italian-style ballet or solo Spanish stampings, they were a sensation – the five heads turning as one, the legs all raised to exactly the same height, the regimented gestures cued-in precisely to the music. And their little-girl voices, equally drilled and automated, oddly at variance with their ripe young bodies, brought to Paris a touch of the better-class New York burlesque house that rapidly increased the number of 'stage-door Johnnies' at the end of each performance. Brisson in his magazine *La Revue Illustrée* described them in 1896:

> Their gallant exercises performed each evening at the Folies Bergère attract the crowd. What do people like most about them? The pale gold of their hair, the litheness of their bodies, the whiteness of their teeth, the carmine of their smile, the slightly acid freshness of their voices, their mechanical toy waddle, the gracefulness of their slender legs, the sensuous seething of their frilly and beribboned underwear – this kind of charm cannot be explained – it must be experienced.

Chand d'habits (The Apparel Merchant), a pantomime by Catulle Mendès (an important theatrical personality and, without doubt, one of the greatest beer drinkers of his time) with music by Jules Bouval, was the Folies Bergère's most successful pantomime. Staged in the year that the Barrison Sisters were first to appear at the Folies, it was revived in 1905. It was a drama in which Pierrot kills a clothes merchant so that he may accompany Musidora to a party. He is haunted by the merchant's ghost who, disguised as Pluto, takes Musidora's place in the bed where Pierrot thought he would find her and carries him away to hell.

This pantomime in four scenes was written for a

mime artist from Marseilles, Severin. He became
famous and followed in the footsteps of the most distinguished French mimes, Debureau and Rouffe.
According to Catulle Mendès's own notation in the
Journal (17 May 1896): 'It is indeed one of the
proudest moments of my career to have given
this admirable mime the opportunity to offer himself to Paris, to the enthusiastic public and to a fair
critique.'

Loïe Fuller was another one of the artists to have
made her mark at the end of the nineteenth century.
Born in 1862 in Fullesburg, Illinois, she began her
career as an actress and dancer. She had an unattractive figure and no particular choreographic ability.
She would probably never have encountered fame
had it not been for an accident one evening: draped
in an overly large stage costume which continually
had to be pulled up, she got caught in the projector's
multi-coloured light beam, to the delight of the
public. From that evening on she arranged her
number (with huge veils on which the fans blew and
light played) and appeared in this manner for the first
time at the Folies Bergère in November 1892. By
1897 she was topping the bill at the Folies in a production entitled *La Danse du Feu* – The Dance of Fire.
The serpentine dance was a triumph: she arrived just
in time to dazzle the aesthetes of the era who discerned in her veils the arabesques of 'Art Nouveau'.
Jean Lorrain saw her as 'a human flitter-mouse
wrapped in a shroud' and Robert de Montesquieu
as 'a conflagration in the heart of a convolvulus' (the
flitter-mouse and the convolvulus being two decorative elements often used in 'Art Nouveau' design).
Loïe Fuller regularly appeared at the Folies Bergère
and was paid the fabulous fee of 24,000 francs a
month. There she created the violet, the fire-dance,
the dance of the flowers, the butterfly and the mirror.
The lady who said, 'I chisel the light' was a pioneer
of the newborn music-hall: she opened the way for
the light effects of the great stage revues.

At the back of the stalls, where standing spectators 'promenaded' during the show, and from where they had ample sight of the stage, the notorious 'ladies of the town' were attracted, and plied their trade. This practice thrived for half a century until it was curtailed to a certain extent for the sake of respectability.

Until Paul Derval ended one of the Folies Bergère's oldest traditions, the patrons of the Folies could find certain 'available' women in the *promenoir* who came not for the spectacle of the show but for the enticement of their customers. The show could be seen just as well from the *promenoir*, a vast circular area at the back of the stalls, as from the first rows of the circle, and for a modest price, provided they were prepared to stand. The spectators who wished to see the show crowded up to the barriers that separated them from the stalls, leaving a large empty space at the back; this was the girls' traditional pitch. They had formerly conducted business outside the doors of the Folies, taking their custom to the numerous little hotels in the district which did a roaring trade letting rooms by the hour without questions asked.

Noticing two of the frozen, wretched 'girls' outside the theatre one winter's night, the kindly doorman allowed them into the *promenoir* to keep warm – and so a tradition began. But it soon got out of hand when their 'sisters' learnt of the 'shop-window' of illustrious prospective 'clients'. The girls squabbled over one another's 'catches' and soon embarrassing incidents resulted in the management regulating what it could not eradicate – drawing up a black list eliminating the most objectionable characters. Cards were printed and distributed to the prettiest, best-behaved and best-dressed of these women, and ladies unaccompanied by gentlemen were not admitted to the *promenoir* except on presentation of these cards. The passes were valid for two weeks only, and every fortnight the general manager of the Folies Bergère received the '*promenoir* ladies', as they were called, and held a parade to decide which of them he would allow to renew their cards – a sort of organized form of prostitution.

'They are extraordinary and magnificent when they walk in pairs along the hall's semi-circular promenade,' J. K. Huysmans, a noted critic of the day, recorded, 'powdered and rouged, their eyes drowned in a blur of pale blue, their lips shaped in a loud red, the bosom projected forward over a tightly-laced waist, blowing a wisp of *apopanax* – while they fan themselves – which blends with the powerful aroma of their underarms and the very delicate perfume of a dying flower in their corsage.'

Charlie Chaplin, who at the age of fourteen appeared at the Folies Bergère in 1909 with the Fred Karno Troupe from England, recalls in his autobiography his first impression of the Folies Bergère – and his encounter with one of the *promenoir* ladies:

Sunday night was free, so we could see the show at the Folies Bergère, where we were to open the following Monday. No theatre, I thought, ever exuded such glamour, with its gilt and plush, its mirrors and large chandeliers. In the thick-carpeted foyers and dress circle the world promenaded. Bejewelled Indian princes with pink turbans and French and Turkish officers with plumed helmets sipped cognac at liqueur bars. In the large outer foyer music played as ladies checked their wraps and fur coats, baring their white shoulders. They were the habituées who discreetly solicited and promenaded the foyers and the dress circle. In those days they were beautiful and courtly.

The Folies Bergère also had professional linguists who strolled about the theatre with the word 'Interpreter' on their caps, and I made a friend of the head one, who could speak several languages fluently.

After our performance I would wear my stage evening-dress clothes and mingle with the prom-

enaders. One gracile creature with a swan-like neck and white skin made my heart flutter. She was a tall Gibson Girl type, extremely beautiful, with retroussé nose and long dark eye-lashes, and wore a black velvet dress with long white gloves. As she went up the dress-circle stairs, she dropped a glove. Quickly I picked it up.

'*Merci,*' she said.

'I wish you would drop it again,' I said mischievously.

'*Pardon?*'

Then I realized she did not understand English and I spoke no French. So I went to my friend the interpreter. 'There's a dame that arouses my concupiscence. But she looks very expensive.'

He shrugged. 'Not more than a louis.'

'Good,' I said, although a louis in those days was a lot, I thought – and it was.

I had the interpreter put down a few French *phrases d'amour* on the back of a postcard: '*Je vous adore*', '*Je vous ai aimée la première fois que je vous ai vue*', etc., which I intended to use at the propitious moment. I asked him to make the preliminary arrangements and he acted as courier, going from one to the other. Eventually he came back and said, 'It's all settled, one louis, but you must pay her cab-fare to her apartment and back.'

I temporized a moment. 'Where does she live?' I asked.

'It won't cost more than ten francs.'

Ten francs was disastrous, as I had not anticipated that extra charge. 'Couldn't she walk?' I said, jokingly.

'Listen, this girl is first-class, you must pay her fare,' he said.

So I acquiesced.

After the arrangements had been settled, I passed her on the dress-circle stairs. She smiled and I glanced back at her. '*Ce soir!*'

'*Enchantée, monsieur!*'

As we were on before the interval I promised
to meet her after my performance. Said my friend:
'You hail a cab while I get the girl, then you won't
waste time.'

'Waste time?'

As we drove along the Boulevard des Italiens,
the lights and shadows passing over her face and
long white neck, she looked ravishing. I glanced
surreptitiously at my French on the postcard. *'Je
vous adore,'* I began.

She laughed, showing her perfect white teeth.
'You speak very well French.'

'Je vous ai aimée la première fois que je vous ai vue,'
I continued emotionally.

She laughed again and corrected my French,
explaining that I should use the familiar *'tu'*. She
thought about it and laughed again. She looked
at her watch, but it had stopped; she indicated she
wanted to know the time, explaining that at
twelve o'clock she had a very important appointment.

'Not this evening,' I said coyly.

'Oui, ce soir.'

'But you're fully engaged this evening, *toute la
nuit!'*

She suddenly looked startled. *'Oh, non, non, non!
Pas toute la nuit!'*

Then it became sordid. *'Vingt francs pour le
moment?'*

'C'est ça!' she replied emphatically.

'I'm sorry,' I said, 'I think I'd better stop the
cab.'

And after paying the driver to take her back
to the Folies Bergère, I got out, a very sad and dis-
illusioned young man.

Guy de Maupassant in his novel *Bel-Ami* sets one
of his scenes in the same environment. When Duroy
(Bel-Ami of the title) comes on bad times he resorts
to accepting money from his mistress, Madame de

Marelle, 'a real Paris society woman'. Madame de Marelle is unaware of his relationship with Rachel, one of the Folies Bergère's *promenoir* ladies, and when he is approached by her in the company of his new-found love, de Maupassant describes the scene:

One evening she [Clotilde de Marelle] said to him:

'Would you believe it, I have never been to the Folies Bergère? Will you take me there?'

He hesitated, afraid of meeting Rachel. Then he reflected: 'Pooh, after all it's not as if I were a married man. If Rachel sees me, she'll understand the situation and won't talk to me. Besides we shall have a box.'

Another reason influenced him. He was very glad of the opportunity of offering Madame de Marelle a box at a theatre, without having to pay for it. It would be some light compensation.

When they arrived at the theatre he left Clotilde in the cab, while he went for his pass, so that she should not see that it was presented to him free. Then he came back for her and they entered and were received politely by the man at the door.

The promenade was packed. With difficulty they made their way through the crowd of men and women. At last they reached their box, mid-way between the orchestra and the restless throng in the gallery. But Madame de Marelle did not cast a single glance at the stage; her whole attention was attracted by the women who were roaming about behind her, and she turned round continually to watch them. She wanted to touch them, to feel their clothes, their faces, their hair, to discover what those creatures were made of.

'There's a stout dark woman,' she said suddenly, 'who keeps on looking at us. I thought just now that she was going to speak to us. Did you see her?'

'No,' he replied, 'you must be mistaken.'

But he had noticed her long before.

It was Rachel who was prowling round them angrily, with violent words on the tip of her tongue.

Duroy had brushed against her just as they were making their way through the throng, and she had said, 'Good evening,' in a low voice, and with  a wink of understanding. But he had not replied to this civility for fear of being seen by Clotilde; he had passed her by coldly, his head held high, and a disdainful expression on his face. Stung by unconscious jealousy, Rachel retraced her steps, and once more brushed up against him, exclaiming in louder tones, 'Good evening, George.'

He still made no reply. Then she determined to force him to recognize her and greet her, and she kept returning to the back of the box, waiting for a favourable opportunity.

Rachel

When she noticed Madame de Marelle looking at her, she touched George's shoulder with the tip of her finger.

'Good evening. How are you?'

But he did not turn round.

'Well,' she continued, 'have you suddenly become deaf since last Thursday?'

He made no reply, and affected an air of disdain, as if he would not compromise himself by as much as one word with a baggage like that.

She burst out into angry laughter.

'You're dumb, are you? Has Madame there bitten out your tongue?'

With a furious gesture and in an exasperated voice he broke out:

'Who gave you permission to speak to me? Get out of this box or I'll have you arrested.'

Then with flaming eyes and heaving bosom she screamed:

'So that's it, is it? You silly mug! If you carry on with a woman, the least you can do is to say, "How do you do" to her. Because you happen to be with someone else today isn't a reason for cutting me. If you had only made a sign when I passed you just now, I'd have left you alone. But you meant to give yourself airs. You wait. I'll pay you out. What, you can't even say good evening to me when I meet you –'

She would have kept it up, but Madame de Marelle had opened the door of the box, and was escaping through the crowd, frantically looking for the exit.

Duroy had darted after her and was endeavouring to rejoin her.

Rachel, seeing them in flight, shouted after them triumphantly:

'Stop her! Stop her! She has stolen my man.'

The spectators began to laugh. Two men, for the joke of the thing, seized Clotilde by the shoulders, and endeavoured to bring her back, at the same time attempting to kiss her. But Duroy, who had caught her up, pulled her roughly away, and dragged her out into the street.

Despite these two accounts, one fact and the other fiction, discretion was the chief quality required of the *promenoir* ladies; direct soliciting was out of the question. But the ingenious system that worked well for years was brought to an end when Paul Derval became proprietor of the Folies Bergère in 1918. This move might well have been prompted by an incident that took place in the *promenoir* of another theatre, as recalled by the British entertainer Billy Milton who had partnered Mistinguett:

In those days the *promenoir* was not confined to the activities of women alone. It was an absolute meeting place for the homosexuals too. One day the police stepped in and arrested a man who had seen the show at least a hundred and fifty times! The homosexuals at the Folies Bergère, the Casino de Paris and the Palace theatre always used the *promenoirs* until one managing director of the

Palace, who had his offices at the back of the theatre, on the ground floor by the *promenoir*, was murdered by a young sailor. He was stabbed in the face and the body was covered by the office carpet until the police were called. The murderer was finally traced and sent to Devils Island.

Paul Derval maintained that his job was to run a theatre, not a house of assignation, declaring that people came to the Folies Bergère to see the show; if they had anything else in mind they were to seek it elsewhere. His decision to cast the *promenoir* ladies 'back from whence they came' – the streets – was met with outraged indignation, and although some of them managed to slip through the net using in-genious ploys to get back inside, the oldest profession in the world was eliminated from the promenade of the Folies Bergère (although some people claim to have been propositioned by them during the Second

Manet's celebrated 'Bar at the Folies Bergère' study of the Folies Bergère barmaid asking: 'What would you like to have, Sir?' 'M'dear, I simply daren't tell you,' the silk-hatted roué replies.

World War) – but not from its stage.

The practitioners of this time-old tradition continued in even greater glory and glow from behind the footlights. The stage of the Folies Bergère became the spring-board for the public charms of the notable courtesans of the day. During the last two decades of the nineteenth century and the first of the twentieth, France enjoyed an upsurge of artistic flourishing that became known as *La Belle Epoque* and the four women who symbolized this period on the stage of the Folies Bergère, as well as in the bedchambers of the crowned heads of Europe, were the celebrated – or notorious – Liane de Pougy, Emilienne d'Alençon, Cléo de Mérode and La Belle Otero.

It was a time of change that heralded both Art Nouveau and Post Impressionism, when painters as diverse as Monet, Cézanne and Toulouse-Lautrec worked. It was an age of extremes, when Proust and Anatole France were fashionable along with the notorious Monsieur Willy, Colette's husband. In the decorative arts, Mucha, Gallé and Lalique were enjoying success; and in the theatre Lugné-Poe was introducing the grave works of Ibsen at the same time as Parisians were enjoying the spectacle of the can-can of Hortense Schneider. Paris was the crossroads of a new and many-faceted culture, a culture that was predominantly feminine in form, for, above all, *La Belle Epoque* was the age of women. Women dominated the cultural scene. On the one hand there were the Comtesse Greffulhe, the patron of Proust and Maeterlinck, who introduced greyhound racing into France; Winaretta Singer, Princess de Polignac, for whom Stravinsky wrote *Renard*; Misia Sert, the discoverer of Chanel and Diaghilev's closest friend. On the other were the great dancers of the Moulin Rouge, immortalized by Toulouse-Lautrec – Jane Avril, Yvette Guilbert, La Goulue – as well as such celebrated dramatic actresses as the great Sarah Bernhardt. But it would not be possible to speak of *La Belle*

Epoque without mention of the four great courtesans who, in many ways, perfectly symbolized the era.

Mistresses were not unknown in France, of course. In the past there had been the great royal mistresses – Diane de Poitiers, the Marquise de Pompadour and the Comtesse du Barry. A royal mistress was an accepted position in court circles and many vied for the coveted title of *maîtresse en titre*. They were a different breed from the four courtesans who dominated the press – and the stage of the Folies Bergère – during this period: the mistress had her own establishment, her illegitimate offspring often acknowledged by her lover; the courtesan had no such rights. Hers was a more independent existence, for she had numerous admirers who vied for her favours and paid dearly. Earlier in the nineteenth century, during the Third Empire of Louis Napoleon III, were women such as the famous courtesan Léonide Leblanc, who later graduated to become mistress to the Duc d'Aumale, King Louis-Philippe's son. Another was La Barucci who, arriving an hour late for her meeting with the Prince of Wales to whom she was presented as the most unpunctual woman in Paris, turned her back on him, bent down low, swept up her skirts, revealing a pair of large rounded naked buttocks and said, 'I show him the best part of me and it costs him nothing.'

Other celebrated courtesans were Marie Duplessis, who inspired the younger Dumas to write *The Lady of the Camellias*; La Païva, who rose from a Jewish ghetto in Moscow to die one of the richest courtesans of all time; and the great Cora Pearl who introduced modern make-up to Parisian women. Thus they forged their lucrative careers. These women were followed by the courtesans of *La Belle Epoque* whom audiences flocked to see on the stage of the Folies Bergère.

Although in very much the same profession as their sisters conducted from the *promenoir*, theirs claimed a more celebrated clientèle bringing with

Liane de Pougy

them higher stakes. The crowned heads of Europe (as well as our own Prince of Wales, before becoming Edward VII) came to see and escort these great courtesans, lavishing money and jewels on them in return for their favours; many lost their fortunes and were ruined by them.

Liane de Pougy, after an early marriage at sixteen had, when the marriage failed, launched herself into a brilliant career as a courtesan which led her eventually into marriage in 1910 with the Roumanian Prince Ghika of Moldavia, a nephew of the Queen of Greece. They lived happily for twenty-seven years until his death when she donned the habit of Sister Mary Magdalene of the Penitence and entered a Dominican convent in Lausanne where she died in 1950. For her first performance on the stage of the Folies Bergère in October 1896 she chose Jean Lorraine's *L'Araignée d'Or* (The Golden Spider). Liane de Pougy had as confidant and accomplice throughout the years the celebrated Lorrain, a decadent writer and flamboyant homosexual who numbered among his friends Proust and the poet Comte Robert de Montesquieu.

Among the celebrities to whom Liane de Pougy owed her success was the Prince of Wales. For her début at the Folies she wrote to him simply: 'Sir, for tonight I make my début in Paris. I would be established if you would condescend to come and applaud me.' And that is exactly what he did. From then on she obtained quick success in Parisian society, something which was made easy by her background; she was an officer's daughter and had benefited from a first-class education. Moreover, her stunning beauty was her passport to eternity in her chosen field. She led, until 1910, an elegant and sophisticated life in her private house in the rue de la Néva. She remained faithful to Prince Ghika throughout their marriage despite her reputation.

Her compatriot, Emilienne d'Alençon, whose real name was Amilienne André, had made her entrance into Paris in the *demi-monde* with the help of the young Duc d'Uzès, whose family promptly packed him off abroad before she succeeded in adding him to the list of suitors she had managed to ruin (he died at twenty). She first appeared at the Cirque d'Eté in 1889 where she performed with tinted rabbits dressed in paper ruffs. The public was enraptured more by her tight-fitting bodice and her low cleavage than by her act. From that moment on she appeared everywhere, playing in such evocative shows as *Paris Boulevard, Tara Boum Revue* and *Emilienne aux Quat'zarts*, and not only from bed to bed but from crowned head to crowned head. It was, in fact, at the time that she appeared at the Folies Bergère that she first met King Léopold II of Belgium with whom she conducted a lengthy *liaison*.

Emilienne d'Alençon

Cléo de Mérode commenced her career in the *corps de ballet* at the Paris Opéra where she rose to become prima ballerina. One of her performances was attended by Marchand, director of the Folies Bergère, always on the look-out for new talent. He persuaded her to accept his invitation to appear in the leading role at the Folies in a ballet-pantomime entitled *Lorenza*. None could have been more surprised by the invitation than the dancer herself, who describes the proposal in her memoirs:

In Paris, a letter from Monsieur Marchand, the manager of the Folies Bergère, was waiting on my desk. He invited me to stop at his office. I was intrigued. What might he want from me? Surely, he didn't expect me to perform an exotic number in his music-hall? Between M. Marchand and me there was no discussion of a 'number' but of an important production. I was offered the main role of a ballet-pantomime in three acts by Rodolphe Darzens and Franck Affano, the very young Italian composer whose opera 'Resurrection' had recently been recreated in the Salle Favart.

Cléo de Mérode

Cléo de Mérode became known to the Parisian public when she was introduced to King Léopold II of Belgium. He expressed his surprise that she had the audacity to bear the name of a princely Belgian family. She replied that it was her true name (it was, indeed). The king took her aside and chatted with her for a good fifteen minutes. The following day all Paris spoke of him as *Cléo*pold. In her memoirs Cléo de Mérode denies that anything whatever had happened and this seems true since Léopold courted Emilienne d'Alençon at the time.

Caroline Otero was among the most dazzling figures in France between 1889 and 1914, one of those incredible women who symbolized *La Belle Epoque* and emerged as one of its most flamboyant characters – La Belle Otero. At the height of her fame, or notoriety, this spectacular Spanish dancer was described in the press as 'the most scandalous person since Helen of Troy'. During the twenty-five years of her reign she enjoyed the patronage of such men as Kaiser Wilhelm II, Edward VII and Grand Duke Nicholas of Russia. At one time she lived in a sumptuous establishment near the Bois de Boulogne, built for her by a French duke in gratitude for a champagne supper she had given for him, and was waited on by a staff of seventeen. Of her multitudes of admirers, she reduced some to near ruin, a few to suicide and many to their knees in proposals of marriage. Several duels were fought over her and, never afraid of violence herself, she even fought one with an actress who had ridiculed her. Although she was regarded as one of the most acquisitive courtesans of all time, a reputation she enjoyed with former French royal mistresses, she was essentially a dancer, a Spanish dancer, whose sensuous performances had won her international acclaim.

This Spanish dancer from Andalusia burst onto the Parisian stage at the Cirque d'Eté for a season where Marchand – ever eager for new talent to appear at the Folies – saw her perform and followed her to Berlin where her next engagement had taken her to the Wintergarten Theatre. There, he signed her up on a ten-year contract for 5,000 francs a month, rising to a fabulous monthly salary of 35,000 francs. She became one of the most enduring stars of the Folies Bergère, winning for her début, in which she was brought together with Loïe Fuller and the Barrison Sisters, the following notice from *Figaro*:

> We had seen quite a few things in Paris, but we had to wait until She came to see this: a woman with Andalusian eyes, of which the poet speaks, blood-red lips, a magnificent head of wavy, raven-black hair, a rearing-up and throwing her head back like a young thoroughbred. The gyrations of her hips and legs drive the public crazy. She is loaded with jewels like an idol: diamonds, rubies and emeralds whose sparkle dazzles the audience. Her bosom is more covered with jewels than a Chief of Protocol's chest is with medals and crosses, they are in her hair, on her shoulders, arms, wrists, hands and legs, and dangle from her ears, and when she ends her dance, the boards continue to glitter as if a crystal chandelier had been pulverized on them. And she is watched by two guards who protect her millions.

The great French writer Colette, who together with Mata Hari appeared at the Folies Bergère, became a close friend of La Belle Otero. She met Otero during those six years she spent on the stage following her divorce from Monsieur Willy. In her books *My Apprenticeships* and *Music-Hall Sidelights*, Colette recalls:

> Madame Otero, upright in the middle of that period of my life when I was exploring the possibilities of earning my own living, had not the faintest resemblance to a coconut tree. She was purely ornamental. Like all luxuries, she was

curiously and variously instructive, and merely to hear her made me rejoice that the early stages in one of my careers should have set her in my ways.

'You look a bit green, my girl,' she once said to me. 'Don't forget that there is always a moment in a man's life, even if he's a miser, when he opens his hand *wide* ...'

'The moment of passion?'

'No. The moment when you twist his wrist.'

She added: 'Like this,' and made a screwing movement with her two clenched hands. You seemed to see the blood flow, the juice of the fruits, the gold and goodness knows what else; to hear the bones crack. Can you picture me twisting the miser's wrist? I laughed, I admired; there was nothing else for me to do. Magnificent creature!

Another incident illustrates Otero's wily avarice. Lunching at the Palais de Glace one day, Jacques Riberner (a friend and confidant of Otero's) introduced her to a stolid, red-haired, north-country Englishman called Thompson. His bluntness disturbed her but when Riberner explained that he was immensely rich she decided to accept his invitation to lunch the following day at Durand's. That evening Riberner called in at her dressing-room at the Folies Bergère and said that Thompson had been greatly impressed with her. If she played her cards right he would buy her the moon.

The next day she kept her rendezvous with the man and their meal passed satisfactorily. But when she got up to leave he asked her why she had to go so soon.

'I have an urgent appointment,' she said apologetically.

'Please stay with me. Your appointment cannot be more important than I am.'

'It is very important indeed. It is to collect a 40,000 francs advance with which to pay a dressmaker's bill.'

He seemed bemused. 'If all you need is 40,000

francs I shall give them to you, but only on condition that you do not keep this appointment and come with me to London tonight.'

'To London! Tonight! That is impossible.' She laughed. 'You know that every night I play at the Folies Bergère. If I am absent I have to pay a forfeit and that can be very expensive.'

'I will pay your forfeit,' he said without hesitation.

'Very well. But it will cost you another 50,000 francs.'

He did not seem to mind.

'Then if you will excuse me I have to make a telephone call, to tell them I will not be at rehearsals today.'

She rose from the table leaving Thompson puffing a cigar. First she telephoned her dressmaker.

'Now you know that I do not owe you anything,' she said to her, 'but I want you to make out a bill for 40,000 francs at once, and I shall come round and pay it. But the money is mine; you understand?'

Having fixed the dressmaker she then rang the Folies to speak to Edouard Marchand, the manager. With luck her trip could net her an extra 90,000 francs; but it would mean involving Marchand. 'Tell everyone I am ill,' she said to him, 'and that I cannot play for a week. I shall come round presently with my 50,000 francs forfeit. Naturally, it will be mine.'

Returning to the table, she told Thompson that all was in order for the trip to London. They then called on the dressmaker, for whom he wrote out a cheque for 40,000 francs, whilst she slipped Otero a note confirming that the money was in fact hers; and afterwards went on to the theatre where Thompson paid Marchand the 50,000 francs forfeit in cash, which Marchand managed to hand to Otero behind Thompson's back.

Aside from Colette, Mata Hari was another friend of La Belle Otero's, and one of her music-hall contemporaries who appeared at the Folies Bergère. The notorious spy began as a dancer whose act was to

La Belle Otero. A painting by Charles Blanc, 1926.

perform before an altar centred between the pillars of a vast white hall, supported by a group of coloured attendants. She was Dutch, her real name was Margaretta Geetruida Zeller, later Macleod, and her appearance was described as 'snake-like'. She purported to be an Indian dancer and her mouth and nose, which were rather thick, together with the brilliance of her eyes, lent credence to the belief.

The great Russian-born designer, Erté, who created costumes and settings for the Folies Bergère between 1917 and 1930, worked in Paris for the French couturier Paul Poiret until the *maître* closed his salon towards the end of the First World War, and Erté's first venture into theatrical design was to create a costume for Mata Hari:

> Mata Hari was always very charming to everyone, and she was also very fashionably dressed. Nobody would ever have thought she was a spy! But she imagined many things that didn't exist. For instance, she thought she was an Indian dancer from the temples of India and tried to persuade everyone into believing it, but it wasn't true. She was Dutch. And then I think that when she was accused of being a spy, she played the part of being a spy! She was always very keen on publicity, so that people could talk about her, and would do almost anything to attract attention. Her talent was not much, in fact it was not enough, so she fabricated this aura of mystery around her in order to conceal any lack of it.

Erté's costume design for Mata Hari, 1913.

> The costume I did for her was for the part of an oriental dancer in a play which was called *Marie Marais*, and Paul Poiret, who had been commissioned to do the costumes and settings for the production, asked me to design it for her – and that was the first theatrical costume I ever designed.

Many years later, long after Mata Hari was dead, Otero was asked about her. 'Leave her alone. She

10 Costume for Mata Hari, 1913

has suffered enough,' she replied sympathetically.

The Great War brought La Belle Otero's career to an end just as it also affected many of her European patrons. An era was ended, a way of life destroyed, and with it the fortunes of her lovers and suitors. However, though it may have forced her abdication it did not extinguish her legend.

These artists, however, were the exception to the rule at the Folies Bergère. The majority of the girls were – and still are – respectable with high moral values, and shun 'stage-door Johnnies' whom they feel degrade both themselves and their profession. The Folies Bergère and the other leading establishments that boast the most beautiful and elegant girls in the world seek this talent in Britain. The English girls have not only the haughty, defiant 'cool' that is required of a statuesque beauty with long, shapely legs, but a friendly 'look, but don't touch' arrogance which, like a thoroughbred, is decidedly in-bred. One such beauty, who appeared at the Folies Bergère before the First World War, when she was only just sixteen, was to become Britain's most popular pantomime principal boy: Dorothy Ward. She remembers that she and the rest of the English contingent at the Folies Bergère were protected by an English governess, had regular private tutelage, lived together in a private girls' hostel and learnt enough French to see them through the day. She also remembers the lyrics of a song she sang at the Folies:

I like it best of all
– on the sunny side of Bond Street.
There are ladies short and tall
– on the sunny side of Bond Street.
When it is the season, I get my call
– on the shady side
– on the lady side of Bond Street.

On one occasion the young Dorothy Ward and her chaperone were passing Maxims when the manager stopped her and remarked, 'You must be English.'

'What makes you say that?' asked Miss Ward.

'I can tell by the way you wear your hair – long, blonde and natural; you have no need of make-up because of your lovely complexion; and by your pretty dress and long white socks.' Enchanted by the naturalness of the English rose, he invited them to luncheon as guests of the restaurant, with an open invitation for them to return there whenever they wished – *gratis*.

Another admirer of Dorothy Ward's was Bend Or, the Duke of Westminster, who found her to be even more enchanting and refreshing and presented her with a black leather jewel-casket with her initials studded in diamonds on the lid. She has that jewel-casket to this day – but the diamonds, alas, have gone the way of the world.

2

Revue Extraordinaire

1900! The Great Exhibition. The middle of the period known as *La Belle Epoque*. Paris was truly the centre of the world, and, as if to prove the point, everyone in the world, or so it seemed, was visiting the World's Fair and enjoying the delights of a city which had never offered so much. That year saw the inauguration of the first lines of the Métro and the first petrol-driven vehicles. The first moving picture show was held in the basement of the Grand Café. There were princes to be met on every street corner – Serbs, Croats, Russians – and many of them went to the theatre.

For this occasion the Folies Bergère staged a *Spectacle Varié – Tous les Soirs*: Variety Show – Performances every Evening. At the beginning of the following year, a ballet-pantomime, *Napoli*, was created for the Folies. With a tableau by Paul Milbiet and music by Alphano, the plot was, as usual, banal and unlikely, and served only as a pretext for the dance:

> Act I: 'The Parisian Girl' and her friends wait at the Lyon railroad station for 'The Banker'. He arrives too late and the train leaves.
>
> Act II: On a terrace over the Gulf of Naples, a singer in love is being mocked by all in the group except for the Parisian Girl. He notices it and sings for her.
>
> Act III: 'The Blue Grotto' where the two declare their love for one another.

Act IV: A song contest, the singer wins the first prize ... but 'The Banker' arrives – 'The Parisian Girl' introduces the singer to him – 'Let him come to Paris,' says The Banker. 'No,' she answers. 'I am staying in Naples with him.'

The Folies Bergère's company of dancers was large in number and directed by an outstanding person, Mariquita, the ballet mistress, who staged *Napoli*. Born in Algeria, an orphan picked up by travellers, she arrived in Paris at the age of six. After having starred in children's roles, she quickly won acclaim. Then, even though she was married to the director of the Porte Saint-Martin Theatre, she continued to work – until she died. As the ballet mistress of the Folies Bergère and, later, at the Opéra-Comique where she directed the dance company for nearly twenty years, she was described in Cléo de Mérode's memoirs: 'This small little woman was imposing despite her physical scantiness. She carried herself very straight, thus not losing an inch of her height. ... Two accessories never left her: a fan and a lorgnette. The fan she held continually in her right hand: it was her staff of authority.'

By the turn of the century Marchand, who had brought such change and excitement to the Folies Bergère, fell ill and was forced to give up the management of the theatre, dying soon afterwards. He was succeeded by two illusionists, the Brothers Isola, who took over the Folies Bergère in 1901, mercifully saving the house from bankruptcy. Emile and Vincent Isola had been presenting shows for some five years before finding themselves in the exalted position as heads of this great institution. They were inseparable and devoted to one another. Courteous and friendly, they were known for their generosity and kindness and it could be said that this added to their success, for no one could refuse anything they asked. It was, in fact, their only trump card as they were neither cultured nor had they any specific knowledge of the rudiments of theatre production. Moreover, their grasp of any matter concerning money was negligible. They were driven by naive ambition through their desire to succeed with integrity and it was perhaps these virtues that won them their goal; in their relations with their artists their word was their bond; there was no need of contracts. While on the one hand they lacked business acumen, on the other their very kindness was the key to their success.

Emile and Vincent Isola had begun their careers as conjurers with a juggling act and had formerly appeared on the boards of the Folies in 1886. Their rise to riches was rapid. They were born at Blida in Algeria, a small town which was damaged by an earthquake in 1867, as a consequence of which the Isola family left Algeria and settled in Paris. Their father ran a saloon and occasionally presented little shows in the evenings for the entertainment of his customers. As youngsters the Isola brothers mastered the art of conjuring and did so well as to feel confident enough to try their luck in Paris.

They had been given a ten-minute spot in a variety show at the Lancry Theatre, where they performed a shooting act on the lines of William Tell's historic exploit, except that their gun fired blanks and the apple fell of its own volition, deftly exchanged for another pierced with an adequate bullet hole.

On the first night Emile got tangled up with his rifle and the shot was fired while the gun was still pointing skywards. Vincent, who had his back turned and had seen nothing, did his rapid manoeuvre as rehearsed; the apple fell at the given signal and he tossed it to the audience for them to admire the bullet hole. The apple came smartly back, along with other fruits and vegetables in varying stages of decay. Save for a miracle that was to take place soon after, their destiny could have meant a hasty retreat to Blida.

A small boy lay dying of an unknown illness and

his mother, seeking to brighten his last days, came to see the Brothers Isola and asked them to give a private conjuring act at the child's bedside.

Their compassion aroused, the brothers gave not one but several shows for the young invalid. For three days they virtually lived in the sick-room. The child's eyes filled with wonder at the sight of so many marvels. But he died, and although the Isolas had no money they refused to accept payment for their services.

After the funeral the bereaved mother again sought out the Isola brothers. She was anxious to give them some reward for all they had done, in memory of her only son. The brothers protested but the lady was insistent. She was also very rich. It was not long before they bought the Théâtre des Capucines, which they renamed the Théâtre Isola, where they presented magic acts. They eventually leased their theatre to Max Maurey and Alphonse Frank and in 1897 took over the directorship of the Parisiana, a small music-hall in the Boulevard Poissonnière which specialized in revues. Their success with the Parisiana enabled them to acquire the Olympia the following year – and three years later they found themselves in charge of the Folies Bergère.

The transition to spectacular revue in Paris did not happen overnight. In 1899 and 1900, it was the *cafés-concerts* alone which presented revues. Most of the better-known music-halls at that time were offering a programme very similar to those produced by provincial English variety theatres before World War Two; a kind of music-hall stock or repertory, with a permanent company changing the whole show each week or two. Basically the programmes were still a series of *tours de chant*, seasoned with specialities and followed by a comic playlet, the whole in some cases still being linked together with specially written material. Comparison with the standard American museum show or burlesque is inescapable. But once more the parallel is misleading.

The *form* of the entertainment might have been similar but its content was not. Turn-of-the-century burlesque shows were described by Fred McCloy, press agent for the Columbia Amusement Company, as:

> ... a conglomeration of filthy dialogue, libidinous scenes and licentious songs and dances with cheap, tawdry, garish and scant scenery and costumes ... in or near the slum spots in the larger cities ... dirty and unkempt, dismally lighted, and with no attempt at ventilation. They were allowed to exist without police interference along with the bawdy houses that infested the neighbourhoods. No woman ever crossed the thresholds of their doors, and male patronage was confined to shameless degenerates and to that other species of degenerate that sneaked in with concealed faces.

This describes 90 per cent of the burlesque business up to about 1900.

The Isola brothers continued to engage variety acts in the Marchand tradition, but in 1902 they commissioned Victor Cottens to write a revue. It was the first modern revue to be presented at the Folies Bergère and was billed simply as *La Revue des Folies Bergère*. This was the start of revue at the Folies Bergère as we know it today. The Folies Bergère began acquiring an international reputation as one of the major Parisian attractions, second only to the Eiffel Tower, and this could be directly attributable to the Isola brothers' innovation. It was a revue in six tableaux (there are over forty nowadays) in which the stars were La Belle Otero, Marguerite Deval, the comic Fugère, Maurel, Clémence de Pibrac, Anne Dancrey and the crooner Fragson, the pride of the *café-concert* (who was tragically murdered by his father). The revue was a triumph. Whilst some of the press announced that it was the first spectacle since *Place aux Jeunes* (Make Way For the Young) years earlier, other critics took unkindly to the advent of revue at the rue Richer. 'A *revue* at the Folies Bergère,' sniffed *Le Rire*: 'Ah, well, as far as revue goes, we've seen it all before.' But Cottens contradicted him by announcing a month later after the nightly packed houses that the new revue at the Folies Bergère was a work of art and that this time it had surpassed itself. Thereafter, the Isola brothers decided to repeat the formula each year by mounting similar revues in the spring, all of which turned out to be box-office successes. The rest of the season was given to variety for which the directors engaged the most famous personalities of the day.

The Isolas, who had always been driven by ambition, set their sights on a richer, more prestigious prize: they would be content with nothing less than the Paris Opéra itself. They sold the Folies to their administrator, Clément Bannel, made a gift of the Olympia lease to Jacques-Charles, and finally – because they sensed the music-hall image might spoil their chances of getting the Opéra – returned the Parisiana to Ruez from whom they had acquired it. The Isolas were granted directorships of the Opéra-

Comique. But, uneducated as they were, they were obliged to leave their affairs in the hands of their trusted accountant, Boucheron. All went well until he died – and then his successor absconded with millions and ruined them. Sacha Guitry, at that time married to Yvonne Printemps, organized a benefit performance to raise funds for the Isolas and, touched by his gesture, they offered him a gift of inestimable value – they revealed to him the secret of the Indian rope trick, which Guitry, together with the rest of the theatrical profession, had known for years. The Isolas were last heard of on the stage of the ABC music-hall in Paris between the wars, working as conjurers and jugglers.

Jacques-Charles, then working as general secretary for the Isolas, received the Olympia as a gift because the Boulevard des Italiens rents were so high that the lease was virtually unsalable. Having acquired the Folies Bergère's goodwill for a capital sum, for example, Clément Bannel, the Folies's company secretary, paid an annual rent of 78,000 francs (about $12,500 or £3,120 at the exchange rate then current). The Olympia, with far less accommodation in a smaller space, cost 360,000 francs (£14,400) a year – a prohibitive sum at a time when an income of 25,000 francs (about £1,000) secured for a senior French executive a large house in the country with a carriage, horses, a gardener and several living-in servants.

Jacques-Charles, who accepted this heavy commitment because it would give him the chance of staging his own revue (and because he had private information that a street-planning change would make the Olympia a more desirable site), was a complete man of the theatre. Some of his contemporaries worked like producers of films, assembling the finance, the creative talent and the performers, and letting them get on with it; others confined themselves to the director's role, imposing their own artistic concept on a prepared package. But Jacques-Charles had to be

ANNE
DANCREY

RE

in at every level of the production, advising, suggest-
ing, insisting. In his books on the music-hall, he
describes how the Isolas would make informal and
unexpected visits to their theatres on most nights – but
this was just to check that everyone was on his toes
and earning his money. It had nothing to do with the
quality of the show. He recalls his astonishment when,
shortly after he began working for the brothers,
'P. L. Flers came into the office one day carrying
three bound manuscripts. "I have brought you the
new Folies Bergère revue," Flers announced.' Shortly
afterwards, Landolff, the famous costumier, and
Menessier, the set designer, were ushered in. Jacques-
Charles expected the five men – the author, the two
designers and the Isolas – to sit around a table and
go through the book together, scene by scene, line
by line – the usual custom. But Vincent Isola simply
stood up, handed a copy to each of the new arrivals,
and said: 'Here, Messieurs, is the new revue. We
open in one month. Be sure everything is ready. So
far as money is concerned, pray discuss this with our
cashier, Boucheron.'

The third manuscript was given to Jacques-Charles
to pass on to the musical director – and the 'con-
ference' was at an end.

Jacques-Charles himself, formerly a cartoonist, a
theatrical gossip writer for *Gil Blas* and then a press
agent, favoured an approach that was very different.
His passion for personally supervising every detail
of a production infuriated many of the people he
worked with when he first began to direct. Costumiers were affronted when he insisted on accom-
panying them to choose materials; *décor* specialists
became irritated at his perfectionism. Even on first
nights, unlike his fellow impresarios, he was to be
seen, resplendent in white tie and tails, accepting
congratulations in a stage box.

Before the performance, however, he would be
found back-stage in his shirt-sleeves, overseeing the
show himself. 'Pace is everything in a revue,' he

would say. 'When *I* am in charge, I find on average that I can cut six minutes from the running time established by a stage manager.'

The curtain did not rise on Jacques-Charles's first revue at the Olympia until 1911. Before that, all the Parisian music-halls with properly equipped stages had switched to the extravaganza formula. Thus between 1901, when the Isolas took over the Folies Bergère, and 1906, when Chaveau and Cornuché transformed the Alcazar d'Eté and reopened with the revue *Vive Paris!*, the city was scintillating with talent of all kinds.

In 1905 the lease of the Folies Bergère fell into the hands of Paul Ruez, and in 1908 it went to Clément Bannel. The artists to appear at the Folies during Bannel's six years in office included Mistinguett, Yvonne Printemps, Charlie Chaplin, Antonet, Grock, Little Tich – and the youthful Maurice Chevalier. Chevalier had already started to make his name at the Eldorado and was classified as a comic. But the Folies Bergère was another matter and Bannel knew that he was taking a chance. A venue of international standing to which the public came from the four corners of the earth was hardly a testing ground for an easy comic capable of pleasing the patrons of L'Eldo, as it was known. After his début at the Folies Bergère, Chevalier was slated by Nozière, the critic of the *Figaro*: 'Who has engaged this laborious and painful comic to appear as the lead in first class production numbers?' Chevalier was saved by P. L. Flers, who took him under his wing and directed him in the winter revue in which the star was Jane Marnac. There, Chevalier was no longer subjected to criticism and began learning his job and building his act.

Before the 1914–18 war, a smart, ambitious youth was selling programmes at the Paris Olympia at which Jacques-Charles was presenting revue. A sympathetic personality, he would offer his programmes to ticket-holders as they entered the foyer. '*Il me coûte cinquante centimes,*' was his plaintive cry, and then he would continue, 'That is the price I pay, and that is the price I sell at. Nobody works without *some* profit; I leave it to your generosity to give me what you think I deserve – for the programme and my sweet smile!'

At the beginning of the First World War all the theatres in Paris closed, but after the battle of the Marne, Raphael Beretta took over the administration of the Folies Bergère as Bannel's successor. Beretta was said to have a flushed face, noble bearing, a large mouth – and little, if no means. He had been the conductor at La Scala music-hall in Paris and at the Ambassadeurs, and now war was over, having been *chef d'orchestre* of the Olympia, he conceived the idea of reopening the Olympia Theatre and called on the services of the astute young programme seller, Léon Volterra, who had saved a few thousand francs and became the backer of Beretta's enterprise. At the start, the landlord, the artists, and all concerned shared on a percentage basis, but within a very few weeks Beretta and Volterra were able to pay regular salaries, and within a year they bought the Olympia with their profits. A year later they took over the Folies Bergère as well as the Casino de Paris.

Before the war ended, the partnership split, and Volterra, with a fat sum of money in his pocket, deserted the Folies Bergère and took over the sole ownership of the Casino de Paris, in direct opposition to Beretta and the Folies Bergère, installing Jacques-Charles at the Casino de Paris as author and artistic director. First with Gaby Deslys, later with Mistinguett, Maurice Chevalier, Jane Marnac, the Dolly Sisters, and sumptuous spectacles, the Casino developed into a formidable rival to the Folies Bergère, and Volterra made a large fortune. He later took up racing in a big way with considerable success, having acquired *en bloc* from a bank the horses they held as security for a businessman whose empire had crumbled. It was Volterra, together with Jacques-Charles, who was to put pay to Beretta's reign at the Folies in 1917.

At the beginning of his spell with Volterra at the Folies Bergère, Beretta had succeeded in presenting sumptuous shows to which audiences arrived in abundance. He had financial security in the form of a sleeping partner, Jules Dumien, who backed his every move to the hilt. A bookmaker who was both uneducated and illiterate, Dumien had a remarkable penchant for figures. He had made his fortune on the tracks and established his theatrical connections as the Isola brothers' sleeping partner. It was through him that they had been able to build their empire so rapidly. But gullible as they were, the Isolas had decided to abandon Dumien when they moved over to the Opéra-Comique, considering this new, respectable venue to be out of his league. Dumien was vexed at the departure of the disloyal Isolas from the Folies Bergère, but they in turn were unable to coerce him with their customary camaraderie. Beretta himself refused to listen to Dumien, treating him with a certain disdain but continuing all the while to profit from his financial support.

Gaby Deslys

It was in 1917 that Volterra opened the Casino de Paris under his own management, with a spectacular revue written and staged by Jacques-Charles, entitled *Laissez-le Tomber!* (Drop him!), featuring the return to Paris of the exceptional Gaby Deslys. This revue proved to be such a triumph that the Folies Bergère audiences flocked to see it, resulting in a rapid fall in box-office receipts for the Folies. Dumien, who was naturally put out by the Folies Bergère's current financial decline, turned on Beretta, accusing him of mismanagement and of being incapable of presenting a revue to compete with the Casino. He set about removing Beretta from his post and suggested in no uncertain terms that he find a successor.

Paul Derval, under his real name Paul Pitron, had been a comedian but because of his passion for

spectacle had presented provincial theatre tours. He
had met Beretta by chance through their mutual
friendship with a pretty young comedienne who had
been Beretta's protégée. Derval engaged the young
lady for one of his tours and Beretta joined them.
After the tour had ended they went their separate
ways, but their friendship was cemented. When
Beretta took over the management of the Folies
Bergère and needed an assistant, he remembered his
young friend and over coffee in a restaurant drew
up an agreement with Derval:

> 'I want you to be my second-in-command,'
> Beretta said to me. 'What do you say?' He offered
> me a regular monthly salary, plus a percentage of
> the profits. I accepted. Over our coffee we ex-
> changed a little letter in lieu of contract and
> M. Beretta handed over the keys of his office.
>
> So it was that the next morning, to the stupe-
> faction of the entire staff, I walked into the offices
> of the Folies Bergère and briefly introduced myself
> as the new Assistant Director.

Paul Derval was elevated to administrator in 1918.
Thirty-three revues at the Folies Bergère were to be
staged in the fifty or so years of his reign until his
death in 1966. He enlisted the services of the brilliant
producer and author Louis Lemarchand, who continued in office until his retirement in the early 1930s.
Lemarchand was succeeded by Jean le Seyeux and
the former musical director of the Casino de Paris,
Maurice Hermite, in 1932.

Lemarchand gave the Folies revues an extraordinary luxury which could not be equalled
through the years. Even Ziegfeld in America, who
perhaps surpassed the revues in elegance, could not
attain their sumptuous look. Luxury became their
hallmark.

The Folies Bergère had a penchant for discovering
new talents and presenting them so fabulously as to
make stars of them, many of whom, as a conse-

FOLIES BERGÈRE

Y. PRINTEMPS

LA REVUE

quence, became national institutions. It attracted many 'straight' actresses and singers as well – artists such as the great prima ballerina Anna Pavlova, Yvonne Printemps, Gaby Deslys, Alice Delysia and Yvette Guilbert who were lured to the Folies by its glamour and high fees.

Yvonne Printemps, whose style of singing was the antithesis of Yvette Guilbert's, was one of the greatest French operetta singers. She began her career as a chorus-girl at the Folies Bergère at the age of twelve and became a unique singer who attracted world-wide recognition for her unfaltering vocal range. Her real name was Yvonne Wigniole and she was living alone with her ruined mother when P. L. Flers's wife managed to get her into the Folies Bergère where she was spoiled and coddled by the actors (Flers was one of the revue writers at the Folies). There, her career began and blossomed into fame as the audiences became charmed by her. Mistinguett remembers in her memoirs that in 1912, while she too was appearing at the Folies Bergère, little Yvonne 'came to my dressing-room for a snack and told me stories as delicious and dizzying as Yvonne herself'. That same year a critic who had heard Printemps sing, wrote: 'A nightingale does not a spring make but Miss Printemps sings like a nightingale.' *Conversation Piece*, a sentimental extravaganza set in the Regency period, was written and composed by Noël Coward for Yvonne Printemps. In it, playing in English for the first time, she portrayed Melanie, the little girl who falls in love with her elderly guardian, Paul. The latter was to be played by American actor Romney Brent until Noël Coward himself took over the role. The cast included Louis Hayward, George Sanders playing a Regency Rake, and Valerie Hobson was in the chorus. The successful run in 1934 only ended when Yvonne Printemps returned to Paris to fulfil a film commitment. Despite such enchanting music as 'I'll Follow my Secret Heart', sung by Printemps, it

Yvette Guilbert wearing the famous long black gloves.

closed after six months, still playing to packed houses, as no substitute for Printemps could be found. The entire production transferred to New York later that year with Pierre Fresnay (who subsequently married Yvonne Printemps after her marriage to Sacha Guitry had been dissolved), co-starring in the role of the guardian and Printemps in her original role.

But one of the most enduring figures of the stage to have evoked the spirit of Paris and the *vulgarité* of its inhabitants was Yvette Guilbert, the French *diseuse* who won an immense vogue by rendering songs drawn from Parisian lower-class life and from the humours of the Latin Quarter. She became the greatest singer of the period 1894 to 1914. The poet Aristide Bruant wrote many of her argot songs. Toulouse-Lautrec and Chéret created posters for her.

She won great acclaim at the Folies Bergère and continued her career well after World War One, at an advanced age still encountering success at the Alcazar and the Empire in Paris.

Before her début at the Folies Bergère in the early 1900s, she had appeared at the Ambassadeurs where the greatest names of *café-concert* appeared. 'She was number one and all the others more or less followed in her train,' recalls the critic Louis Léon Martin in his memoirs. 'She is the one who created the contemporary song. She sang without the explanatory gestures of her colleagues, immobile, underlining only the expression of her mouth from whence came an original diction, sharp, staccato yet clear, fascinating, carrying far, never letting a single syllable be drowned out.' After a modest beginning at the Eden and then at the Moulin Rouge, she enjoyed her first successes at the Divan Japonais, and in 1891 at the Petit Casino where she was depicted in posters by Toulouse-Lautrec and Chéret shown with her customary chignon and her traditional stage attire, including her famous long black gloves. These gloves, if we are to believe Xanroff (the author of *Le Fiacre*, which she performed later at the Folies in 1903), were adopted by her only to 'avoid periodic cleaning which she considered exorbitant' – at the time all singers wore white gloves.

She began at the Variétés as a show-girl, together with Cécile Sorel, later to become the famous Célimène of the Comédie Française. 'We were rich in hope and youth,' Yvette Guilbert wrote in her memoirs. Sorel was always given a costume which displayed her superb *poitrine*, but Yvette, thin as a rail above her waist, had shapely legs, so her costumes were carefully designed to show them.

'How long does it take an actress to get somewhere – to be able to make a decent living, as well as play good parts?' Yvette asked Zidler of the Moulin Rouge, who was her kind and wise friend and adviser from the earliest days of her struggle to keep her mother and herself until his death, by which time Yvette had become internationally famous.

'From ten to fifteen years,' came the discouraging reply.

'Your voice isn't good enough for operetta,' she was told by an actor named Barol when he asked her one day why she didn't try the *café-concert*. 'But you could start with four times your *théâtre* salary at L'Eldorado,' often styled *La Comédie Française de la Chanson*, where later Mistinguett became and remained the darling of the establishment for several years. And so Yvette gave an audition to the directress of L'Eldorado, Madame Allemand, who was to take over the Folies Bergère and to install Edouard M. Marchand, as artistic director. She offered to pay Yvette six hundred francs per month.

Waiting in the wings for her first appearance, Yvette heard the tremendous applause for a very gross comedienne, the last word in banal vulgarity, who was at thàt moment on the stage. At the end of the turn, the more the applause gained strength, the more Yvette's courage failed her. There was a male singer before her, and then Yvette took the stage, to be greeted with yells of: 'Oh! Oh! She's skinny – she looks as if she's left her tits in her trunk!'

The uproar was so bad that she had to quit the stage without getting through one song. The director was kind but endeavoured to impress upon her that the music-hall was not the Comédie Française. 'My stage isn't a drawing-room. You can't sing in a music-hall standing still, without moving your arms or legs.' She took his advice.

The history of Yvette Guilbert in the music-hall is unique. She invaded a territory where grossness and vulgarity were rampant, with songs of Xanroff, Richepin, Aristide Bruant, Jean Lorrain, Maurice Donnay, and other men of letters, and she certainly made no concessions to her audiences.

For the last years of the nineteenth century Yvette Guilbert exercised her supreme art, mostly in establishments controlled by such people as a butter merchant, a *limonadière* from Marseilles, a washerwoman from Montmartre, an ex-dishwasher, a former tailor, and a bricklayer, who, on paying her, commented sadly: 'A thousand francs for singing thirty minutes! How many bricks would I have to lay for that price?'

She referred to this period of her life as martyrdom. Her success with the public left her cold, and when illness enabled her to cancel her music-hall contracts she determined to realize her ambition to put, at last, *la chanson de France* on its proper pedestal, thus beginning, after much study and research, those unforgettable renderings by the supreme artist.

In complete contrast to this artist whose *vulgarité* was her hallmark, came another great star of the period who was one of the few of this era to have made her reputation for chic. Alice Delysia appeared at the Folies Bergère in the 1908/9 season, five years after Yvette Guilbert's début there. Born in Paris in 1889, Delysia made her first appearance at the Moulin Rouge, in 1903, in the chorus of *The Belle of New York*. She played in various Parisian variety theatres before leaving for New York where she appeared at Dalys Theatre with Edna May, and returned to Paris for a series of revues including those at the Folies Bergère. She left the stage for three years after her Folies Bergère triumphs, returning only for a few Olympia revues before making her London début.

She became an overnight star in the West End in 1914 at the Ambassador's Theatre in the C. B. Cochran revue *Odds and Ends*, with Mistinguett's former partner Max Dearly, where she was received by audiences and critics alike as 'incomparable'. She continued to appear at this theatre – in 1915 in *More* and in 1916 in *Pell Mell* with Nat D. Ayer (the actor and famous composer of many hit songs including 'If you were the only girl in the World') – and elsewhere in London and New York for the next few

years. While in New York in 1925, Cochran wired
asking whether she would appear in his forthcoming
revue at the London Pavillion, *On with the Dance*,
and she wired back, 'Of course I play at dear old
Pav. How funny man you to ask. Pay me what you
like.' Among her fellow artists in this show were
her friend Douglas Byng, Ernest Thesiger, Hermione
Baddeley and the all-famous Cochran Young Ladies.
The hit number (a 'first' for a young composer
named Noël Coward) in this revue was 'Poor little
Rich Girl', which she put over superbly. Her delightful sense of comedy, her essentially Gallic charm, her
'naughtiness' which today would hardly cause the
flicker of an eyelid, her wonderful voice with its
ringing high notes, and above all her indisputable
'star' quality appealed enormously to British
audiences. She was perhaps the only French star to
have been taken to the hearts of a British public who
have seldom warmed to French entertainers.

The great danseur noble and international choreographer Sir Anton Dolin, who was a member of
Diaghilev's company and appeared for many seasons
in Paris, remembers Alice Delysia with affection:

Alice Delysia

I adored Delysia. She was a divine artist. I saw
her in practically every show she was in, in
London. I was playing in Brighton for a Christmas
season in 'Alice Through the Looking Glass' and
afterwards we had the most lovely supper at the
hotel where I was staying. I ordered lobster which
she loved even at that time of night; she sang at
that table, and even in those last years of her life
she still had the most beautifully pitched voice.

She tried to commit suicide not long before she
died. She was found in her little flat in Brighton
(where she lived throughout the seventies after
the death of her husband Rene Kolb Bernard at
their home in the South of France), luckily by
Douglas Byng, who was very kind to her and
looked after her. She had been despondent and

felt she didn't want to go on with life. Evelyn Laye and I went to see her in the Brighton hospital and we asked her how she felt.

'*Très mal,*' Delysia replied.

'What would you like?' I asked.

'I would love to eat caviar,' she said simply in her engaging French accent. I telephoned Fortnum and Mason when I got back to London and they sent some along to her. Douglas Byng, thoughtful as ever, provided the lemon.

As a performer she had great sex appeal. She was a professional in every sense of the word. She had a lovely voice, was a fine actress and a great beauty. She had it all. When Cochran went bankrupt she sold all her jewels and gave all the money to him. People don't do things like that these days – but she did.

In the song Evelyn Laye sang in *Phil the Fluter*, the sentiment applies: 'They don't make them like that any more!'

After Delysia's 1908/9 season at the Folies Bergère, Paris was invaded by the much-acclaimed and welcomed Russian ballet. The company was headed by Nijinsky, Karsavina, and the great prima ballerina Anna Pavlova, who was to appear at the Folies Bergère shortly afterwards.

Anna Pavlova was born in St Petersburg on 31 January 1881. Her Jewish mother was a laundress and her unknown father a peasant. She was a graduate of the Russian Imperial Ballet School and one of the last five ranking ballerinas of the Maryinski Theatre. Only after seven years of study and triumphing in *Swan Lake* and *Giselle* was she named 'prima ballerina' (nowadays a term loosely used to describe almost any ballerina who appears as soloist). Pavlova was the first great star to leave the Tsarist confines and toured Scandinavia one summer, forfeiting her pension for so doing. The Scandinavians had never before seen such exquisite dancing.

The short tour through Scandinavia gave her a taste for the outside world and in 1909 she followed Diaghilev to Paris to dance opposite Nijinsky in the initial, legendary season at the Théâtre du Châtelet. Their waltz in *Les Sylphides* was the lightest, most aerial and brilliant dancing ever to be seen by the human eye. But, dissatisfied with her position in the company, she soon withdrew. Her reception in Paris, however, was rapturous.

No one was prepared for the overwhelming success of that first performance of Diaghilev's Ballets Russes on 19 May 1909, despite the advance rumours, the feverish anticipation and the general excitement of the proposed season. Diaghilev had decided to bring the magnificent dancers of the Imperial Russian Ballet, then at its height, to Paris, where ballet had become a trivial appendage to the Opera House. But with the unexpected death of his patron the Grand Duke Vladimir, his Russian subsidies evaporated. The problem was money, a problem that was always to haunt him. Diaghilev set out to conquer Paris; but to realize his dream he bargained, lied, broke promises, stormed, bullied, cajoled, charmed and mesmerized. He guaranteed money he did not have, then scurried about to raise the money he had guaranteed. The magician did it all with mirrors. Even before the money was in his hands, he grandly ordered the Théâtre du Châtelet to be redecorated from the proscenium arch to the topmost gallery.

But Diaghilev's financial machinations were trivial compared with the pure gold he produced that night. It was a revelation to see the swift beauty of the young ballerinas and the challenging strength of the male dancers as they stamped out the rhythms of the Polovtsian Dances from Borodin's *Prince Igor*.

An eye-witness recounts Pavlova's performance:

She was small, about five feet. She wore a size one-and-a-half slipper, but her feet and hands were large in proportion to her height. Her hand could cover her whole face. Her trunk was small and stripped of all anatomy but the ciphers of adolescence, her arms and legs relatively long, the neck extraordinarily long and mobile. All her gestures were liquid and possessed of an inner rhythm that flowed to inevitable completion with the finality of architecture or music. Her arms seemed to lift not from the elbow or the arm socket, but from the base of the spine. Her legs seemed to function from the waist. When she bent her head her whole spine moved and the motion was completed from the length of the arm through the elongation of her slender hand and the quivering, reaching fingers. I believe there has never been a foot like hers, slender, delicate and of such an astonishing aggressiveness when she arched as to suggest the ultimate in human vitality. Without in any way being sensual, being, in fact, almost sexless, she suggested all exhilaration, gaiety and delight. She jumped, and we broke bonds with reality. We flew. We hung over the earth, spread in the air as we do in dreams, our hands turning in the air as in water – the strong, forthright, taut, plunging leg balanced on the poised arc of the foot, the other leg stretched to the horizon like the wing of a bird. We lay balancing, quivering, turning, and all things were possible, even to us, the ordinary people.

Like Nijinsky, but in a very different way, Anna Pavlova has become a unique figure in the twentieth-century ballet. Although to this day her name is synonymous with 'Russian Ballet', she was never a member of the Diaghilev Ballet in the true sense. She made a few appearances with it as a guest artist. Technically she was flawless. As an actress-*danseuse* she was unsurpassed, and this was no doubt the reason for the legendary '*Dying Swan*' solo, created for her in 1905 by Michel Fokine to the music composed by Saint-Saëns. She shared with Nijinsky that rare ability of *becoming*, instead of *acting* the character, but she also had tremendous theatrical flair.

Forming her own company, Pavlova began the series of world tours which she continued until her death. Before World War One, she returned regularly to the Maryinski Theatre in St Petersburg. She appeared in all the principal countries of North

Anna Pavlova with her beloved pet swan, Jack, in 1925.

and South America, Europe, Africa and the Orient, bringing the art of ballet to numerous communities where it was unknown, inspiring many young dancers who have become international stars of the ballet today. This travel, however, was an essential part of the dancers' survival, for opera houses throughout the world in those days had very short seasons – perhaps six weeks a year – and the artists had no alternative but to travel if they wished to continue their craft – and to eat. Pavlova was acclaimed wherever she went. She was, however, canny enough to surround herself with inferior (and lowly paid!) dancers in order to appear even greater than she really was. When she drew all London to the Palace Theatre in 1910, Pavlova continued to remain aloof from the Diaghilev Ballets Russes, and with the then unknown Mikhail Mordkin as her partner, and a small *corps de ballet*, she proved one of the greatest attractions in the history of the Palace Theatre.

Her appearances at the Folies Bergère were received with similar enthusiasm, but she suffered immeasurable pain when she came off stage: 'Many is the time I saw the great Pavlova in her dressing-room at the Folies Bergère,' Paul Derval remembered, 'her face twisted with pain, not daring to remove her ballet shoes, so bruised and bleeding were the feet inside them.'

Erté recalls working with her:

I designed Pavlova's costumes in Paris, in 1918, for a *divertissement* in which she danced the role of Autumn in 'The Four Seasons'. I also designed her costume for a gavotte in that same production. This was after she had left Diaghilev and formed her own company. Her Dying Swan was absolutely divine. I first saw it from my mother's box in Russia at the Maryinski Theatre. Her movements were so continuous and fluid that she appeared to have no bones! She was the only ballerina who was the *real* Dying Swan; she was, without doubt, the greatest dancer I've ever seen. She was much better than Ulanova, and although Karsavina was superlative, she was not as fantastic as Pavlova, whom I saw for the last time at the Pavilion d'Armide dancing one of her most famous roles, *Sylphides*.

As a person, working with her, designing her costumes and conducting her fittings, I found her to be perfectly charming. She had a very gentle, soft nature.

Her repertoire consisted chiefly of classic ballets, including *Chopiniana*, *Don Quixote* and *Coppelia*, but her favourite ballets were *Giselle* and *The Dying Swan*.

The few ballets Pavlova herself created were neither greatly received nor, unfortunately, have they lived on.

She made her home in London with her husband and manager, Victor Dandre, and died at The Hague at an early age – a week before her fiftieth birthday – on 23 January 1931.

The French revue singer and dancer Gaby Deslys made her début in Paris in 1898. By 1903 her reputation had become firmly established, rendering 'point' numbers, and she became the greatest French music-hall star of her day, with Mistinguett alone as her closest rival. She triumphed at the Folies Bergère, personifying the period with her geniality and stylishness. After her New York début she returned to Paris in 1917 with a fortune in jewels (donated largely by her greatest admirer, the King of Portugal).

Her brown hair dyed a conventional blonde, her Marseilles accent sprinkled with English intonations – a new snobbery – she was heralded by a fanfare of publicity. She also brought back several of her successful New York musical numbers, and that February the Folies-Marigny won her from compet-

Erté's costume design for Gaby Deslys.

ing music-halls at a cost of 200,000 francs, an enormous salary for Paris. She became the first American jazz-band exponent to appear in the French capital, succeeded years later by Josephine Baker in *La Revue Nègre*.

Together with her jewels, Deslys brought along with her a dark-haired young man who danced as naturally as most people breathe – and with tremendous style. This young American of Hungarian descent played an important part both in her career and her affections. They became the most celebrated couple ever to appear on the music-hall stage (with the major exception of Mistinguett and Chevalier). His name was Harry Pilcer of 'I'm just wild about Harry' fame. Their act was the first battery of jazz to appear in Europe when they appeared in a rag-time band with the enthusiastic ballad, 'Allo, my Dearie'. The band's instruments ranged from saxophones to revolver shots. And for the first time a music-hall actress appeared on stage, smothered in plumes and feathers, bejewelled like a queen, performing dances 'of an almost insane ferocity'. Her Gaby Glide swept through Paris over-night.

Jean Cocteau was present at one of their perform-ances:

> On the right of the little black-coated group there was a barman of sound effects in a gilt pergola full of bells, triangles, boards and motorcycle horns. With these he mixed cocktails, adding from time to time a dash of cymbals, all the while rising from his seat, posturing and smiling vacuously. Mr Pilcer, in tails, thin and rouged, and Mlle Gaby Deslys, like a big ventriloquist's doll, with a porce-lain complexion, corn-coloured hair and a gown with ostrich feathers, danced to this hurricane of rhythm and drumbeats of a kind of domesticated cataclysm which left them completely drunk and dazzled under the streaming glare of six air-raid searchlights. The house stood and applauded, roused from its torpor by this extraordinary number, which is to the frenzy of Offenbach as a tank is to an 1870 *calèche*.

The performance described by Cocteau took place at the Casino de Paris in the revue *Laissez-le Tomber!* which was nicknamed 'The Ladder Revue' because for the first time nudes climbed up and down a ladder thirty feet high. This was a far cry from the first appearance of a nude at the Folies Bergère five years earlier, in 1912.

When Gaby Deslys left the revue for another engagement, she was succeeded by Mistinguett who not only inherited her role on the stage with Harry Pilcer, but the one in his affections as well. They were to become inseparable when her affair with Chevalier broke up. It was said that she took him on the rebound. Mistinguett was greatly impressed with Gaby Deslys, as well as with the profusion of ostrich feathers, satins, nudes, monumental sets and spectacular transformation scenes in the show, as she records:

> Though it is true that I never imitated anybody, this did not prevent me from eyeing what Gaby Deslys bought, and buying what she had her eye on. It began with her chemises in the rue de Douai, and ended up with her dancing partner. He had caught my eye when I first saw him, very much as he had caught hers in New York. Pilcer was very much in love with her by this time, but Gaby was never short of swains. The most famous of her loves was Manoel of Portugal, who lost his crown for her, so they say. However, there is a story that Manoel suddenly put in an appearance at a restaurant where Gaby Deslys was dining with a party of friends. Gaby turned white.
>
> 'What do I do now?' she muttered. 'We've never even met. They're going to call my bluff.'
>
> Manoel walked calmly over to the table and addressed one of the party.
>
> 'Will you introduce me to Mademoiselle Deslys?' he said. 'I should be happy to ratify this most entrancing of falsehoods.'
>
> Poor Gaby, she died, still in her thirties, leaving all her money to the poor of Marseilles. Harry Pilcer never forgot her. He had a chapel built to her memory in his villa and on the altar lit by candles and heaped with flowers could be seen a portrait of Gaby Deslys.

Sir Anton Dolin also remembers her:

> I saw Gaby Deslys at the Globe Theatre, which was a rather daring thing to do, but my mother thought it would be good for my education to see Harry Pilcer do his drunkard's dance on the staircase, which was very famous. Afterwards, allowed by my mother who waited at a café around the corner, I went back and waited outside

the stage door for Gaby Deslys to come out. There
was this great white Rolls outside the door and
out she came; it was after a matinée and she was
screaming for Harry who was dallying in the
theatre somewhere. They were going back to the
house they had in Knightsbridge. I was lucky
enough to get her autograph before she swept off
in the Rolls.

But I knew Harry Pilcer well. When Gaby died,
he was left a little money. He was a great favourite
in Cannes. He ran the Palm Beach Casino and
whenever I wanted a table I just rang and he gave
it to me, but as I couldn't afford to pay those
prices I always went as his guest. He was a very
kind person, and we could all see exactly why she
adored him.

Of the great clowns, Footitt, Chocolat, Antonet,
Grock and Bagessen were the most popular to appear
at the Folies Bergère. The first permanent duo of a
clown and an Auguste was probably the twosome
of Footitt and his partner Chocolat. They first
appeared at the Nouveau Cirque in 1889 and remained successful there for fourteen years, followed
by a season in 1905 at the Folies. Henri Thétard, in
his history of the circus, described Footitt as, 'dressed
in a bouffant costume and a pointed hat, gaunt,
athletic, a hard look on his face, his hair on end, a
grimacing mouth, he was the accomplished Anglo-
Saxon clown, the king of violent burlesque, the
"knock-about". Chocolat, his partner, a great bewildered black man, was the most fantastic receiver
of slaps and kicks on the behind one could imagine.'
After twenty years of this routine, Footitt tried with
his sons to open a circus, and later a bar, but both
ventures failed. He died in 1921 at the age of fifty-
seven.

Antonet occupies a central place in the annals of
the circus. 'The very utterance of his name brings
to mind the superb elegance and demeanour of the

white clown,' notes Tristan Rémy. This opinion was shared by Henri Thétard: 'His play was subtle, burlesque without being ludicrous, cutting but not nasty. He seemed to be a well-bred eccentric, a somewhat extravagant fellow, viewing his partner's doltishness with an excess of indulgence.' The jaunty clown (that is how Serge salutes him) was born in Brescia, Italy, in 1872. His real name was Umberto Guillaume. The third generation descendant of a great circus family, Antonet was at one time or another a circus rider, jumping jack, clown and even a bull-fighter. It was in America, while he was the artistic director of the San Martin Theatre, that he met Grock, who became his partner for seven years.

They first appeared together at the Folies in 1910.

A keen theatre-goer describes Grock's performance:

> He took a minute violin out of an enormous violin-case, played a few delightful variations on it and sat down at the piano. From then on, things started happening. The piano stool was set too high and too far away, so Monsieur Grock had to tug painfully at the massive grand piano to bring it closer to the stool. Then he sat down and played beautifully. After that, he quarrelled with his partner, tore off the piano-top, slid around on it like a toboggan, sat down on the back of a chair, fell off and got up again.
>
> Grock's voice seemed to wander about inside him. Sometimes it was in his nose, sometimes in his throat, sometimes lower down; he had all the ventriloquist's tricks at his finger-tips. *'Pourquoa? Sans blague! . . .'* was the famous catch-phrase in his French act which he toured for several decades and brought to a pitch of rare perfection. The character he portrayed was his own double. He didn't have to act a part. He was the character, the part himself. There were Polichinelle, Arlequin and Pierrot: now there was Grock.

Born Charles Adrien Wettach in 1880 near Reconvillier, Switzerland, Grock's blunders with piano and violin became proverbial and many clowns adopted his format. His father, a watchmaker, was an amateur acrobat, and his son grew up with such a love of the sawdust ring that he was allowed to spend each summer with a circus, where he performed first as a tumbler and then as a violinist, pianist and xylophonist. When he was nineteen, Grock clowned in a café, but the draw of the circus proved irresistible, though it brought him a wandering life of hardship from Hamburg to Bucharest. He then became a partner of a clown named Brick, and changed his name to Grock in 1903. Together they appeared in France, North Africa and South America. When Brick married, Grock joined the celebrated Antonet. In Berlin, appearing on a stage instead of in an arena, they failed at first, but by mastering the stage technique they obtained, through C. B. Cochran, an engagement at the Palace Theatre, London, in 1911. Two years later, Grock, with an anonymous partner, perfected those adventures of a simpleton among musical instruments that made audiences in many cities laugh – at his wonder as to where the strings had gone when he held his fiddle the wrong side up, and at his labours to sit nearer the piano by pushing it toward the stool.

Grock, passionately devoted to the profession which he entered at an early age, had been a tumbler, tight-rope walker, juggler and snakeman. Besides his remarkable talent for mime, he was a musician, acrobat, actor and author, and he could speak a dozen languages. He left his audiences convulsed with laughter. His act was the longest ever seen, either on stage or in the arena, but no one ever objected.

After their separation and until his death in 1935, Antonet continued his career in the circus. Grock left the circus proper to stage his celebrated musical clown act, a number which made him famous world-wide. Between the two wars Grock returned to the stage of the Folies Bergère. His farewell performance took place in Hamburg in 1954 and he died at Imperia, Italy, in 1959 at the villa he had built for himself – the most eccentric place imaginable.

Another great clown to appear at the Folies Bergère was Bagessen, a Dane, who was billed as '*Le Casseur d'Assiettes*' and originated the act involving the breaking of dozens of plates. There was no act in circus, music-hall or theatre which provoked such continuous laughter as Bagessen's. He was a sad figure in his shabby frock-coat and little bowler hat as he started to tidy up the room in which there stood a dresser. A comfortable-looking, plump housewife gave him his instructions and he started to arrange the plates and dishes. In his two arms he lifted a huge pile of plates and hugged them to his chest. As he staggered across the room, one plate started to slide from the pile; an agonized expression came over his face, and, horror upon horror, another slid out. His efforts to recover them were frantic, and he was successful, but, in saving them, a cascade – seemingly never-ending – flowed from his arms and crashed onto the floor in hundreds of pieces. By this time the audience was rolling with laughter. Bagessen drew himself up, glaring furiously at the audience for laughing, and then, further enraged by his wife, who raised a broom as if to strike him, he took the two plates he had saved and deliberately broke them. The laughter became a roar of thunder. Bagessen dashed for another pile of plates, higher than the first, but he slipped, and his hands stuck to a fly-paper. His efforts to extricate one hand – then the other – sometimes both, worked up to a one-man all-in wrestling match. He must have established a record for continuous laughter for the two or three minutes of this fly-paper routine. The act got funnier; ridding himself at last from the fly-paper, he seized pile upon pile of plates. By this time the plates seemed alive – possessed by the devil. The more he attempted to balance the pile or to recover one escaping, the more acrobatic the plates became; they danced, they slid, they pirouetted, they turned somersaults. Despite the audience's laughter, they prayed that he might be spared further disaster. Momentarily there seemed a glimmer of hope as he almost rescued a plate; of pride, as he appeared to save a pile from cascading; of despair and sheer humility. When at last the poor little man, hypnotized as if by a superb set of china on the top of the dresser, advanced towards it, the audience choked – it had reached the limit of laughter.

Although the plate-smashing and the fly-paper incidents were copied, and variations of the fly-paper are current in shows today, none could be funnier than the original. No imitation of Bagessen has ever approached his act.

Bagessen travelled all over the world, breaking thousands of plates and getting stuck to fly-paper, and earning a fortune for his efforts. He ultimately reached the goal of so many clowns: he retired to a farm in his native Denmark.

Little Tich, who was more of a clown and a comedian than Bagessen or Grock, was one of the great figures in the early days of music-hall. His long-soled shoes, one of his cleverest inventions, enabled him to bend over and almost touch the ground. He was a deformed dwarf whose fantastic tramp's get-up was the delight of Paris music-hall audiences. Pieral, another dwarf, dressed up, like Little Tich, as a *prima donna* or Spanish dancer. Joe Jackson, a clown who was one of the greatest victims of plagiarism, played a tramp who stole a bicycle, but maintained his high salary despite cheap copyists; he used to appear on stage alone, using objects as partners, in the way that Little Tich did. But the artist who was more influenced by Little Tich than anyone else was Charlie Chaplin.

Touring with Fred Karno's Troupe, Charlie Chaplin made his début at the Folies Bergère in 1909 at the age of fourteen, where he was paid £6 a week for the ten-week season. He was a small, thin lad, almost cadaverous, with long hair and a sulky expression. He staggered about the stage in a frock-coat several sizes too large for him, tripping over himself in a frenzy of inspired buffoonery, and soon all Paris was flocking to see him. It is no exaggeration to say that but for that visit to the Folies Bergère, Charles Chaplin would not have become the Charlie Chaplin the world came to know and admire. It was in Paris that he met the two men who had a predominant influence on his career: Max Linder and Little Tich. Max Linder was the greatest French comedian of his day. Chaplin would dash in to see his act whenever he could. He learnt all his gags, his wistful good humour, his pathetic helplessness, and when Hollywood made him an offer two years later, he declared, 'I want to be America's Max Linder.'

Chaplin adopted Little Tich's walking stick, his enormous boots and his little bowler hat. In fact, it was at the Folies Bergère that Chaplin discovered his famous silhouette.

A few years later, after the first war, Little Tich returned to appear at the Folies Bergère. In the meantime, Charlie Chaplin's antics had set the whole world laughing and the dwarf who had been so adulated ten years before was slated for imitating Charlie Chaplin!

To give an insight into the appearance, performance and appreciation of Little Tich's impact at the Folies Bergère, we have the recollection of the great showman and impresario, the late C. B. Cochran:

> I have thought that the French went to excess in their extravagant acclaim of Little Tich. It should be realized, however, that Paris saw Little Tich at his very best: as an incomparable gnome of fantasy. Even in England he had not then begun to follow the technique of Dan Leno and other comedians of this epoch by making a long monologue between a short verse and a short chorus the outstanding feature of his turn. Although he chatted away glibly in French, with the accent of Birmingham, he relied mainly on indescribable and truly inimitable movements. Got up as a grand lady, in court dress with a long train, he hurled himself upon the stage of the Folies Bergère.
>
> '*Je m'appelle Clarice,*' said Tich, with that chuckle which I recall when I hear Charlie McCarthy, the human wooden doll of Edgar Bergen. Continuing, in French – more or less: 'I am an admiral's daughter – I've just come from the court ball – oh, my success! – what a *succès fou! – beaucoup de succès* – very nice!' – the 'very nice!' always in English.

Charlie Chaplin adopting Little Tich's image.

Little Tich, slated.

Little Tich, the
originator of the
Chaplin silhouette.

By this time the customers in the seats of the
Folies Bergère were rolling in the aisles, and the
ladies of the promenade had left the bars and
crowded to get a view of the stage. Tich waved
his large feather fan, got tied up in his train (as
Lupino Lane did in the peer's robe in *Me and My
Girl*), and by this time everything done or said
by the strange little figure was greeted with shouts
of laughter. Old Parisians tell me that the success
of Tich as a laughter-maker has never been
equalled in Paris.

To the Parisian, Tich was the reincarnation of
the dwarf court jesters of the Middle Ages – the
little English Don Antonio of Velasquez; the poet,
Jean Lorraine, saw in him all the grotesquerie of
the low-life characters from the novels of Dickens.
Toulouse-Lautrec drew him in his costume of a
danseuse espagnole; it was in the epoch of La Belle
Otero, which intensified the drollery of the
inhuman caricature. La Loïe Fuller had recently
captivated Paris with *La danse serpentine*, and when
Tich, at the end of his turn, appeared in the
voluminous skirts of La Loïe, chasing the coloured
lights from the projectors, the delight of the spectators surpassed all bounds.

Tich was the King of Paris.

Other great stars to have appeared at this amazing
Palace of Pleasure include Mistinguett and Maurice
Chevalier – about whom more later; female imper-
sonator Barbette; Raimu, a singer from Marseilles
who was to become the resident comedian at the
Folies and subsequently to achieve fame in the plays
and films of Marcel Pagnol; the Hungarian girls
known as The Dolly Sisters; Fernandel, who became
one of Mistinguett's partners and whose toothy grin
was to become as well known as the Eiffel Tower;
Jean Gabin, who started as a chorus boy at the Folies
Bergère in 1912; Arletty, who began her career as a
model with Poiret; and Josephine Baker, the *célèbre*

UNE REVUE
AUX
FOLIES
BERGÈRE

Artists appearing at the Folies Bergère during La Belle Epoque.

noire, the greatest female since Mistinguett to appear at the Folies Bergère.

But with the advent of the First World War came change – change even at the Folies Bergère. Audiences began to seek new and different approaches to entertainment. The stars began to diminish and were to be replaced by mammoth, extravagant spectacles comprising breathtaking tableaux – and the fabulous nude dancers and show-girls who were to introduce to the audiences escapist glamour seen only in their dreams. Although shocking through their unexpected, surprise appearances, they were *never* vulgar or offensive in their presentations to either locals or tourists from that day to this.

A new style evolved through Derval; he abolished the ladies of the *promenoir* and introduced the nude. From programme notes we find recorded some of the artists to have appeared at the Folies Bergère by the turn of the century:

JUGGLERS: Minquevalli, Kara; *ACROBATS:* Leona Dare, the Scheffers, the Kremo, the Craggs. *CLOWNS:* Griffiths, Huline. *COMEDIANS:* Little Tich, Bagessen and more recently, Grock. *PANTOMIMES:* Hanlon-Lees and their famous pantomimes. Martinetti with Robert Macaire. *DANCERS/SINGERS:* La Tortajada, Guerrero, Cavalieri, the Barrison sisters, Judic and Yvette Guilbert. La Belle Otero. Severin.
A particular notice for Loïe Fuller, who for two years attracted all of Paris to the Folies Bergère. The ballets leave their important mark on the Folies from the reign of Sari: Carbagnatti, Brambilla, Stichel, Pauline Leveque, Lola Rouvier, Campana follow the grands ballet of Désormes and Louis Ganne which starred Margyl, Cléo de Mérode, Yetta, Rianza, Napierkowska, Pavlova and the fabulous tableaux which included Liane de Pougy, Emilienne d'Alençon and the protégées of Charles Desbecque, all of whom are part of the history of the Folies Bergère.

3
The Nudes

The Folies Bergère was the first music-hall in the world to present a naked woman on the stage, and thus shocked – and excited – a nation, and attracted visitors from all over the world.

Under the management of the Allemands, their nephew Edouard Marchand introduced the first 'girls' to the Folies. In 1894 the vogue of the strip-tease seized the music-halls of Paris and the Folies took it over and elaborated on it to the extent that, in the twentieth century, its reputation for 'les girls' overshadows its many other beautiful performances.

It was on 30 November 1886 that Madame Allemand, the proprietor of the Folies Bergère, staged, at a relatively modest outlay, the first music-hall revue entitled *Place aux Jeunes* (Make Way for the Young). But it was in fact only at the beginning of this century, especially at the Folies Bergère under the direction of the Isola brothers, that the revue developed and led to the advent of the first nude to be seen on stage by the public.

The origin of striptease is said to be the *Bal des Quat'z Arts* at midnight on 9 February 1893. A group of Paris students had rented the Moulin Rouge for their celebrated Four Arts Ball, by tradition a night of orgiastic frenzy, drunkenness and pandemonium. On this occasion the personal attractions of two girls were debated by their admirers. The girls then stood on tables for their ankles to be judged. Competition extended to their legs, thighs, hips, buttocks, breasts and shoulders. One girl ended up completely naked.

Next morning, however, Senator Béranger, a rather pompous, lugubrious fellow whose main aim was to question the morals of the inhabitants and who had formed a League of Decency to prevent dogs from urinating in the street (not on the grounds of sanitation so much as an example of indecent exposure), set to work to trace those responsible for the display at the Moulin Rouge. Several weeks later, Mona and two or three of her admirers were brought before a Paris court. The magistrates were lenient and fined them a mere 100 francs each. The Latin Quarter, however, was not amused.

Hearing that effigies of himself (labelled 'The Father of Decency') were hanging from lamp-posts on the Boulevard St Michel, Senator Béranger summoned the police and in the fracas that followed an innocent young man quietly drinking Pernod at a pavement café on the Place de la Sorbonne was fatally wounded. As a result of the ensuing riots, the Chief of Police was dismissed, and the students decided that it was their inalienable right to enjoy the sight of a naked woman if they so wished.

The following day the entire Latin Quarter was up in arms. Gangs of students bore down on the Prefecture of Police and laid siege to it. The youth of Paris was in open revolution. Troops were called in from the provinces; the police, vastly out-numbered, held off the assailants as best they could; the Prefect of Police was dismissed. Order was restored, but in championing Mona, the first 'nude' in Parisian show business, the students had proved once again that the French capital had the democratic right to choose *liberté* – in any sense it wished.

Paul Derval takes up the story:

Mona's lovely body had fired other imagina-tions besides those of her student audiences. Direc-tors of music-halls suddenly woke up to the fruitful possibilities of a new form of entertainment of which the public would never tire – the nude. The stumbling block was, of course, the ubiquitous Senator Béranger. How was one to safeguard oneself against the fulminations of the League of Decency?

The answer to this teasing question was forth-coming the following spring. On 13 March 1894, in a poky little music-hall in the rue des Martyrs boasting the exotic name of Le Divan Fayouau, a short sketch entitled *Le Coucher d'Yvette* (Yvette Goes to Bed) was hailed with uproarious en-thusiasm by an excited house.

The stratagem was a simple one. Since it was out of the question to exhibit an entirely naked woman, and since an almost naked woman is never quite naked enough, evidently the thing to do was to rely on the spectator's lubricous imagination by presenting him with the spectacle of an artist undressing by easy stages. Imagination being always one jump ahead of reality, the spectator would see her as already naked when she had not yet removed her last drapes.

Striptease was born; the vogue caught on like wildfire and soon every variety house in Paris had its own version of *Le Coucher d'Yvette* and titles like *Le Bain de Maid* (The Maid Takes a Bath), *Suzanne et la Grande Chaleur* (Suzanne in the Heatwave) and *Liane chez le Médecin* (Liane at the Doctor's) on the bills were enough to pack the house.

In a sketch called *La Puce* (The Flea), at the Casino, Angèle Hérard went so far as to present herself as the victim of a tiresome itch, the cause of which she proceeded to investigate with the thoroughness her audience expected of her. The popularity of this somewhat repulsive little mime was enormous: Angèle Hérard went on a tour of Europe, where her success varied with the dictates of each country's laws of decency. In Berlin she was allowed to remove her stays, but was obliged to keep them on in Vienna. Munich permitted her to scratch her knee: Budapest forbade it.

'The Folies Bergère,' Derval continues, 'naturally enough, had its own variation of *Le Coucher d'Yvette*, but the shows never sank to the level of *La Puce*. Little by little a revue formula was taking shape, embracing all kinds of acts from singers to prize-fighters, without putting so much emphasis on the nudist aspect.'

Shortly before the turn of the century, French bourgeois society had been moulded by an academism enamoured of antique culture. In the salons as well as the brothels were reconstructed scenes of Greek Shepherds or the rape of the Sabine women; all this, admittedly or not, was just a pretext to reveal a calf, a thigh or a bosom. In short, the *tableaux vivants*, 'living pictures' as they were called, consisting of scenes presented on stage by costumed actors who remained silent and motionless as if in a picture, were an astute way of satisfying the admirers of antique sculpture and of boys and girls. They were shown on several stages, including that of the Folies Bergère, where in 1894, for an 'exclusive engagement', they showed the marvellous *tableaux vivants* of London's Palace Theatre. The public was offered Gibson's Venus, Bouguereau's Aurora, E. M. Bredt's Moorish Bath and other marvels. This type of spectacle, however, was undoubtedly the most dreadful that had been invented, both in terms of bombast and voyeurism. Despite the advertisements for these

The *tableau vivant* 'Naughty Nights in the Bois' – a reference to the notorious all-night parties in the Bois de Boulogne – from *Les Nuits du Bois*, 1923.

displays as seen in the posters of the period, their promise was unfulfilled, for the spectators did not see much. Skin coloured outfits were *de rigeur*!

Bare breasts first appeared at the Folies Bergère in 1907 in a pantomime entitled *La Chair* (The Flesh) in which a cuckolded husband, played by Georges Wague, tore the clothes from his wife's body. The ensuing scandal was enormous, particularly since the breasts in question belonged to Colette. She was to become the second woman in the history of France to achieve the rank of *Grand Officier de la Légion d'Honneur*. Maurice Chevalier, who had fallen head over heels in love with Colette in 1908 – three years before he met Mistinguett – wrote in his memoirs: 'Colette was a superb example of the 1908 beauty. Plump, broad shouldered, a trifle stocky. Yet without surplus fat, and with a high, full, shapely bosom, a bosom which is – oh, here goes – the most exciting, appetizing bosom in the world!'

But he was still a shy lad at that time and he never dared tell her. However, he did manage to pluck up the courage many, many years later to confess his youthful passion to the great writer. She answered in her rich Burgundian accent: 'My dear boy, why didn't you tell me at the time? What a waste. I'm a fat old woman now. It's much too late!'

She was appearing at the Folies Bergère because she had just left her husband and was obliged to earn her own living, choosing the stage for this purpose. However, she kept a small pile of lined exercise books in her dressing-room at the Folies and in between scenes she would lock herself in and scribble away interminably in her small, close handwriting. A novel, *La Vagabonde*, and a series of remarkable pen portraits entitled *L'Envers du Music Hall* were written in this way at odd moments during the show.

Colette's nakedness, however, was not entirely of her own choice, but was forced on her by the pressures of her new-found profession and of the persuasion of her theatre director who had his eye on

Colette with Georges Wague.

box office returns while on tour, prior to opening in Paris. She had been ousted from her marital home by M. Willy and was destitute. She was living under the patronage of her lesbian protectress the Marquise de Belbeuf. Colette describes the scene in *Les Vrilles de la Vigne* with a good deal of humour: Colette and her partner Wague are in the midst of rehearsal with the theatre director, Jadin, in attendance. Colette's costume is being discussed while, as Colette describes, she averted her eyes and said nothing, devoutly wishing for a ham sandwich, or perhaps two – or three, with mustard.

'Well,' the boss sighed, 'let's see it ... Go on, Wague, begin the scene where you tear off her dress.'

He rushed toward the famished [Colette] with dagger drawn, and she suddenly turns into a pursued and panting child, claws bared ... for an instant, they struggle, the dress rips from the top and [Colette] is revealed half-naked, her bosom bared to the knife.

'Oops! Stop there, my dears. It's a fine effect, but, wait ...' The boss mediates, smacks his lips, mutters.

'Of course, of course it's not ... it's not naked enough there!'

The bored filly jumps as though bitten by a wasp.

'Not naked enough! What more do you want?'

'Well, I'd like ... I don't know ... I'd like ...' Inspired, he steps back a few steps and stretches out his arm; with the voice of a pilot taking off, he says:

'Let out a breast!'

Colette dwelt very little on the audience, aware only of its omnipresent, mocking picturesqueness. She wrote that, 'the minute I step onto the stage, I no longer belong to myself,' which simply meant that the only important thing was not to fall down when dancing, nor to catch her heel in the hem of her dress. The audience was a popular one, easily amused. It consisted for the most part of children of paradise, the public of the upper balconies. Dressed in sweaters, colourful collarless shirts, their hands thrust into the pockets of their tight jackets, berets on their heads, unlit cigarettes hanging from their mouths, 'pimps' filled the theatre on weekends. Saturdays were always sold out, but as Jadin rather crudely put it, 'What the hell do I care – I don't get a percentage of the take.' Some shell out 2¼ francs to reserve one of the cane-bottomed chairs close to the stage. These are the faithful passionate fans, the ones who talk back to the artists, who boo them or applaud them, who make scatalogical remarks or shout obscenities that break up the entire audience. Sometimes, they get carried away, they go too far, and the whole thing turns into a real brawl.... The artist onstage had best wait with deadpan expression, stock-still, until the storm rolls over – unless he wants to become a target for the oranges, rolled-up programmes and coins flying through the air.

Colette goes on to describe the cashier of the day:

Watch-dogs, in a kennel with its back turned to the west wind, are better housed. She has her lair, from eight in the evening till midnight, and from two till five for matinees, in a damp recess under the stairs leading down to the artistes' dressing-rooms, and the battered little deal pay-desk is her sole protection against the brutal draught directed at her whenever the constantly opened and shut iron door swings back into place. Alternate hot and cold gusts, from the radiator on one side and the stairs on the other, slightly ruffle the curls round her head and her little knitted tippet, whose every stitch carries an imitation jet bead.

An electric bulb hangs above her head like a pear on a string, petti-coated in green paper, and at first all that can be distinguished is a small yellow hand emerging from a starched cuff. A small yellow hand, clean, but with the thumb and fore-finger blackened from counting coins and copper tallies.

After a short while of attentive scrutiny, the features of the cashier can easily be discerned, among the many green shadows cast by the lamp, on the shrivelled face of a pleasant, timorous old lizard, devoid of all colour. Supposing her cheek were prickled, would there spurt from it, instead of blood, pale globules of the anaemic juice used in bottling brandied cherries?

I know nothing of the cashier except her bust, always bent forward from her habit of writing and her desire to please. . . . She arrives long before me and leaves at midnight. Does she walk? Has she legs and feet, a woman's body? All that must have melted away, after twenty-four years behind her battered little pay-desk!

A lizard, yes, a nice little wrinkled lizard, old and frail, but not so timorous after all: her tart voice has a shrill ring of authority, and to one and all alike she exhibits the equable kindliness of one whose power is undisputed. . . . The chief stage-hand, grey-haired, blue boiler-suited, speaks to her as would a small boy: he has been on the house staff for a mere eighteen years!

Fortunately, the head cashier was there to maintain order. She presided over the box office and was able to wither any tough guy or real *apache* who tried to purchase a ticket to one of the special front-row seats:

'Keep your forty-five sous and get out!' Colette writes of a *contretemps* between cashier and trouble-maker.

'But why, Madame Barnet? What did I do?'

'Oh, sure, "What did I do?" You think I didn't see you last Saturday – you were in number one in the gallery, weren't you?'

'Who says so?'

'You're the one that stood up during the panto-mime and yelled, "She's only showing one tit, I want to see both of 'em – I paid two bits, one per tit!"'

'Me? Come on, Madame Barnet, I behave my-self, I don't do things like that. I swear, it wasn't me.'

'Don't give me that, I saw you, didn't I, and that's it! You can't have a seat for another week. Put away your money and get out!'

Colette describes the appearances of another nude and the audience's reaction:

A shattering storm of applause greets – but why? – Gemma la Bellissima, a flaccid dancing-girl in green gauze. She is the 'Dancer in the Nude', whose bashful antics are noisily acclaimed and accompanied, while her reserved smile acts as an apology for having to display too much! At one moment, turning her too white back to the audience, she goes so far as to attempt a lascivious wriggle; but she quickly turns round again, as though wounded by the glances, to resume, eyes suitably lowered, her little game as a modest washerwoman, wringing and shaking her spangled veil.

The Folies Bergère was passionately addicted to suspending nude girls from scenery of all kinds.

A new chapter had begun in the history of the Folies Bergère. The nude personified the goddess of love and her acting was confined to the shooting of one or two arrows from a jewelled bow.

'Nudes are, today, the *sine qua non* of the shows at the Folies Bergère,' Derval explains, 'and if I ventured to dispense with them I might as well shut up shop. Yet it is not so very long ago that I presented for the first time the audacious spectacle of a nude on the Folies Bergère stage.' Before that, the only bare flesh to be seen in the theatre was the small area between the cancan dancer's silk stocking and her frilly drawers – and even *that* created unheard-of protest and excitement in the house.

In some countries, such as England, nudes were not really part of the show proper. Naked women were not allowed to move on stage but had to stand transfixed, like statues. This, of course, had a distinct advantage: breasts of minimum aesthetic quality were at least given the benefit of immobility. In the days of the Ziegfeld Follies and George White's

Scandals in New York there was very little nudity
on the stage. Excessive prudishness seemed part and
parcel of American morality. American obscenity
laws forbade even the showing of the navel, although
it has never been explained why that particular part
of the female anatomy should be quite so shocking.

In America, Florenz Ziegfeld was the first producer to put nude models on the stage. From the
opening of the Ziegfeld Follies in 1907 until his last
show in 1931, Ziegfeld launched over 3,000 beauties,
girls who lived in the headlines and went on, some
to triumph, wealth and peerages, others to poverty,
scandal or suicide. However, he used the undraped
figures only in the designer Ben Ali Haggin's
tableaux. The nudes were scattered among the laces,
rosebuds and spangles of his fabulous settings, as part
of the scenery, but the nude girl was never allowed
to move as much as her little finger. It was not done
merely to display nudity, as Ziegfeld carefully explained, nor was it merely an excuse for exploiting
it. If a chosen masterpiece showed an undraped figure
it was represented faithfully, as it was in the original
painting. When other producers later copied him,
Ziegfeld announced to the world: 'These orgies of
nakedness are disgusting, worse than one can find in
the lowest dives in Europe and they make one
ashamed of ever having anything to do with revues.'
But that they were both shocking and delighting a
slightly jaded Broadway, Ziegfeld had no doubts.
He had only to listen to the names called out to
chauffeurs by the stage doorman nightly – Guggen-
heim, Rhinelander Stewart, Vanderbilt, Biddle,
Hutton – to know that his daring artistry was paying
off.

The first nude at the Ziegfeld Follies in about 1918
had to be asked to volunteer for the role by Ben Ali
Haggin, who warned that any girl would seem over-
dressed in that first tableau if she wore as much as
a string of pearls around her throat. Kay Laurell
stepped forward, and after her début as 'September

Morn', in which she posed sitting undraped on top of a huge globe with soft lights playing over it, her name became synonymous with undraped feminine loveliness; and she was more than willing to have it remain as such. She knew she had a beautiful figure, slender as a boy's, but softly rounded, and that it was her greatest asset on the road to fame. Ned Wayburn, who staged many of the Ziegfeld Follies shows, called Kay 'the original American Venus'.

But it was only in Paris in 1918 in the operetta *Phi Phi* by Willemetz and Christine that breasts, the famous 'little heathens', first appeared bare on the legitimate stage. As for total nudity, it became a practice for the first time in 1919 with *Paris qui Danse* (Paris is Dancing) at the Casino de Paris, arousing the ire of the moralists, whose 'league against street licentiousness' protested with indignation against the posters showing such graphic detail as the nude form.

Paul Derval recalls that 'the first nude at the Folies Bergère was an adorable little blonde, exquisitely made and as curly as a lamb. The day she appeared on the stage for the first time, a mesmerized hush fell over the house, followed by an immense sigh of admiration.'

A new chapter had been written in the history of the Folies Bergère. As Derval adds:

> This pioneer never realized her historic significance. Perfectly content to make her appearance every night, on a flower-decked float, wearing nothing but a crown of flowers and her own enchanting smile, she illustrated to perfection the truth of the old adage, 'Be beautiful and hold your tongue' – for she had not one line to speak. She personified the goddess of love and her acting was confined to the shooting of one or two arrows from a jewelled bow.
>
> One of these darts must have found its way into the heart of a regular patron for she married a short time afterwards and bore her husband two adorable children.

Those darts, however, failed to find their targets in the hearts of the great French institutions such as Mistinguett and Maurice Chevalier, for with the introduction of the nude came the steady decline of a star personality attracting audiences. This change was more lamented by the stars themselves than by the public, notably Chevalier himself:

> The truth of the matter is that, round 1918, the nude show-girl quietly took possession of the Folies Bergère's stage, thus dispensing, by her own unrivalled and perennial appeal, with the need for highly paid celebrities.
>
> Production numbers featuring beautiful, animated tableaux of nude figures rapidly became the real draw in Grand Revue and managers were no longer forced to bow down before the hitherto implacable star system.
>
> Instead of spending their capital on astronomic salaries, they found it more profitable henceforward to concentrate their resources on the richness and magnificence of the production. In this amicable struggle between the spirit and the flesh, there is now no possible doubt as to the victor, and it is in this respect that the great music-halls of Paris have developed with the times, to become the first port of call for all those foreign visitors who come in their thousands to feast their eyes on splendours unknown in their own countries.
>
> The Parisian revues of P. L. Flers [at the Folies Bergère] and Léon Volterra [at the newly opened Casino de Paris which was proving to be the Folies's greatest rival], with their star-studded casts, have seen their glory dimmed by the magnificence of the undraped female form whose language is universal.
>
> Directed on these lines, the Folies Bergère has attained an international reputation which neither the rise and fall of régimes nor the fluctuations of national prosperity have yet managed to tarnish.

Chevalier did not give up hope, though, of returning to the Folies Bergère, starring in one such revue:
'We could call it, say, *Maurice en Folie*. After all, I
did introduce the striptease to Paris some years back
in one of my shows. I can see myself, in nothing
but my little straw hat, cavorting to great effect
among the nude lovelies of the Folies Bergère – but
I do insist on my hat; dammit, a man has his modesty!'

Not only was the nude capturing the imagination
of the public, but her sister the chorus-girl was
increasing in popularity – starting with the Barrison
Sisters, there were later the famous troupes of the
John Tiller Girls followed by the Jackson Girls and
finally the Bluebell Girls, first introduced to the Folies
Bergère by an Irish dancer.

The difference between the nude, or the show-girl,
and the chorus-girl was at first well-defined: the
chorus-girl danced and the show-girl moved, showing, rather cautiously, as much as she was permitted
to reveal. But the caution of the earlier revues, in
which the nudes might occasionally sway to the
music, or move carefully two or three steps across
the stage, was eventually thrown to the wind, gradually giving way to a more adventurous period during
which apart from the sixteen or twenty show-girls,
there would also be sixteen to twenty nudes, some
of whom would be professional dancers.

During the First World War, the breasts of the
girls at the Folies became a sort of symbol of what
a great number of troops briefly on leave from the
agony of the front line thought they were fighting
for. There are few descriptions available of the shows
of that period, though we are told that Italy's entry
into the war was greeted by a parade of 'twenty
magnificent girls, dressed in Italian military uniforms, each with one fair breast exposed'.

With the end of the first war came the completely
nude show-girl of the Folies (nude, that is, except
for her *cache-sexe*, a more theatrical version of the
once-favoured fig leaf).

JOHN TILLER'S FOLIES GIRLS

It was soon discovered that while individual stars might come and go to more or less acclaim, the nudes alone, together with the magnificently gowned *mannequins habillés*, were capable of bringing in the crowds. Derval never hesitated in taking advantage of the fact. Conscious of the time being right, he introduced the first nude into one of his early post-war revues without any previous announcement.

Derval's attention to the morality of his girls, while never perhaps as strict as that of the Tillers in the early years of the century, was necessarily careful. He had to recruit many of his dancers from the dancing schools of England, and the chances of getting really accomplished girls would have been much less if the Folies had been known as a thoroughly disreputable theatre. Derval assures us that:

When in Paris, the girls are under constant supervision by the English authorities. Most of

them live in a hostel run by an English padre. This
good churchman does his best to be both father
and mother to his girls, but it is not always easy
to keep a regiment of grown-up young women
in order. Many is the storm in a teacup over a
mislaid bra or a misappropriated lipstick which
the 'captain' cannot always settle on her own. The
Reverend is then called upon to arbitrate in these
little disputes, a task which he fulfils, I am sure,
with the same commendable dignity he brings to
other and more serious matters.

The hostel is comfortable. The girls have their
own refectory and common-room, where they
take their traditional cup of tea together, and once
a week the padre gives them a little talk. The girls
are naturally free to live on their own if they
choose, but they almost invariably prefer to share
in the life at the hostel.

On the American stage, uniformity appears to be a
necessity in the chorus line, notably the early Ziegfeld
Follies and the more recent Radio City Rockettes,
but at the Folies Bergère greater stress is directed
on the personality of each individual member of a
troupe. Derval was a firm believer in the French
maxim that uniformity breeds boredom and he
therefore selected his dancers in the hope that each
one would claim the attention of a certain number
of spectators. He applied the same principle to the
selection of the show-girls. Patrons often write in to
the Folies Bergère commenting on the girls: 'Your
latest show-girl, sixth from the right in the finale,
has great style – the soubrette in the Persian scene
is too affected – Paloma is clumsy on her feet.' Derval
had no hesitation in passing on these comments to
the girls in the firm belief that they were artists in
their own right and not rubber-stamped effigies.

Many of the nudes consider their work a stepping-
stone to either stardom or marriage. Colette Fleuriot,
for instance, started in the chorus and bit by bit she
worked her way up until she gained well-deserved

success both in Paris and America. Others are content with their work, given, for example, that they have a secure job. The current Folies Bergère show needs to run for five years in order to be profitable, thereby assuring the girls steady employment.

'One day a ravishing young woman was engaged to make an appearance of a fairly unusual kind,' Derval recalled. 'Her costume consisted of an evening dress reaching from her ears to her feet in the front but steeply cut away at the back, in a *décolleté* that began at the waist, and ended . . . considerably lower down.

'At the first fitting she blushed crimson and stammered, "Oh, Monsieur Derval, I'm sorry but – I don't think I could . . . not every day . . . you see, I'm married . . ."'

Derval took pity on her. He kept her in the number as the costume suited her so well, but they came to an arrangement. Her skirt was fitted with 'a little curtain' held in place with two hooks and eyes, which she was allowed to put on whenever her husband was in front. She was in the show for a whole year. 'I would like to take the opportunity of making my excuses to the unlucky patrons who saw the show on "curtain" days,' commented Derval in his memoirs.

There were nearly always one or two students in the cast of every Folies revue. One studied law, for instance, surrounded by text-books in her rather crowded dressing-room, and another of eighteen studied to be a doctor. She was showing great promise as a student at the Lamartine Lycée when her parents suddenly lost all their money and she was obliged to start earning a living. Anxious to continue her studies, she decided to take a job which would leave her free to attend the Faculty of Medicine in the daytime. There was only the theatre to choose. Her parents naturally opposed her choice of the Folies Bergère but she succeeded in convincing them that she was able to behave properly no matter where she chose, assuring them that the Folies was not the den of iniquity which many people supposed. The family acquiesced and the girl got the job – and subsequently, her degree.

But some girls did have problems in the nude scenes. Paul Derval records an incident on a first night during one of the big production numbers. Yvonne Ménard was to become a major revue star but was still in the chorus at the time:

Yvonne Ménard

> Yvonne, who is an exceptionally attractive and shapely young woman, was dressed in that little triangle of fabric known as *cache-sexe* which must be gummed on before appearing on stage.
>
> That evening Yvonne, in the general excitement of a first night, must have dressed rather carelessly – either that or the spirit gum was of poor quality, for her costume suddenly showed unmistakable signs of coming adrift.
>
> Hot with embarrassment, Yvonne did her best to play the scene as much as possible with her back to the audience. There would come a point, however, when she would be obliged to face the front and lean against a set piece with the lights full on her. The costume was now hanging by a thread.
>
> The stage manager could stand the suspense no longer. Creeping behind the set piece against which Yvonne had taken up her position, he seized the moment when the dancer was temporarily in shadow to repair the damage.
>
> The poor fellow mistimed his gesture badly. The spotlights swung back on to Yvonne Ménard, and the audience saw a large male hand, armed with a tiny glue-brush, groping towards Mlle Ménard's costume. There was a shriek of delight from the house, followed by a round of applause.
>
> It is only fair to add that the applause redoubled when it was seen that the glue-brush had finally managed to do its work.
>
> What was even more amusing was that some

spectators thought the incident intentional. A flushed-looking gentleman came to me in the interval.

'Congratulations, Monsieur Derval!' he beamed. 'That bit of business with the fig leaf is a real stroke of genius.'

Indeed, some patrons came back several nights running in the fond hope of seeing the trick repeated. They did not, I regret to say, get their money's worth. Yvonne Ménard had changed her brand of spirit gum.

Apart from the leading lady, herself an accomplished dancer, the company under Derval's management consisted of sixteen show-girls, ten chorus-boys and sixteen nudes, two of whom were *premières danseuses*. The casting of a show-girl presented no great difficulties to him. So long as the girl had a good figure and a pretty face, nothing more was required of her except the ability to dance a few elementary steps. 'The nudes are another matter. They must be flawless, and, unlike my American colleagues, I do not have battalions of girls at my disposal. The casting of nude dancers is even more difficult. Two or three are needed in each revue and for them the Folies Bergère applies at various dancing schools. Suitable candidates are few and far between.'

Derval had often been asked to present male nudes at the Folies Bergère but as he could never be sure whether or not this was an indication of a secret desire on the part of the fair sex for equality symptomatic of that era he was reluctant to add to the existing scheme of things. The tableaux featuring the semi-nude male dancer would invariably involve a cage in which the 'old Adam' lay imprisoned. But the naked male figure had none of the features of the traditional Tarzan. The ladies in the audience, it seemed, preferred the lithe and slender body of Adonis. The man remained a prisoner in his cage while a few dancers, naked to the waist, pirouetted around him. Then one of them darted past the wings,

deftly unhooked her skirts and reappeared, completely nude.

Billy Milton recalled that:

> In my day in the French theatre it was customary
> for girls to ice their breasts and their nipples to
> make them stand out and for the chorus young
> men to pad their jock-straps with silk socks in the
> hope that the *haut-monde* would reach for their
> opera glasses and possibly lead them to a future of
> luxury and comfort on the Riviera or in the
> States . . .

> As it happened, Mistinguett was invited to a
> preview of the new show at the Folies Bergère, and
> she invited me to accompany her. For quite a
> while she sat placidly watching each item as they
> followed one after the other in rapid succession
> until a certain scene in which sixteen beautiful
> girls lay in abandoned pose on a tilted rostrum
> covered with black velvet. The devil, dressed in a
> red-lined cloak, with horns, of course, fluttered
> sexually over each one of them in turn. He was
> wearing red silk tights with a formidable bulge in
> front. Well, as it happened, this artist had been
> discovered by Mistinguett and had become what
> is known as a protégé of hers. He had a superb
> body, but when 'Miss' caught sight of this big
> '*arrangement*' she cried out involuntarily:

> 'Oh, no! He's a lot smaller than that!'

LES CEINTURES DE CHASTETÉ

Derval goes on to assure us that in art, nudity is
only indecent if indecency is the intention. The
British and American theory, which used to impose
a statue-like rigidity on this kind of exhibition, was
sensible and effective, but the fluidity of the dance
achieved the same result. He recalled a time when
French law insisted on the issue of an invitation to
the superintendent of police, who attended the public
dress rehearsal of the show to make sure that the
Folies Bergère kept within its bounds. This rule,
however, has been rescinded, but as there is no aspect

1925

of the show that could possibly offend public morals or taste, there is hardly the need for an imposed censorship. Any censorship remains in the taste of the management and its designers and performers.

However, the wearing of a diminutive triangle of fabric is still *de rigueur*. 'I once had, for the whole run of a show,' Derval recalled, 'a star dancer who persisted in appearing, night after night, as undraped as her mother Eve. She merely took care not to face the front, and as far as I am aware, no one in the audience ever suspected that the young lady had an allergy to spirit gum.'

'The Folies Bergère has some very prudish patrons,' Derval continued. 'They have only themselves to blame; nobody, after all, forced them to come. The reputation of our theatre is too widespread for them to plead ignorance; they can therefore have none but the worst reasons for their hypocrisy. The man who secretly enjoys the sight of a bosom fairer than that of his own wife feels bound, I suppose, to manifest his disapproval, if only out of concern for what the neighbours will say.'

There are, of course, other men who, on a visit to the Folies Bergère, attempt to go as far as possible. The great star Josephine Baker had gone up to change when sudden piercing screams were heard coming from her dressing-room. His heart in his mouth, the manager tore along the corridor to find the star, completely unclothed, screaming abuse at some obscure photographer who had slipped into her room, hidden behind a curtain and snapped her just as she had stepped out of one costume and was about to put on another. The film, of course, was promptly confiscated by the management and the intruder thrown out.

Josephine Baker took a considerable amount of calming down, which was odd considering that the costume she had just been photographed without consisted only of three roses.

The designer Erté finds that show-girls fall into two categories:

> The first consists of girls who approach the job as if they were working on an assembly line in a factory. They are mechanical and bored, thinking only about when they can leave. Those who qualify for the second category are unfortunately rare. They are the ones whose love of the theatre and of clothes is sufficiently well developed for them to enjoy dressing up in sumptuous costumes, even if it is only for three hours a day. I have always been astonished that so few show-girls ever seem to realize that each evening they appear could be the most important of their lives. Yet I have heard many fairy stories in which the 'prince' (of finance) ended up marrying the 'show-girl' (from the Folies Bergère).

One cannot talk of show-girls without paying tribute to one of the legendary figures of the chorus line, Miss Bluebell, who appeared at the Folies Bergère in the 1930s. Nowadays her troupes of dazzling show-girls appear not only at the Lido in Paris, but in Las Vegas, Buenos Aires, Tokyo, Nairobi, Geneva and Barcelona. The Bluebell Girls are as well known now as the Tiller or Gaiety Girls were in their day.

The widowed Miss Bluebell now lives in a penthouse in the ambassadorial quarter south of the Avenue Foch. She was, as befits the legend, born in poverty in the Rotundra Hospital in Dublin in 1912. Her mother, an unknown Mrs Kelly, gave her away a fortnight later to a spinster, Mary Murphy, who was to raise her. Margaret Kelly was a thin, delicate girl with matchstick legs. A doctor, mesmerized by her clear blue eyes, had nicknamed her 'Bluebell' – the name that has brought her fame. Once asked if she had ever traced her real parents, she replied with the directness for which she is respected: 'I never wanted to. After all, they never did anything for me. I've never been curious about them.'

Dancing classes were prescribed as therapy for the spindly limbs. Bluebell turned out to have a natural talent. Mary Murphy, unable to hold things together in Ireland, migrated with her adopted daughter to Liverpool, where the rest of her family had settled, and most of Bluebell's upbringing was in West Derby. Her dance lessons were partly paid for through newspaper rounds and caddying on the golf courses where plus-foured players, alarmed by her slight frame, would on occasion lug the heavy irons around themselves and still fork out the caddie's tip.

'I never considered that I had a deprived childhood. I was always well dressed. Mary Murphy saw to that. And I had enough jam butties to eat.'

At thirteeen, she got her first stage job; predictably as a pantomime 'babe' in a production at the west-country seaside resort of Newquay. Her salary was five shillings a week, and she sent Mrs Murphy half of it. Her 'Auntie' realized that the stage was clearly the only career for which Bluebell would be suitable and removed her from school at fifteen, encouraging her to join The Hot Jacks – a little troupe of half-a-dozen girls of the same age who performed mad gyrations in organdie blouses and blue bloomers. From The Hot Jacks, Bluebell made a giant step by becoming one of The Jackson Girls, under the aegis of Alfred Jackson, who was to provide a permanent troupe of dancers for the Folies Bergère.

Three somewhat stunned sixteen-year-old girls set out from London to work as the Alfred Jackson Girls at the Scala, Berlin – the start of a teenage career that was to take Bluebell around Europe, culminating in the Folies itself – then the Mecca for every chorus-girl. It was 1927. But any idea that Bluebell might have taken any part in the scandalous night life of the capital can be dismissed: for one thing, after a day rehearsing and an evening performing the kind of routine the Alfred Jackson Girls were famous for (thirty-two girls in a row kicking higher and higher, faster and faster, to the beat of a tambourine), she would have had no energy for it, and for another, the girls were so heavily chaperoned that the opportunities never existed.

Bluebell was appearing as one of the Alfred Jackson Girls on tour in Germany when Paul Derval went to see them in Hamburg. He was impressed with the troupe and engaged them for the new Folies Bergère revue, *De la Folie Pure* (Pure Folly), which was to open at the end of 1929. A *Spectacle en 60 Sensations*, it was produced by Louis Lemarchand, with costumes created by half-a-dozen designers including Erté. So Jackson formed another troupe for the Folies Bergère show and included in it a couple of the girls from the German tour. And that was the start of the Folies Bergère group, The Alfred Jackson Girls.

Although now seventy years old, Miss Bluebell looks a spry fifty. Her hair trimmed close to her nape, she could easily be mistaken for a Frenchwoman; the possessor of chic and simplicity. But this is hardly surprising since she has lived in Paris for the past fifty years and frequently travels all over the world. On 5 November 1982 she celebrated the fiftieth anniversary of the inauguration of her now famous troupe of Bluebell Girls dancing at the Folies Bergère. Tracing her actual arrival at the Folies Bergère, Miss Bluebell says:

> While on tour in Germany, Alfred Jackson asked me whether I would replace one of the girls at the Folies Bergère who was going on a month's holiday and as I couldn't afford a holiday of my own, I went to the Folies Bergère to earn the extra money, and went back to Germany after that month. I learnt to speak German during that time and thought I'd really like to learn French too, so I asked Alfred Jackson whether I could return to the Folies Bergère, and he agreed. We were a sixteen-girl precision, speciality act, in the John

Tiller high-kicking tradition – but we were much quicker!

When I first came over to the Folies Bergère I was paid £2 a week and the management provided meals and accommodation. We all lived together in a big apartment, 50 rue de Paradis, which is around the corner from the stage door of the Folies Bergère. Mrs Jackson used to stay with us and Alfred Jackson used to travel with the German troupe. There were two maids who looked after us, and we used to get up at nine in the morning, have breakfast at quarter to ten and leave the house at quarter past ten for the theatre where we had class every day except Saturday and Sunday – we had matinées on those two days. We used to go to the theatre two by two and return to the apartment two by two. We weren't allowed to speak to anybody.

Bluebell became captain of the Folies Bergère troupe two months after joining the company, but this was not to last for long. Business dropped considerably by the following January and Derval asked the company to take a cut in salary, as she explains: 'Alfred Jackson told Derval that he wouldn't agree to the cut, thinking that they wouldn't actually let us go. But they did. I was obviously out of a job but I didn't want to go back to Germany to join the other troupe.' So Miss Bluebell returned to England, where on a visit to friends appearing at the Leicester Square cinema she met Alfred Jackson's brother, John William, as she was going through the stage door.

'What are you doing here, Bluebell?' J. W. Jackson asked her. 'I thought you were with Alfred at the Folies Bergère.'

She told him the tale and explained that she was looking for work.

'Well, as it happens I'm looking for a girl for my new show in Paris at the Casino de Paris.'

Bluebell willingly accepted his offer to return to

Paris to join his troupe, the J. W. Jackson Girls, even though it meant spending her hard-earned savings on the fare:

> We started rehearsing but nobody seemed to be working very hard, which I wasn't used to. When they got on stage for the opening, it obviously showed and I gave my notice in after the first night. I said, 'I haven't paid all that money to come over to do this silly kind of work.' The captain of the troupe telephoned J. W. Jackson, who called me and asked what was the matter. I told him that the work was terrible and that I couldn't work like that. He asked me to stay on for at least two months, offering to make me captain of the troupe, but I told him that it had gone too far to remedy.

Present at the Casino de Paris at the time was a former Harrods salesman, a Londoner named Arthur Rowe. He had taken dancing classes in his spare time and auditioned for the role of one of the famous Eight Lancashire Lads (the troupe in which Charlie Chaplin had begun his brilliant career). Rowe was sent on tour to Germany and the troupe finally ended up in Paris where Rowe became captain of what became the J. W. Jackson Boys at the Casino de Paris:

> Although Bluebell complained that the girls didn't work very hard, my troupe of boys certainly did. This was no doubt because we were part of Mistinguett's act, and she was the task-master of all time. We worked every night and had matinées on Saturdays and Sundays, plus rehearsals for the new show. We would rehearse for three months and as all the theatres in Paris were closed for the month of August, that would be the last month of our rehearsals for the new show. We worked right through the night until the following morning.

The 'Boys' act, however, did not require the

precision of thirty-two high-kicking girls and the disciplines imposed on their speciality numbers.

After leaving the Casino de Paris revue, Bluebell visited her friends at the Folies Bergère the following day in the hope of getting back into the company. Paul Derval learnt that she was in the theatre and sent for her. 'Would you like to form your own troupe at the Folies Bergère?' he asked Bluebell. She could hardly believe her ears. She had hung her hopes on, perhaps, being asked to take over as Principal dancer, but being asked to form her own troupe of twelve dancers was unbelievable. She accepted the offer – more than willingly – and lost no time in contacting her friends, inviting them to join her at the Folies, and, indeed, seduced many others away from shows they were already in.

It is no wonder that Miss Bluebell has kept among her treasured mementoes the Folies Bergère programme of that first performance at the Folies, in which she headed her own troupe of girls under her own name for the very first time – a troupe that was to culminate in the formation of many other Bluebell troupes throughout the world during the next fifty years. Her first Folies Bergère programme billing announced:

THE BLUE BELL'S GIRLS

That first troupe of Bluebell Girls danced happily through the 1932–3 season of *Nuits de Folies* (Nights of Folly). But their hopes were to be dashed by the intervention of the formidable Mistinguett who had been contracted to star in the revue *Folies en Folie* which was to open the following year. Her agreement had provided for her approval of the entire cast, and she arranged with Derval to attend a performance one evening to see whether she liked the new Bluebell Girls' work.

The dancers were rehearsing underneath the stage, but in their anxiety to please the visiting star, they over-rehearsed, lost track of time and missed the cue for their first entrance on stage. Chaos ensued, and Miss Bluebell recalls that 'Mistinguett, who was a stickler for discipline, had us sacked on the spot. But the real reason was because she wanted to bring over a black American fellow, Buddy Bradley, and his troupe, who were in London at the time. So Derval called me and said, "I'm terribly sorry, but Miss wants to bring her own people in."

'And I thought, "Where do I have to go from here?" '

She did not have far to look for she decided to turn adversity into advantage. She went to see the Buddy Bradley Girls at work. They were tall, and had broken away from the very simple kicking routine which was the rule with the Tillers, the Rockettes at the Radio City Music Hall in New York, the Jacksons and most other chorus lines, but moreover, they broke the line and did tap-dancing and other production numbers. Miss Bluebell decided to take this even further. She too would concentrate on engaging for her troupe the taller girls, on average five foot nine inches – which has remained the minimum height requirement for a Bluebell Girl to this very day – and who, like fashion models, would show off to better advantage whatever clothes or costumes were designed for them. And she decided also to give them more interesting work to do which would enable them to develop their own individual personalities within the discipline of the troupe.

Meanwhile, Miss Bluebell had eleven girls on her hands, and for whom she was obviously responsible – but for whom she had no work. She trundled along from theatre to theatre, agent to agent, and eventually ended up in the office of Jacques-Charles, who was producing stage shows to complement the showing of films at the vast new Paramount Cinema in the Boulevard des Italiens. He agreed readily to the idea of a troupe, but he explained that as his stage was so enormous Miss Bluebell's twelve girls would be lost on it. She would have to provide a troupe of twenty-four instead. This she agreed she could do. And did.

Their billing, 'The Bluebell Girls', went up in lights for the very first time. But in the meantime all was not well at the Folies Bergère and Mistinguett and Derval began casting somewhat envious eyes on the Paramount Cinema. Paul Derval telephoned Miss Bluebell to say that they were not happy about the Buddy Bradley situation and asked her to return with her troupe for the 1934 Mistinguett revue which was to feature Fernandel.

But in common with so many others, Miss Bluebell did not feel well disposed to Mistinguett by now.

Mutual admiration, however, does exist between Miss Bluebell and another great dancer and entrepreneur, Sir Anton Dolin, who first met Miss Bluebell in Monte Carlo in 1950. He had danced in Monaco on many occasions – as well as in practically every other part of the world – and says of her:

> Miss Bluebell is a very quiet person. She's enormously strict too. They all love her, the girls. But she's a very hard business-woman and that frightens people. I love her real name, Margaret Kelly. Nothing could be prettier than that. Bluebell is a lovely name but Margaret Kelly is even prettier. She told me that her greatest ambition was to be a ballerina, but that, 'We lived in Liverpool and had no money to come to London to study, so I became a Jackson girl at the Folies Bergère instead.'

Miss Bluebell remembers that first encounter with Sir Anton. He said to her, 'Hello. You don't know who I am but I know who you are. I want to say how wonderful I think the girls are.'

'My God,' she replied. 'As a kid I used to go and see you at the Hippodrome in London. I used to sit up in the gods and see you with Markova. You were a sensation.'

They met again in April 1982 at a celebrity

luncheon hosted by the Variety Club of Great Britain
in celebration of Bluebell's golden anniversary mark-
ing her unique contribution to show business. She
brought along with her the show-girls from Paris
to share in her glory. They travelled in full costume
and feathers.

'The Charles de Gaulle and Heathrow Airports
will never be the same again,' she laughs. 'The
passengers had never seen such a sight; these tall
show-girls in sexy show-costumes. They thought
they were dreaming!'

Sir Anton Dolin believes that 'the Bluebell girls have a quality of their own. They are dignified. You can tell a Bluebell girl just as you can tell a Balanchine or an Ashton ballet. At Miss Bluebell's luncheon, I said, 'I wasn't a Bluebell girl, unfortunately. Firstly, I was the wrong sex – and secondly, I wasn't tall enough.'

When Sir Anton suggested that Miss Bluebell was a hard business-woman, he might easily have had in mind two incidents, recalled by Miss Bluebell herself, to justify this remark:

When I did the Ken Dodd show at the London Palladium in 1967, Bernard Delfont asked me to go and see him. I went to his office over the Prince of Wales, and he asked whether I'd be interested in doing a show at the Talk of the Town. As he showed me around the Talk of the Town theatre himself, I said, 'I usually work with Donn Arden,' [who produces the spectacular Lido show in Paris, and the MGM Hotel show in Las Vegas where the Bluebell Girls appear] and Delfont said, 'Well, we have our own producer, Robert Nesbitt.' And I said, 'In that case, I'm afraid that I'm the wrong person for you. There can only be one captain on the ship.'

Robert Nesbitt and I nearly got into a big fight. When I did the Royal Command Performance, my head-girl called me and said, 'You'd better get over here. He's shortened one of our numbers.'

So I took the 'plane to London the next morning and went into the Palladium, and found him there. So I said, 'How do you do, Mr Nesbitt. I'm Miss Bluebell. I believe you want to shorten one of my numbers and I don't agree. They were constructed like that and I want to keep them like that.'

'I'm afraid we've got trouble with the television people,' he replied. I understood perfectly and said, 'Fine. I'll go and talk to them.'

It turned out that there were one or two problems. A curtain came down at a certain point and got in the way of the camera shots. So I modified the routine to fit in with the composition of the shots, but I didn't allow them to cut it. We very nearly had a fight but I'm glad it was averted. I have great respect for Mr Nesbitt and his work.

A man who has great respect for Miss Bluebell is Bernard Delfont, who was knighted and then later given a peerage for his great contribution to the British theatre both as one of the most important impresarios and for his dedication to theatrical charities. He remembers the first occasion on which he visited the Lido some years ago:

> I saw these lovely-looking Bluebell girls and thought how well they were groomed; everything about them was beautiful – coiffure, costumes and presentation. I said to the person who was with me, 'I wish we had girls who looked like that in England. Why can't we have that sort of perfection in our English girls?'
>
> Later, Miss Bluebell asked whether I would like to meet one or two of the girls and I said that I would love to. I realized that I would have to speak to them in French, but when I met them they turned out to be girls from Blackpool, from Liverpool – from all over England! And that was a big laugh for me. They all turned out to be from home.
>
> I admire Miss Bluebell's work tremendously. She's a remarkable person.

It is a fitting tribute to Miss Bluebell that a troupe of show-girls who appear in Paris and other great capitals of the world and who seem so essentially French, personifying all that France has to offer – chic, design, art, culture – should, by and large, be English, the product of an Irish woman's great industry.

Most of the girls are from lower-middle-class backgrounds, their parents unconnected with show business. The British overcame their reticence at putting their daughters on the stage a long time before the French, as well as producing more tall girls. Today, the question of toplessness, which may have seemed an element of traditional Parisian naughtiness in grandfather's day, evokes little excitement in an age of naked beaches from St Tropez to Brighton, and when even Julie Andrews can flash her *poitrine* in the cinema. One grows so accustomed to seeing the nude or topless artists on stage at the Folies Bergère that when, for instance, the current star of the show, Norma Duval, appears never revealing her bosom, there seems to be something strangely missing or prudish, even though it would

Norma Duval

be as unthinkable to expect a star of her calibre to reveal all as it would have been in the old days to have expected Mistinguett to appear nude – her fabulous legs and personality were enough to excite generations of audiences.

Miss Bluebell, however, is amused at the attitude to the state of nudity by her young dancers nowadays. Her observations are shared by Donn Arden, author and artistic director of some of the most fabulous floor shows in the world.

These days there's such an awareness of nudity that if the girls have a pretty body they don't mind going nude at all. That is the way the world has changed. It's amazing though the amount of girls who want to go nude when they have such ugly bodies. They don't realize how unattractive their bodies really are.

And Miss Bluebell echoes this thought:

There's a girl been writing to me since last December. She's six feet one inch tall, but as she wasn't due to be sixteen until March, there was nothing I could do as the law does not permit us to employ girls until they are sixteen. Aside from her persistent letters, her father has been calling me all the time to say how much she would like to be a Bluebell girl. So eventually, when she was sixteen, her father brought her to see me. We talked for a while and I finally said, 'You know, with your height you really would do better in the topless production numbers than the "covered" ones. You see, we have chorus lines and you may be a little tall for the other girls,' and she replied immediately:

'Oh, I don't mind going nude,' she said rather casually.

I looked at her father who said, 'No. She's okay. We don't mind. She goes nude on the beach.'

Sixteen years of age, she goes nude on the beach with Mummy and Daddy. Can you imagine how surprised I was?

Another girl came to me one day, one of the 'covered' dancers in the current show, and said she would like to appear topless. I felt that was very encouraging and so two months later I told her a place had come up and that the change would be good for her, too. In a long-running show it's good for them to do something different. Granted, they are paid more when they go nude, but that is not always the reason. So she said, 'Thank you very much. I'm going to ring home tonight to tell Mum that I'm going nude. I can tell Mum, but I couldn't possibly tell my father. I'll let Mum do that.'

After the show she came along and said to me, 'Something terribly funny's happened, Miss Bluebell. I 'phoned home, Mum wasn't in, so I plucked up the courage and thought I'd better tell him instead, so I said, "Daddy, I'm going to appear nude in the show," and he said: "Ooh! For God's sake, don't tell your mother! She must never know!"'

Donn Arden remembers that 'There was one girl who wanted to go nude, and as she didn't have much "up there" she asked my advice about having the operation or having the silicone injections and I said, "O.K. As long as you don't end up with a top like Jayne Mansfield; that would be too much." Well, she went ahead, and ended up with two tennis balls! And they don't move at all!'

Sometimes the girls have operations twice or three times over in order to achieve the desired results, but does the management help to finance these operations? 'No!' says Miss Bluebell.

I would never do that and neither would Donn Arden. We help with noses, the chin, teeth, but not breasts, because if anything went wrong, they'd say, 'Well, you gave us the money for it.' I never encourage them to do it. We say, 'We can't hire you as a nude right now. If you want to be a covered girl, that's possible,' and maybe the next audition the following year they return as a nude, having had something done to their breasts of their own accord.

We're not too concerned about small imperfections on the body as all the topless girls have body make-up. Take one of the girls who worked for me for a long time. She couldn't go topless because she'd had a bad operation and it showed. But she appears nude in the Las Vegas show because she had a skin graft and she's fine now.

Donn Arden feels in any case that it is more exciting and provocative to have the nudes semi-covered, with, say, a lace garment, instead of the 'here's two tits syndrome', and does not like to have all the numbers nude or all the girls topless.

Interestingly enough, the two most spectacular production numbers at the Folies Bergère have been 'covered'. The last show, *Folie je t'adore*, presented a production number entitled 'Mazel Tov', set in historical Israel, without a single nude on stage. It proved to be the highlight of the show. The current production at the Folies Bergère introduces a Hungarian tableaux in three acts to music influenced by Emmerich Kalman, consisting of the most exquisite costumes with embroidery and applique, and head-dresses of such beauty that they ought to be on show in museums. This, too, is the highlight of the show – and it does not have a single nude in it.

Miss Bluebell's troupe continued to appear each season at the Folies Bergère until the outbreak of war: *Folies en Folie*, for the 1934–5 season, when Mistinguett starred, and all was forgiven; *Femmes en Folie* for the 1935–6 season which starred Jean Sablon, Betty Spell, Irène Hilda and Randall; and the following year, *En Super Folies*, which heralded the return of Josephine Baker. *Folies en Fleur* in 1937 presented the great comedian Dandy and featured a discovery of Mistinguett – Frédéric Rey, the male nude, who was to appear in the nude adagio section of the Folies Bergère shows for many years to come.

While appearing in Vienna in 1933, Mistinguett was intrigued at the appearance of a mysterious young man of about seventeen, very fair, rather pale and extremely handsome, who sat, motionless, in a box throughout every performance. Mistinguett could not help noticing the silent stranger, who attended her performance night after night until, unable to contain her curiosity any longer, she sent a member of the company to find out who he was. His name was Frédéric and he wanted to meet her. This was dutifully arranged, but although he spoke not a word of French, nor Mistinguett a word of German, he conveyed through an interpreter that he was in love with her – and with the 'Music Hall'. He implored her to find a part for him in the show, assuring her he was a good dancer. Mistinguett was impressed with his enthusiasm and his eagerness to leave Vienna, which he had found boring:

Frédéric ('Fritz') Rey

> To see what he had in him, I decided to set him the 'Music Hall' entrance exam. 'Fritz,' I said – that was his name – 'If you can walk down the staircase properly you can come with us.'
>
> Walking down the staircase was one of the most difficult things one could ask of a boy. It was women's work that very few women ever managed to do really well.
>
> Fritz came down the staircase with the skill and style of a veteran show-girl. We were open-mouthed. Fritz had passed the test with flying colours. He came with us.
>
> He was the company mascot. We nearly lost him when we got back home though. A portly little man, connoisseur of lovely boys, found him to his taste and nearly spirited him away. Fortunately I had already introduced Fritz to Derval, the director of the Folies Bergère, who engaged him for his new revue.

4
The Chevalier/
Mistinguett Merger

Although the Folies Bergère had become as well known as Paris itself by the turn of the century, it also became one of the most sought-after theatre dates for any performer to play. To secure a season at this amazing music-hall carried with it the same mark of achievement as it does for stars who nowadays top the bills at the London Palladium or the Palace Theatre in New York. But famous as it may have been at that time, it was now to gain even greater recognition by bringing together as a team, for the first time, two of the greatest star personalities that France was to produce. It would enjoy for all time the distinction of launching together on the same stage the greatest female entertainer of the period – and for many, many years to come – Mistinguett, who was to be partnered by an unknown young comic who was on the threshold of stardom, and who was to reach it shortly after as the result of his appearance with Mistinguett on the stage of the Folies Bergère in 1911.

Mistinguett was born Jeanne Bourgeois, of a Belgian father who was an upholsterer, and a French mother, at Enghien, on the outskirts of Paris, on 5 April 1873. She was always guarded about her age and reputed to be considerably older than she really was, but never, for an instant, did she look it. She was the most famous and popular French comedienne of the first half of this century and became regarded as a national institution in France.

Her first contact with the entertainment world

had been to lend a hand with the washing-up in the caravan of the owner of the visiting circus in return for seeing the shows for nothing. She realized very early on that the music-hall was to be her domain. She cajoled her parents into letting her have singing and violin lessons as an excuse to travel up to Paris twice a week. The local schoolboys used to follow young Jeanne through the streets on her way to the station and nicknamed her Miss Helyett after the title role of a well-known operetta of the period, because she resembled the picture on the playbills.

'Miss Helyett! Miss Helyett!' the boys chanted and teased her on the way to the station, and it was on a train on one of these journeys that, while travelling in the carriage each week with a revue-writer called Saint-Marcel (who was later to give her her first job), she was to inherit her famous stage name.

Saint-Marcel had just written a new song called *La Vertinguette*, and he was humming it to himself as she climbed into the carriage:

'Why, Miss Helyett – hullo.' He smiled vaguely and went back to his song, teasingly including her nickname in the lyrics:

> *C'est la Tin-tin-guette*
> *C'est la Miss Helyett*
> *C'est la Miss-tin-tin*
> *C'est la Miss Tinguette.*

'Do you know,' he said, turning to her, 'if you ever go on the stage, you must call yourself Miss Tinguette.'

And that is exactly what she did when she began her apprenticeship at the Eldorado night-club in the Boulevard de Strasbourg, opposite the famous Scala Theatre, in 1897. She started there as a nobody, and left after ten years, fully prepared for stardom. During that period, she earned little and had an illegitimate child who was seized by his father, a Brazilian aristocrat, who returned to Brazil with the baby.

At the Eldorado she performed in a simple black *crêpe* dress (all she could afford), singing her songs, as she had always done before, sitting on the prompter's box, and carrying on spirited altercations with members of the orchestra. Her person seemed charged with electricity as she sang *'Je suis une gamine'*. 'She embodies all that is best in my city,' wrote Cocteau. 'She flatters the patriotism of which I am not ashamed. And I bow down before that implacable determination to shine with that light, so long in reaching men, which is the essence of the stars...'

'Soon after my début at the Eldorado, I made a slight alteration to my name,' Mistinguett records. 'As I was addressed as Mlle Miss Tinguett by people who thought Miss was a peculiar kind of Christian name and as Mlle Tinguett by the few who disliked what they took to be my Anglomania, I combined the two and called myself Mistinguette. Later I dropped the final "e".'

After leaving the Eldorado she secured an engagement at the Moulin Rouge where all of Paris flocked to see her dance the *Valse Chaloupée* with Max Dearly. The forerunner to the evocative *apache* dance, the *Valse Chaloupée* caused a considerable sensation as it swept across Paris to the Left Bank. It was another waltz, the *Valse Renversante*, which was to mark the beginning of her career at the Folies Bergère – and her long association with Maurice Chevalier.

Mistinguett became the symbol of Paris and the idol of the world. 'Miss', as she was to become known affectionately, of the fabulous legs, the gamine personality, the elaborate costumes, has been described as one of the most dazzling stars of the entertainment world. There were few to equal her, none to surpass her glamour.

Her audiences, from kings in the Royal Box (and later on in her dressing-room) to urchins in the gallery, all adored and admired her. Her best-remembered songs were *'Mon Homme'* (which was

Mistinguett

specially composed for her when she was deeply in love with Chevalier) and '*J'en ai Marre*'.

Even in advanced years, Mistinguett prided herself on her fabulous legs. They were reputedly insured for a million dollars. She was not highly talented as a dancer, nor did she have a good voice. She could never be mistaken for a beauty by any manner of means, but she had vitality, conviction, an overwhelming personality, a pair of legs celebrated for their beauty, and stunning star-quality. She was dedicated to the theatre and to her audiences, and they, in turn, worshipped her.

For many years she was a great influence on the development of the music-hall in Paris. She was the only French star who could walk down a staircase carrying fifteen pounds of feathers on her head and dragging seven yards of plumes behind her. She was a lithe, acrobatic dancer and had a flair for style, *décor* and production. In fact, she did much to create shows in which she was billed only as a performer. Her life was made up of hard work, precision and devotion to her art. The songs she introduced have been sung the world over.

When she made her entrance, the first thing you saw was her face, and a smile, a huge smile. Her eyes would gleam in the bright lights, but the smile still hovered on her lips, the determined smile of a hostess at a party. She would flaunt her 'nice girl' personality, her immense cheerfulness, weighing up her audience as she went; no swagger, except when she walked her consciously young, tripping walk. As she reached the footlights, she would start to sing, seeming to improvise. She was all too conscious of the fact that forty or fifty thousand francs had to be taken at the box office every night.

The greatest compliment Mistinguett ever received was paid her by the sculptor Rodin: 'If I had to personify the Muse of Music Hall, failing the peplum and the Greek profile, I would give her your legs, Mistinguett.'

So how did a star of such magnitude become involved with an unknown young comic with whom she was to fall desperately in love and guide to stardom? True, like the rest of the population of France, Chevalier had become a fan of this great French institution:

> I worshipped her from afar, never closer than this eagle's nest of a seat for which I had painfully hoarded my centimes. Like so many others in the audiences who flocked to see her, I had been captivated by Mistinguett.
>
> There have been greater comediennes, greater singers, greater dancers – but there has been only one Mistinguett. Complete shows were built around her, she would carry an entire revue on her lovely shoulders, the spirit of the whole evening. Truly, there is no one like her – and if another great personality like hers would come along, she would be a star exploding across the sky.

Chevalier was fifteen-and-a-half when he was introduced to Mistinguett for the first time in 1907. She was appearing at the Eldorado in Paris when she told him that he would succeed because he had 'a handsome little mug'. Accompanied by friends, she later saw his cabaret act in Montmartre one evening and remarked that it was a revelation; he had put the song over as if he were humming to himself for his own pleasure, and with a rhythm and a sureness of touch that took her breath away.

Mutual admiration; but she was a gigantic star and he had only just begun. They met again when he visited the Variétés Theatre, where she was playing. Mistinguett remembered passing him on the stairs. 'He smiled and I smiled back. He called me plain Mistinguett and I called him Chevalier.'

Soon after this meeting, the young Chevalier, who had been working hard, trying to perfect his act in the provinces, travelled to London in the hope of inspiration from the London stage. He was not to be disappointed. On his arrival he went immediately to the Victoria Palace, one of Britain's best Edwardian music-halls at the time, and there he was overwhelmed by the performance of its star, George Robey, with his deep voice, wide smile and giant-sized eyebrows. He also saw performances by Harry Wheldon ('Little Tich' – whose act Charlie Chaplin was to parody and make so famous) and Wilkie Bard, who brought the house down night after night. They were all from poor backgrounds similar to Chevalier's own; each had a unique visual style which, back in his hotel room, the young comic tried to dissect and practised in front of the mirror.

His investment paid off. On his return to Paris, Chevalier had his biggest break to date. The great comic Dranem, whom Chevalier had so assiduously studied and who was now starring at the Eldorado, was taken ill. If Chevalier could take his place, it would mean that for the first time his name would be emblazoned in lights outside a major theatre. He seized the opportunity to replace Dranem, and equipped with his new-found technique, together with bowler hat, skimpy jacket and sailor's jersey, he sang and danced. Hitherto, Parisian audiences were unaccustomed to seeing their singers and comics actually dance as well. He was a sensation.

Present at that performance was one of the most distinguished impresarios of the day, P. L. Flers. He sent a note round to Chevalier, who takes up the story:

> 'Please come to see me tomorrow in my office. Important.' It was signed by the director of the Folies Bergère, the richest, most luxurious and renowned music-hall in Paris. This magnificent theatre, the Mecca for international society in search of amusement, always used spectacular sets on its stage, noisy and brassy enough to command the attention of the world's most famous and often most bored men and women. My act had none of the glitter and dazzle the Folies Bergère

normally employed. What then could they want of me?

He found out the next day. To them, it seemed, he was not a typical singer. They got comedy, dancing and even a boxing skit in which he fought an imaginary bout with himself from his act – and Flers liked what he saw. 'Women sipping champagne in *décolleté* gowns and gleaming jewels, men dressed in evening clothes smoking rich Havana cigars – the typical audience at the Folies Bergère – would like me, too, he said.'

It was not too difficult to convince him. He signed for the winter season, the best contract he had ever had. There was much this job with the Folies could bring him – acclaim, reputation, security and achievement.

But he hardly dreamed it would bring him Mistinguett.

A member of the audience was the famous English impresario C. B. Cochran:

The young Maurice Chevalier.

> I first came across Maurice Chevalier at a *café-concert* in an outskirt of Paris where I had been taken by my old friend C. M. Ercole, P. T. Barnum's agent in Paris, to see a woman perform a dance which had an idea behind its presentation capable of elaboration on a properly equipped stage with an up-to-date lighting installation. While waiting for the dancer I was interested in a young man with his hat pulled down to his ears, very thin and with a long neck, the length of which he exaggerated with a movement of throwing his head forward like a cock crowing. He sang in argot, and the good people who sipped their drinks in the hall from time to time indulged in back-chat with him. He was gay, at ease, and had that 'something'. His name was impressed upon me by his description on the bills:

MAURICE CHEVALIER
Le Petit Jésus

A few years later – it must have been in 1908 or 1909 – my old friend of the Moulin Rouge, P. L. Flers, was producing a revue at the Folies Bergère in which he introduced some tableaux representing English sporting prints, a number of which I had collected for him in London. Invited by him to a rehearsal, I recognized 'Le Petit Jésus'; he had a dance with Mlle Mistinguett, whose position had grown since I had first seen her at L'Eldorado. Three of those taking part in the revue were to become great friends of mine later on. A very young figurante was Yvonne Printemps; Léon Morton, who was to share the success of Alice Delysia in London in 1914 and for several years afterwards, was amusing 'the girls' with conjuring tricks. The very handsome brunette on the stage at the moment I entered the hall was Jane Marnac.

That revue at the Folies Bergère gave Maurice Chevalier a good start. In a year or so I found him again at my favourite revue theatre – La Cigale – off the Boulevard Clichy, where I went specially to see Régine Flory at the suggestion of Max Dearly. This time 'Le Petit Jésus' had summoned up courage enough to discard in one scene the garb of the *café-concert* comic, and had discovered that he could be funny with a clean face and a well-cut suit.

The Folies Bergère represented not just another show, another step in Chevalier's climb to the top. It *was* the top. Two years earlier, Florenz Ziegfeld was claiming that through the portals of his theatre walked the loveliest girls in the world; he omitted to add: 'Except those at the Folies Bergère.' The name had become synonymous with the most magnificent show-girls on any stage – tall and statuesque, draped in silks and ostrich feathers, or merely in rouge and powder – girls whose figures seemed to have been sculpted precisely to Flers's specifications.

Any comedian who could overcome that sort of competition had to be good, and Flers thought Chevalier could do just that. But, unfortunately, he was wrong. The audience sat in stony silence. Chevalier left the stage to less than polite applause. The following day a critic on *Le Figaro* reported: 'Where could they have found this clumsy booby? And who let him loose in our leading music-hall? He is vulgar; beyond belief. His song is nothing but filth.'

In spite of Chevalier's disappointment at his reception, Flers was confident that the young performer was earning every sou of the 1,800 francs he was being paid, and invited him to return to the Folies the following autumn. Chevalier was delighted. But if luck had come his way, good fortune now lay ahead in the shape of his wildest dreams. One day over breakfast he could hardly believe what he read in the newspaper: 'P. L. Flers, producer of the Folies Bergère, announces the signing of Mistinguett to star in his forthcoming season at the music-hall.'

> Mistinguett had been on my mind, in my blood for days, stronger than she had ever been before. I had recently seen her dancing in a show with an urbane, good-looking man named Max Dearly. It was an extraordinary dance which she had created, *La Valse Chaloupée*, a sinuous, provocative, dramatic routine which has since been copied throughout the world as the 'Apache Dance'. She had never looked lovelier or more desirable. How I envied Dearly his chance to hold her long-limbed and supple body in his arms! And now, suddenly, Mistinguett and I were to play in the same show.

Mistinguett was also pleased:

> When I took up my employ as mistress of ceremonies at the Folies Bergère, with the 'girls' and the 'boys', the ostrich feathers and the inevitable staircase, I found, to my delight, that Maurice was also in the cast.

There was a waltz, much in vogue at the time, called *La Valse Renversée*. It was, roughly speaking, a lively, acrobatic '*pas de deux*' and was a feature of every revue. The producers of our show decided to go one better and devised *La Valse Renversante*, an even more tempestuous version of the other. Chevalier was chosen for my partner and together we rehearsed our waltz.

In order to live up to its name, the routine *La Valse Renversante* had to be topsyturvy. As they waltzed around the stage, chairs, tables, stools and all other furniture were sent waltzing too. When every stick of furniture had gone careering into the wings, the couple collapsed on to the carpet and, still dancing, managed to roll themselves up into it as it rolled off stage into the wings.

The planning and rehearsing of the act proved profitable for the artists. Rolled up in their close embrace, with the smell of dust and perfume mixed with warm flesh, they began to tremble at this closeness of one another. Chevalier takes up the story:

Miss was wrapped in my arms as we began to roll ourselves up into the rug. And suddenly my lips were pressed against hers, there in the dark and confining world of that carpet. Passionately, demandingly. Miss answered with an intensity as hungry as my own. We clung to each other as the rug unrolled itself again, still kissing, still caught in the fire that had finally sprung to life between us.

It was at the final dress rehearsal that 'the kiss' took place, and Mistinguett describes her feelings:

I don't think I have ever been so paralysed with first-night nerves as I was before that first revue at the Folies Bergère. I was frightened, not only for myself, but for Maurice. Stage fright is the nearest thing to nightmare that I know. Nothing helps, all confidence drains away, and you are left

Chevalier and
Mistinguett before the
fight.

clutching at a few faint straws of hope. Gamblers
know this feeling, the real ones – those who lose.
But I am not a gambler. I like to win . . . .

That night, wedged in between an arc and a brace,
Mistinguett peered through the curtain to see the
reaction on the audience's faces. Chevalier was
singing and the house sat spellbound, captivated by
his persuasive charm. She herself swooned. She
turned to look at him. He was transfigured, his face
one beaming smile. Sliding his straw hat now down
over his eyes, now on the back of his head, he sang
easily, intimately, gaily, holding the audience in the
palm of his hand.

'He's got them!' she murmured with relief. 'He's
made it. Now I can start teaching him his job – and
first and foremost – how to walk properly.'

And so she did, but her interest was not confined
solely to helping a young, comparatively inexperi-
enced Folies performer to develop his career; there
was the matter of his tremendous sexual prowess
that begged attention.

As their relationship developed, rumours ran riot about the couple, although they tried to keep their romance a secret for as long as possible. She was, after all, a household name in France – and he a mere beginner half her age.

In the privacy of her apartment, she introduced Chevalier to techniques that would have made the women of Montmartre seem like girls newly liberated from convent. But she taught him much else too; how to eat and walk and dress. He would do what she told him, listen to her advice and he would be willing to learn, developing in time a more cultured appearance.

'When I met Chevalier he was wasteful with his money,' Mistinguett complained. 'He would fling it about recklessly and then sleep on a park bench if he felt like it. Since then he has beaten me at my own game. He became more practical than I – and richer.'

During their ten-year romance, he was to learn certain economies that were to be misinterpreted as meanness – a reputation that was to pursue him to the end of his days. He would not tip a waiter, for instance, but shake his hand, considering this to be of more value. The hat-check girl did not receive a tip from Chevalier either; her reward was a peck on the cheek.

But in the early stages of the Folies Bergère, before Mistinguett's tutelage, with his comical costumes on stage there was little about him to which an audience could immediately respond without some additional chemical element. And he could muster that up by simply opening his mouth. But it was Miss who taught him how to exploit it. She instructed him in the way a sophisticated audience like the one at the Folies Bergère needed to be at first teased and then pampered; to be made to feel that it was taking part in something of a love feast. 'Do you want to hear that again?' he would call to them now. He knew they would shout, 'Yes – we do!' The fact that the audience was actually asked made it feel important, vital to his success.

Their Folies Bergère season together was followed by another in 1912, supported by the enchanting singer Yvonne Printemps and the clowns Grock and Antonet. It brought with it a further 500 francs-a-season increase in Chevalier's salary. He once more shared Mistinguett's act, her bed and her excitement with each new success. She knew, too, how nervous the young man was before each show but her worldly ways soon renewed his confidence once they returned to her apartment after the show each night. But they did not live together. Sophisticated though he may now consider himself to be, he still felt his place was with his mother, affectionately known as La Louque, on whom he doted. Miss, on the other hand, enjoyed her independence for quite another reason. All through the first year of their relationship she continued her liaison with another man.

But Chevalier too had other admirers. A famous dramatic singer, Fréhel, had fallen in love with Chevalier and pursued him day and night against his will. There was nothing he could do to free himself from her. She, in turn, realized that it was his affection for Mistinguett that spoiled her chances, and so she lay in wait for Mistinguett outside the Folies Bergère stage door several nights running, with a large kitchen knife hidden in her handbag. Her attempted attack on Miss proved to be as abortive as her determination to secure Chevalier's affection.

It was now Chevalier's turn to be attacked. A rival of his, tired of playing second fiddle in Mistinguett's affections, marched into Chevalier's dressing-room one night and challenged him. They arranged to meet, man to man, after the show that night. At the appointed time, the rival arrived in the rue Saulnier, outside the Folies Bergère stage door. A crowd had gathered, as word had spread of the intended mass-acre. Chevalier arrived soon after, dressed in a sweater and boxing gloves. At first he tried to reason with his rival, but the fellow refused to be placated. Chevalier, who had taken boxing lessons as a boy, gave him a right hook, a straight left followed by a resounding uppercut, and his opponent went sprawling onto the pavement, covered in blood.

Mistinguett emerged from the doorway, clutching her pet marmoset in her arms, and claimed her prize – the victor.

But conflict of a more serious kind lay on the horizon, bringing an end to this great era of *La Belle Epoque*. The period was known as the age of women; Paris was woman and all art during the period was personified through woman – but now it was brought to a bitter end by the 1914 war. It brought an end too to a great chapter in the history of the Folies Bergère.

One Sunday during a full house a rumour spread through the audience: it was the first news of the incident at Sarajevo. Prieuzij, the Serbian student, had assassinated the Archduke Francis Ferdinand, heir to the throne of Austria. The Great War began just over a month later.

The authorities threatened to close the Folies Ber-gère unless it was able to provide adequate shelter for the entire audience in the event of attack, and air-raid wardens visited the Folies regularly to inspect the space available in the cellars. A shell from Big Bertha did land in the rue Joffroy-Marie, smashing all the front-of-house windows of the Folies Bergère. The audience began to panic, but as it was only a few minutes before the interval, the musicians in the foyer were already at their posts, and struck up the 'Marseillaise'. The patriotic audience remained until the end of the performance – with the exception of only two women.

But neither good nor bad news from the front affected box-office takings. The need for escapism remained the same whatever the news. Soldiers on leave, of all nationalities, came to the Folies Bergère for a glimpse of gaiety and happiness before returning to the front. They went back, their pockets stuffed with programmes and photographs which they pinned up in their dug-outs. Often, the last face a wounded soldier saw before he died was that of a chorus-girl at the Folies Bergère.

One of the wounded was to be Maurice Chevalier. He was called up for military service shortly after the start of war, assigned to the French 35th Infantry garrisoned at Belfort. Mistinguett, who had been taken ill unexpectedly, rented a country house nearby where she spent her convalescence; there she was able to see Chevalier periodically when he came off duty. He would call for her and they would dine together.

'Those brief hours were the loveliest I have ever known,' Miss recalled. 'We sat in the late September sun and laughed and talked and lazed as if our happiness could last for ever.'

The idyll was brief. Chevalier was wounded at Cutry, near Melun, and the following day the Germans, who were advancing on Paris, captured the hospital where he had been sent. The young infantryman was sent to the German prison camp at Altengrabow and no further news was heard of him for almost a year. French newspapers reported that Chevalier was dead, but at long last news filtered through – that although he was alive, he was still badly injured. He had, as well, lost his spirit and was to return to Paris a broken man, taking to drink and drugs. But if being a prisoner-of-war did anything for him at all, it provided him with the opportunity of learning to speak English from a British soldier.

Miss had now set out to obtain Chevalier's release, and left for Switzerland, in disguise, to see the Head of the International Red Cross on Chevalier's behalf. But she was arrested on the Swiss border and taken for a spy. She managed, with a certain amount of difficulty, to convince the authorities of her innocence once she was recognized, but was sent back to Paris. There she wrote to the King of Spain, Alphonso XIII, who had been one of her constant admirers before the war. Alphonso brought his influence to bear on the Kaiser, and Chevalier was eventually repatriated in 1916, 'for reasons of health'.

On Armistice night, word spread through the Folies Bergère and before the end of a scene the stage manager went on stage to announce the news. The house became delirious. The audience instantly took up the '*Marseillaise*'; strangers embraced each other; many were weeping unashamedly. A wave of near madness swept through the house. People seized their nearest neighbours and began to dance wildly up and down the aisles, singing snatches of 'God Save the King', 'Tipperary' and '*La Madelon*' in a mad medley of rejoicing.

Chevalier returned from Germany without energy, financial means or that spirit of patriotism displayed by the Folies Bergère audience on Armistice night. 'It's no good,' he told Mistinguett. 'I'll never get my 6,000 francs a month as I did before. I'm finished.'

He felt that nobody wanted him and Mistinguett felt it her duty to get him a chance of a comeback. After several fruitless attempts to find him a job, she appealed to the new director of the Folies Bergère, Beretta, but he was only prepared to offer Chevalier 100 francs per performance. They haggled, but the management refused to offer any more. Mistinguett finally persuaded Beretta to deduct 100 francs from her own 330 francs per performance and to add it to Chevalier's salary. It was done with the proviso that Chevalier was never to know about the deal they had struck.

They were to open the *Grande Revue des Folies Bergère* on 15 March 1917 and took a villa near Deauville for the summer in order to prepare new material for their new show. They invited Maurice Yvain, Albert Willemetz and Jacques-Charles, the best revue writers of the day, to stay with them in order to help create the new revue, and one night, when Jacques-Charles began reading aloud a novel by Carco called *Mon Homme*, it gave Mistinguett an idea. She wanted a song, based on the theme of the novel, dedicated to 'her man' – Maurice Chevalier. The writers worked through the night, and the song they wrote together, with Mistinguett's worthy contribution to the lyric and melody, went into the new revue at the Folies Bergère – and the morning after the first night all Paris was humming it. It was sent to America where the French lyric was translated into English by Channing Pollock for Fanny Brice, who performed it at the Ziegfeld Follies. It became one of Fanny Brice's most popular songs, a heart-felt rendering to her gambler husband Nicky Arnstein, who ended up in prison for embezzlement. Alice Delysia sang 'My Man' in the C. B. Cochran revue, *London Calling!*, in which Noël Coward's name went up in lights for the very first time in the West End of London, and the song was popularized more recently by Barbra Streisand in the finale of the stage and film musical story of Fanny Brice's life, *Funny Girl*:

MY MAN

Costs me a lot
But there's one thing that I've got
– it's my man.
Cold and wet I do get
But all that I soon forget
– with my man.
He's not much for looks
And no hero out of books
– he's my man.
Two or three girls has he
that he likes as well as me
– but I love him.
I don't know why I do!
He isn't true
– he beats me too.
What can I do?

Oh, my God, I love him so –
He'll never know.
All my life is just despair,
but I don't care.
When he takes me in his arms,
the world is bright,
alright.
And what's the difference, if I say
I'll go away
When I know I'll come back on my
    knees some day
For whatever my man is
I am his –
– forever more.

A few years after the launching of '*Mon Homme*',
which became Mistinguett's signature tune, the great
star undertook a South American tour. Unknown
to her, '*Mon Homme*' had been sold to an American
music publisher for 250 dollars, and the first time
Mistinguett sang it in New York a man rushed along
to her waving a document covered in signatures and
rubber stamps and demanded 1,000 dollars from her
and another 1,000 dollars from the Schuberts, for
whom she was working, for the right to sing it. She
was furious. She had created it, helped to write it,
had sung it scores and scores of times – and now she
was being *charged*. She had to pay, but she was bitter.

Soon after the opening of their new Folies Bergère
revue in 1917, Mistinguett and Chevalier reached
the crisis point in their relationship. But before their
next *contretemps* – over star billing – she was to
discover his infidelity.

Chevalier had left his mother's flat and taken one
of his own in the Quartier St Augustin. One afternoon Mistinguett went there while he was out,
intending to re-furnish his drawing-room as a
surprise. But a surprise lay in store for her instead.
She found clothing belonging to his girlfriends
strewn about the place. She remembers that

I was more than vexed. After that I forbade

Maurice to come to my apartment in the Boulevard des Capucines unless a red handkerchief was
seen hanging from my balcony. If the housework
was not done or I had a visitor, there would be
no red flag and Maurice would have to walk round
the block until there was. I never told him why
and I remember he was naïvely puzzled by my
sudden reserve.

But it was not jealousy of an entirely emotional
kind that finally drove them apart. Gaby Deslys and
Harry Pilcer, who were scoring a tremendous success
at the Casino de Paris in the revue *Laissez-le Tomber!*
(Drop Him!) were leaving the show to undertake
another commitment, and Mistinguett and Chevalier
were invited to take over.

But although it seemed like a good idea, Mistinguett, who was accustomed to – and demanded –
top billing, now faced Chevalier's demands for equal
status. Mistinguett dug her toes in, refused his
request and agreed that this is what started the end
of their romance: 'Our success had no doubt gone
to Maurice's head a bit and he probably thought I
was trying to sabotage his performance. He stopped
calling for me at the end of the performance as he
had done every night without fail for ten years. As
to equal billing, I couldn't grant him this. If I had
done so, the other actors would have reacted as only
actors can.'

As the two stars began drifting apart, Mistinguett
found a new partner in the attractive young Earl
Leslie and Chevalier in the charming Elsie Janis, with
whom he undertook to play the Palace Theatre,
London, taking over the lead from Owen Nares in
his show, *Hello America*. Chevalier brought a French
version of this musical back to Paris as a star vehicle
for himself, now determined to break away from
his established partnership with Mistinguett, but the
show failed dismally.

Mistinguett and Chevalier were now invited back
to the Casino de Paris for a new production, but

LESLIE

C. Cosmar.??

agreed only to do one number together as a double act. The Casino had by now become a tremendous attraction for stars and audiences alike, and certainly the Folies Bergère's greatest rival.

Once more Chevalier demanded equal billing, and this time the management agreed. When Mistinguett heard of this, she stormed out and announced that she would not return until the theatre dropped this

Earl Leslie, who succeeded Chevalier in Mistinguett's affections.

stupid arrangement. The management stood firm –
and Mistinguett walked out of the Casino.

For the first time Maurice Chevalier's name went
up in lights outside a theatre – alone; but at a considerable cost to his relationship with Mistinguett, for it
ended their affair.

The indestructible Mistinguett, of course, proceeded with her astonishing successes, but she had
not changed her character with the loss of Chevalier.
She was as earthy as ever. A few years later, when
Paul Derval invited her for a return season at the
Folies Bergère, he met her at the Gare du Nord a
few days before the opening night. Unfortunately,
a railway porter turned on her when she refused to
tip him. He said that she had a face like the back of
a bus. She could swear like a trooper and let out
every invective she could summon up, truly setting
into the porter. The railwayman gave back as good
as he got, and before things got out of hand Derval
abandoned the photographers and pressmen, dragged
Mistinguett through the left-luggage office and
hustled her, screeching like a Banshee, into a taxi
with the press in hot pursuit, photographing her face
distorted with helpless rage.

The following day the film footage was shown,
to the immense amusement of the French public, in
every cinema in France.

Sir Anton Dolin remembers seeing Mistinguett a
good deal during the 1930s when he appeared at the
Mogador with George Milton and Belita, who was
featuring in her first ice-skating half-revue in Paris.
The great ballet dancer had gone over to dance
in the first half. Charles Trenet was making his début
at the ABC Theatre, where Dolin had just finished
playing, and together with Mistinguett he went to
see Trenet's performance which took place after his
Folies Bergère début:

> We were coming out of the stage door; a big
> car was waiting and we were going to dine in the
> Champs Elysées, where Mistinguett was going to

have a free supper. Wherever she went she never paid a bill, according to theatre gossip, but that was not entirely true. When a bill was presented – which was seldom done as her presence was eagerly sought in the restaurants of the Champs Elysées, just as it was in the smart *boîtes de nuit* of Montmartre and Montparnasse; but on the occasions when the bill *was* presented a very large percentage was always taken off. This would appear to be the reason why one used to hear, 'Oh, Miss never pays for anything. She is too mean.' Don't you believe it! She belonged to the days when the theatre had real glamour; and she possessed that same glamour off the stage.

There was an old woman selling flowers outside the theatre and I went over to give her five francs and Mistinguett said: *'Non! Ne donne rien! Elle est beaucoup plus riche que nous!'* ['No, don't give her anything. She is much richer than we are.'] *'Elle est salope!'* ['She's a slut!']

Mistinguett had a notebook with twenty or thirty names in it. I saw this myself in her dressing-room. Against each of these names was so much money listed: 10 francs, 20 francs, 30 francs, and so forth. Meaning that on the Friday or Saturday *that* amount was going to be given to these poor, out-of-work actors. She was not mean at all. In many ways she was very generous.

But Sir Anton's view of Mistinguett is contradicted by the English actor and entertainer who appeared in Mistinguett's act for many years. Billy Milton professes that the book was not comprised of a list of money she gave away each week, but of money she was saving for the artists in the show, many of whom complained that the money they handed over to her each week for safe-keeping was never to be seen again:

Miss was always keen on money; unbelievably so, and when a suggestion was made that I would

Anton Dolin

spend too much money in Paris, she felt it would be her duty to take my weekly salary and then at the end of the engagement she would hand it over to me so that I could come back to England with a substantial amount. And I got a kick under the table from Earl Leslie, her partner and lover at that particular time – but I couldn't understand what he was trying to convey, until later when he warned me about handing over even a *sou* to her.

But returning to Sir Anton who relates his first encounter with the star in 1927:

I had been to a dress rehearsal at the Casino de Paris, and was sitting in a box with the author Rowland Leigh (who many years later was to write the screenplay for *The Charge of the Light Brigade*) and Paul Rocky. [Paul was one of the famous Rocky Twins who were two tall, disturbingly attractive youths who parodied the Dolly Sisters. Mistinguett had discovered them at the Concert Mayol. They were alike as two peas in a pod and so strikingly attractive that they were mobbed each night at the stage door by connoisseurs of the Body Beautiful of either sex. On stage – and off – it was impossible to tell them apart, and their hide-and-seek act behind a tree was a sensation.]

Suddenly a head peered in from the next box.

'What are you doing here, Monsieur?' was suddenly hurled at me in French, in a rather tired, husky voice.

I replied in French, 'Madame, I am here with my friends.'

'You have no right, Monsieur. I must ask you to leave.'

'But, Madame, I think you know Monsieur Leigh.'

'You must go. This is a closed rehearsal. Please, Monsieur, will you leave at once.'

I hesitated, and then came the final outburst

from the box next door. 'Who are you, Monsieur?'

Flustered, and taken aback, I could only reply, 'And who are *you*, Madame?'

I should think that it was the first time in her whole life that anyone had ever dared to say to the great Mistinguett, 'Who are you?'

After the show had opened and Dolin went back-stage to compliment the star on her performance, she said to him, 'And *now* you know who I am, *n'est-ce pas?*'

Mistinguett emerges as a combination between meanness and generosity, but moreover of tremendous professionalism and discipline. At that same rehearsal, when Mistinguett sat in the auditorium clothed in a dressing-gown with a towel draped round her head, she suddenly stopped the rehearsal and the orchestra. She had spotted something wrong with the costume of one of the chorus-girls and pounced on her:

'How dare you put a safety pin in your costume!' she accused.

'Mademoiselle, the button has come off.'

'Don't you know how to sew!'

'No, Mademoiselle, I can't sew.'

'Then you should not be in the theatre. Go immediately. Go and sew that button on. Take it to the wardrobe.'

Sir Anton Dolin, who was there, recalls:

The girl was absolutely heart-broken. Miss kept the whole rehearsal waiting five minutes while that girl went up to have her button sewn on.

On another occasion she showed the other side to her nature when one of the show-girls went into her dressing-room and said, 'Miss – do you have a dress you can lend me tonight? I have a very important date. A charming man. He is very rich and he wants to take me out to supper and I don't have a nice dress.'

Miss got out one of the best dresses she could

find in her wardrobe, handed it to her and said, 'Well, what are you going to wear over it? A cloak? Do you have a cloak?'

'No, Miss. No.'

She gave her the most beautiful wrap to wear and said, 'Now, go out. Have a good time and make sure that you get a lovely diamond bracelet. But! Send me back my coat in the morning! *And* the dress!'

In the same dressing-room, which was long and narrow, the curtain was drawn while Miss changed from the creation of thousands of diamonds and pearls which covered the dress and train she held in her hand during our introduction and short talk. The famous hat of ostrich plumes was already packed away until the next performance. In a few minutes she drew back the curtains, and there she stood, simply but beautifully dressed in a vivid blue coat and skirt, a dark wine-coloured blouse, and hat to match.

To say that her face looked like that of a girl of twenty is an exaggeration, but her figure certainly did. The face was that of a woman of forty or more, but when she smiled and laughed, showing those perfect white teeth of hers, she looked so young that time seemed an unknown thing in her life. For, as I know, and as the world knows, 'Miss is not forty, or even fifty.' At that time, in the thirties, she was closer to seventy, although she had never admitted her age to anyone.

Her amazing youthfulness came from her smile, which I found rather girlish. She was proud of her teeth and allowed me to examine them.

'I have never been to a dentist in my life,' she bragged. 'My teeth are perfect. Look!'

When Mistinguett learned that Dolin was returning to London for a short stay, she asked him to buy her a little Scotch terrier. 'I bought the Scotch terrier for £21 – took it to Paris, gave it to her at the Boulevard des Italiens where she lived, stayed up until five in the morning talking, but she never gave me the £21!'

To illustrate this strange mixture of generosity and avarice that seemed to possess Mistinguett, Billy Milton tells another story. He had commissioned the celebrated photographer Dorothy Wilding to take photographs of him and his leading lady, but having left the negatives with Mistinguett for her approval, he went to ask for their return:

> Imagine my surprise when, as I walked into her dressing-room, I saw laid out on the floor two hundred prints of each negative that Mistinguett had printed privately. I said, 'What's this? I shall get sued by Dorothy Wilding for infringement of copyright!'
>
> And Mistinguett replied rather arrogantly without looking up at me, 'It will be excellent publicity. Worldwide publicity. Big star sued by photographer.'
>
> 'And what about me?' I asked, rather exasperated. 'I paid for all this out of my own pocket.' And then plucking up courage, I added, 'I want two of each photograph.'
>
> 'Very well,' she replied. 'How many do you want? It will cost you twelve francs for each print.' Twelve francs was a lot of money in those days, in 1931.
>
> I had to pay for my own photographs! On top of my paying for the negatives, to which she did not contribute a single sou, she was now charging me for my own pictures!
>
> Of course, she displayed them in the lobby of the theatre. She had a percentage of the takings of the woman in the toilets; she had a cut of the programme girls' sales – she had a cut of *everything*. And now these photographs.
>
> Added to this, she finally used them on all the music covers of the songs we sang in the show!

Milton did, however, get his own back on Mistinguett the night he kicked her up the behind:

I played the barrel organ in one of the scenes with Mistinguett. Apparently when she was at the Folies Bergère with Chevalier there was a face-slapping scene where she slapped his face about twenty times, and he, being a tough young man who'd had boxing training, allowed all this to happen without flinching. Unfortunately, I'm not used to having my face slapped – but she found the excuse to do so.

In playing the barrel organ, when it stops the notes go on; you cannot stop a barrel organ in the way you stop playing the piano, and she thought I was allowing the notes to go on deliberately. So, in the middle of the scene, she came across and slapped my face. I had to give the barrel organ thirty-two turns for it to be ready again for the next chorus for her song – and it happened again. She came over and slapped my face again, but on both sides this time.

So I kicked her. I didn't know what I was doing, it was a sort of reflex action. But I kicked her and she hobbled over to the stage box and sat on the edge of the box, absolutely astounded. I don't think she'd ever been kicked in her life before – and certainly not in front of an audience!

I left the theatre, took a taxi back to my hotel and packed my trunk to go home to England. Two or three hours later I got a telephone call from the company secretary to say that Miss felt I was overwrought with the long and tedious rehearsals, and asked me to play a date with her in Deauville with Jean Sablon. Of course, I agreed, but it was more for the sake of Jean Sablon than Mistinguett.

Her understudy's name was Jade. She was very nice; a sweet woman. Mistinguett was never left to go home alone after the show, and sometimes Jade, who lived in the opposite direction, in Montmartre, would say to me, 'Which of us is going back with the old girl tonight? You or me?'

They were very happy days, but you had to be very alert. I learnt to keep myself to myself because I found that to get too near to the star was a mistake. Take the case of the photographs as an example.

The brilliant designer, Erté, who was ninety years old on 23 November 1982, vowed not only not to get near to the star, but never to work for her again:

> Madame Rasimi had designed Mistinguett's costumes for many years and when Mistinguett formed her own production company she asked me to design one of her productions. So we went to Max Weldy's office where we discussed everything and when all the requirements for the show were noted and ideas exchanged and settled, I said to Mistinguett: 'When can I send my secretary to you to discuss the business aspect?'
>
> Mistinguett said, 'There is no business, Monsieur. I never pay. You will get all the publicity. That is worth more than the money for the costumes.'
>
> 'I'm terribly sorry, madame,' I replied. 'I do sometimes do things without payment for young artists who have no money, but this is different.'
>
> And so we never worked together again.

Miss Bluebell illustrates another aspect of Mistinguett's character:

> In 1936 I got a call from an agent to say that Mistinguett wanted me to bring a troupe of my girls to the Mogador Theatre for her new show, so I said yes. She was going around with a very attractive man at that time, a Brazilian by the name of Carlos Machado, and one of my idiotic girls started going out with him on the sly. Unfortunately, Miss, who seemed to have spies everywhere, found this out.
>
> Mistinguett appeared at the finale of the first

half and then she did practically the entire second half of the show. On this particular evening, when the curtain came down on the first half, she said, 'Stay here for a minute everybody. There's someone I'd like to kill,' and she looked at this idiotic girl who was about seventeen or eighteen years of age. 'And before I do so, she's going to get fired from this show.' Mistinguett left the stage, and did the second half of the show.

The next day I got a call from the agent, who said, 'You've got to fire that girl.' So, knowing how mean Mistinguett was with money, I said, 'Well, you've got a problem.'

He didn't want to hear the problem and insisted that Mistinguett would not work if the girl was to remain in the show. She would have to be fired. So I said, 'O.K. I'll fire her if you like, but she's got a three-month contract. You've got to pay her three months' salary.' He said he would have to confer with Mistinguett and he telephoned me later that day.

'I've spoken to Miss. You can keep the girl.'

Miss Bluebell fell in love and married the conductor of the Folies Bergère, Marcel Leibovici:

My husband used to go and rehearse with Mistinguett when she had her home in the country outside Paris, and he found out more and more about this strange meanness that possessed this great star. Mistinguett used to telephone a handful of friends and say, 'I am rehearsing at home today, come and have lunch with me. It's such a lovely day.'

'Thank you, thank you, Miss. That's very nice of you.'

'Oh, by the way,' she would add. 'Go by the Place de la Concorde on your way here. I've left a packet' – at one of the most expensive delicatessens, containing the luncheon – 'pick it up and bring it to me and we will have a really good time.'

And of course, when they went to pick it up, they had to pay for it!

Arthur Rowe takes up the story:

I was present at one of those luncheons, but on that particular occasion I don't know exactly who paid for it. Mistinguett's château was about fifteen minutes' drive outside Paris. Very French. Louis Quinze furniture. It wasn't a very formal home, but it was very opulent, with eight or nine servants dancing attention.

There were twenty-four of us around the luncheon table, presided over by a very animated Mistinguett. I've never seen such a large, completely round table, and this wonderful meal went on, course after course, for about three hours, ending up with nuts and chocolates.

Aside from being the lead dancer in Mistinguett's act, Arthur Rowe also choreographed her routines. He soon discovered that although she could move well, she was not essentially a good dancer – given that she was over sixty years old by now. Despite the stories about her many love affairs, there remained only one man she really loved to the very end – Maurice Chevalier:

Mistinguett always wanted us to be with her, which was about an hour after the show started. She always opened on this great big staircase; we would wait on the staircase for her to make her entrance, and wave her on. She had masses of feathers and stage jewellery, but she wore only one ring on her hand. It was a huge square emerald which she told us had been given her by the Shah.

One evening when she knew that Chevalier was going to be out front, she sent for all her jewels to be brought to the theatre from her safe-deposit by two detectives. They stood outside her dressing-room, escorted her to the stage and stood on either side of the stage throughout her act. You wouldn't have known they were real because the fake stage jewellery was so marvellous. All this specially for Maurice Chevalier, who sat in the stage box. But she needn't have bothered because he didn't come back to see her after the show. And she was in tears. We tried to console her, and she kept saying she had never loved anyone else.

After the show, the jewels were all taken back to the safe-deposit. In all the years working with Mistinguett that was the only time I saw her real jewels. They were worth a fortune!

And of those famous legs?

She always wore wonderful silk stockings, about two or three pairs, one pair over the other, which gave a magnificent sheen to the legs, and obviously hid any imperfections. She always wore short skirts to show off her legs. She was very proud of them; they graduated down to her ankles in a smooth line; no muscle showed and the knees didn't seem to exist. She was normal height, about five foot five, with perfect proportions. She wasn't beautiful at all though, but on stage she was very heavily made up, and well made up outside the theatre. She was very striking with gorgeous eyes that slanted down. And her voice was rough; it sounded like a concrete mixer!

Mistinguett now began rehearsals for the 1934 production of *Folies en Folie* at the Folies Bergère. The revue was prepared with the greatest of care as it was in direct competition with the opening of the new revue at the Casino de Paris with an unexpected star attraction: Cécile Sorel.

Cécile Sorel, the great leading lady of the Comédie Française, where she reigned for thirty-two years, shocked the whole of France when she made her début in revue at a round figure of two million francs for a ten-month run. One might easily have com-

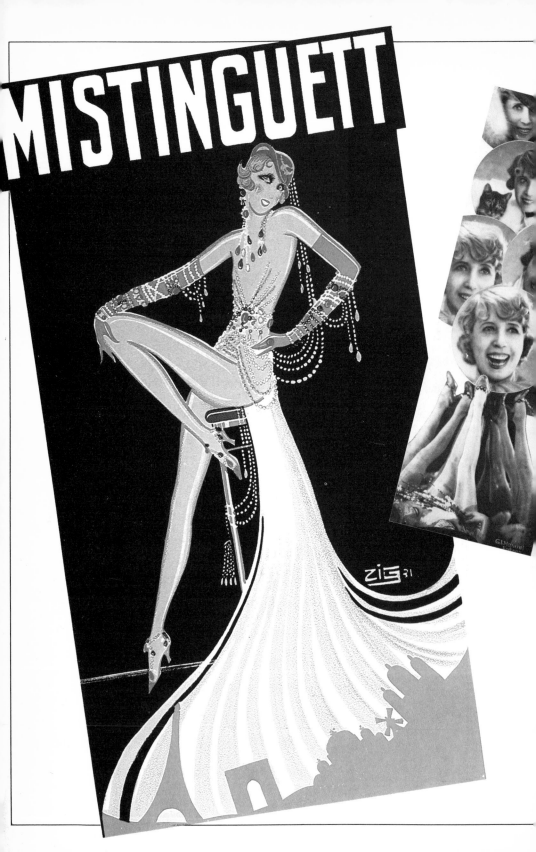

pared the public's reaction to a British outburst had Dame Edith Evans agreed to appear at the old Metropolitan music-hall in the Edgware Road. 'Cécile Sorel leaves the Comédie Française . . . for the Music

Hall!' the newspapers proclaimed. The Casino de Paris had always been the Folies Bergère's greatest rival and remained so until its closure in the 1970s. The Folies, in a counter-offensive to this new move, enlisted the support of Fernandel and Stan Randall, and the show ran for nine months, ending with a tour of Brussels in 1935. The press enjoyed the alleged rivalry between Mistinguett and Sorel.

Cécile Sorel

According to the gossip columns, Mistinguett left a party when Cécile Sorel was announced; Sorel left her table when Mistinguett entered the restaurant. They were, however, the best of friends. On Sorel's opening night, Mistinguett attended her performance and dined with her privately in her dressing-room afterwards. A few days later, Sorel returned the compliment and dined with Mistinguett at the Folies Bergère.

Mistinguett's opening night was greeted with an ovation; her keen reception might easily have been attributed to one of her most famous songs, '*Ça, c'est Paris*', and a new one, '*C'est vrai*' ('It's True'), devised by her and Willemetz, the lyrics admitting to her shortcomings and idiosyncracies:

'*C'est vrai*'
I've enormous great teeth
And three notes to my voice
It's true!
But as I've no wish to steal Miss Sorel's thunder
I'll leave the Lady her Camellias
And sell my humbler blooms instead.
They say that I show off my legs
But I'd not be Mistinguett – if I didn't do that.

They say – that I don't pay the tradesmen
It's true.
They say – I hang on to my shekels
It's true.
But if Monsieur Sarraut the Finance Minister
Took a leaf out of my book
His books might show a credit
And if they put Mistinguett
In charge of France's budget
We'd not be in this mess.

The then critic of *Le Matin*, Colette, described Mistinguett's return to the Folies Bergère in her review of the show:

Mistinguett has re-opened, after her long absence, in all simplicity. Gone, for the moment, are the gigantic feathered head-dresses. Wearing a simple little diamond-studded cap, she made her first entrance. We watched her spellbound as she advanced towards the audience, right to the edge of the proscenium – near enough to touch us, to breathe in with flaring nostrils the dust, the warmth, the heavy mingled perfumes – democratic incense, vital element of Mistinguett. During the long storm of applause, we could all see the blue of her eyes change colour through her tears.

She belongs to the nation. Has she still, this year, that walk so reminiscent of Réjane, those eloquent legs, that gay smile and those sad eyes?

She had, indeed, and so equipped continued to beguile the nation for many years to come, personifying all that Paris evoked. There was a quality of being 'one of us' which endeared her to the bourgeois patrons. She was the Marie Lloyd of Paris. She spoke the language of her own people with a natural charm. Her lively smile was for every individual in the audience; when she sang, the troubles of her listeners vanished, and the world seemed a happier place.

Here was a true artist of the great tradition of the music-hall. But gone from her was the love that she had once cherished.

5
The End of an Era

The end of the First World War brought with it a change in style and tastes. In the mid-twenties Paul Derval had reconstructed the Folies Bergère's interior throughout. He included an upper circle and renovated the walls, ceilings and the foundations, all without interrupting the performances or the run of the show. A new hall and auditorium were constructed in the workshops and brought to the Folies, piece by piece, to cover the old walls.

Having survived the war so well, Derval fell on superstition by having the title of every revue consist of thirteen letters. The only flop of his career at the Folies occurred when he broke away from this tradition, and to this day the thirteen-letter title exists. Even though the word Folies always appears in the title, it is unlikely that the house will run out of titles, thanks to the industry of a regular patron who presented the management with an invaluable list of some 150 titles which should see them well into the next century.

Since Erté's introduction to the Folies Bergère in 1917 by the theatre's costume-maker, Max Weldy, he designed the two major tableaux for the revue each year. Among the most notable during that period were for the 1921 revue. Two years later the Folies presented *En Plein Folies* (The Complete Folies), which starred the seductive Yane Exiane and the athletic dancer Nina Payne. In this revue Erté's tableau *'Grands Fleuves du Monde'* (The Rivers) received a special accolade from *Le Figaro*'s review

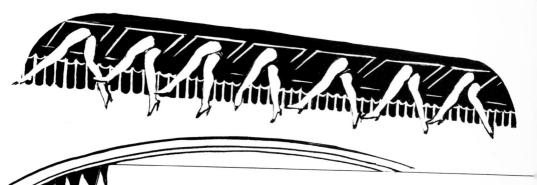

by Jacques Patin, together with his announcement 'that to find a way of describing the marvels of this revue is almost impossible'.

The famous John Tiller Girls (forty-four of them), who were to be succeeded by the Jackson Girls, and the Jacksons, in turn, by the Bluebells, appeared in the 1924 production of *Coeurs en Folie* (Hearts in Folly) with costumes for the exotic 'Legend of the Nile' sequence designed by Georges Barbier, and '*Les Idoles*' (The Idols) tableau by Erté, two of the greatest designers of the period. The following year, *Un Soir de Folie* (A Night's Folly) again presented the popular dancer of the Folies Bergère, Nina Payne. In this production 'The Perpetual Adoration' and

'Chastity Belt' sequences were so sensational as to attract the famous Baron de Meyer to come along and photograph the company.

The 1926–7 season offered a more exciting attraction. The revue *La Folie du Jour* presented to the Folies Bergère audiences for the first time the exotic Josephine Baker, who had scored such an impact in *La Revue Nègre* at the Théâtre Champs Elysées with an all-black cast. The Louis Lemarchand production for which Fréjol was stage director and coordinator had a supporting cast consisting of Chrysis, the Epp Sisters, Dorville, Castel, Alibert, Pepa Bonafé, Maryse and Tymga and the John Tiller dancers. This revue with Josephine Baker as its sizzling star was to cause not only the greatest sensation since Mistinguett and Chevalier's appearance at the Folies, but the greatest consternation Paul Derval had

'The Guadaguivir', one of Erté's designs for The Rivers tableau, 1923.

A design by Erté for
Aphrodite from The
Idols, 1924.

encountered with any of the famous stars to have appeared at the Folies before – or after – her engagement.

Among the most famous of American expatriates, singer and dancer Josephine Baker became a legend in her own time. She had gone to Paris in the 1920s as a variety show dancer and soon developed into a polished music-hall star with an international reputation. Seemingly ageless, she continued to astonish critics and please admirers with her sultry voice, light dusky figure and supple movements.

Illegitimate, half-Jewish and half-negro, Josephine Baker was born in St Louis, Missouri, on 3 June 1906. Her father was a footloose merchant of whom the family saw little, and her mother supported herself and her four children. Josephine left school at the age of eight to augment the family income by working as a kitchen helper, maid and baby-sitter in private homes. In her early adolescence Josephine Baker went at least once a week to watch the dancers in a local vaudeville house and began dancing part-time in a chorus line herself. At fifteen she joined a travelling troupe with the famous Bessie Smith, in Philadelphia, where she was then living with her grandmother. A few months later, in 1923, she was in New York, dancing in the chorus of Noble Sissle's musical comedy *Shuffle Along* at the Music Hall. Placed at the end of the line of dancers, she attracted attention and applause by her flair for improvisation and mimicry. A critic recalled in the *New York Post* that 'there was something about her rhythm, her smile, and her impudent grace that made her stand out'.

After *Shuffle Along*, Josephine Baker appeared in *Chocolate Dandies* on Broadway before joining the floor show at the Plantation Club, where Ethel Waters was the featured performer. With the offer of 250 dollars a week, or twice her Plantation Club salary, she accepted a major dancing part in *La Revue Nègre*, an American production that opened at the

Josephine Baker's Folies Bergère debut, 1926. 'Josephine Baker has it all – class, talent – and ding dong' *Walter Winchell*.

Champs Elysées Theatre in Paris in October 1925.
With this revue, *le jazz hot* invaded France for the
first time since Gaby Deslys's sensational come-back,
and Josephine Baker was, in the eyes of the audience
and critics, its personification.

The first of several law suits in which Josephine
Baker became involved was that filed by the producer of *La Revue Nègre* for breach of contract when
she left the show to take higher pay and star billing
with the Folies Bergère – but not before causing as
much concern for the Folies, when after signing their
contract she undertook a further engagement to
appear in Germany with *La Revue Nègre*, refusing
steadfastly to honour her new Folies Bergère contract. However, Paul Derval finally managed to lure
her back – at a price – and, billed as the 'Dark Star'
at the Folies, she created a sensation by dancing on
a mirror, naked except for a curtain of rubber bananas
strung around her waist. Soon banana-clad Josephine
dolls were selling by the thousands to children and
tourists.

Her first impact on Paris was recorded by André
Daven, director of the Champs Elysèes Theatre who
presented *La Revue Nègre*.

> Opening night was unforgettable. At midnight
> Parisian café society literally invaded the theatre,
> shoving aside security guards. Because of advance
> reviews in the press, the air was crackling with
> tension. Would it be necessary to empty the hall?
>
> At last the curtain rose, revealing a backdrop
> on which Paul Colin had painted a whimsical
> skyscraper. Onto the empty stage behind a colour-
> ful peddler's cart strolled Sidney Bechet, playing
> a poignant, tender melody on his clarinet. The
> pure, spell binding music filled the air and within
> thirty seconds the uproar in the hall had ceased.
> As the last sweet note faded away, the audience
> burst into thunderous applause. Now it was
> Josephine whose presence filled the stage, bringing
> with her a glimpse of another world. As she

danced, quivering with intensity, the entire room felt the raw force of her passion, the excitement of her rhythm. She was eroticism personified. The simplicity of her emotions, her savage grace, were deeply moving. She laughed, she cried, then from her supple throat came a song, crystal clear at first, then with a hoarseness that caught at the heart.

She became an overnight sensation, the darling of Paris, the very essence of the capital in the riotous Twenties, embodying the pain and poignancy of the Jazz Age. One might say that she took over from Gaby Deslys, who was to die early at the age thirty-three. Hemingway danced cheek to cheek with Josephine Baker, proclaiming her to be the most sensational woman anyone had ever seen; Picasso painted her; Colette sent her fan letters. Her name was to be linked with Mussolini, de Gaulle, Peron, Castro, Tito and the Pasha of Marrakesh.

Paul Derval's attention had been caught 'by a wonderful girl, with the proportions of a Tanagra figurine and a personality that seemed to set the stage on fire' when he attended *La Revue Nègre*. He offered her a contract the next day and after discussing terms it was agreed that Josephine Baker would star in the next Folies Bergère revue. The Derval team of experts got down to work. Louis Lemarchand enlisted a team of designers which included Georges Barbier and Erté; the costumes were, as usual, to be made by Max Weldy. Half-a-dozen set designers were commissioned to start work on the sets; wig-makers were enlisted, machinists, seamstresses, shoe-makers; music was composed by precisely a dozen of the most brilliant musicians including Vincent Rose and Irving Berlin. But all this was almost to no avail – for the star had flown.

La Revue Nègre had contracted to play Berlin and there Josephine became captivated by the dazzling city. 'It had a jewel-like sparkle, especially at night, that didn't exist in Paris. The vast cafés reminded me of ocean liners powered by the rhythms of their orchestras. There was music everywhere.' In the audience one evening sat one of the most eminent German directors, the great Max Reinhardt. After the performance he informed her, through an interpreter, that she had tremendous presence and that the only thing that really interested him on the stage was an actor's personality – and she had it in abundance. 'I'd like you to stay here and work with me at the Deutsche Theatre,' he announced. 'With a few years' study, you could become a fine comedienne.'

Josephine Baker before grooming.

Paul Derval had learnt that Josephine was seriously considering the Max Reinhardt offer and, frantic with worry, contacted his agent Monsieur Lorett, who immediately leapt onto the first available train to Berlin. In the biting December cold he waited for two hours outside the stage door of the theatre where Josephine Baker was performing, and he was finally admitted. He was soon to learn that she had no intention of honouring her Folies Bergère contract. He protested. Did she not realize that poor Monsieur Derval had already hired a number of people because of her? Did she not realize what the Folies *was*? That it took three months to rehearse a show, which involved five hundred people and utilized twelve hundred costumes created by famous designers? They were counting on her to be there to inspire the dressmakers and because of her they had built the show around tunes by Spencer Williams and Irving Berlin.

She was almost convinced, and was about to agree to honour her contract, when, putting into practice the financial cunning and insolence she had learnt so quickly in France, she decided to test her essential worth. She had, after all, achieved fame on two continents. She was, after all, introduced in Paris and Berlin as 'the famous' Josephine, and if Paul Derval still wanted her, he would have to pay more.

'Tell Monsieur Derval that if he wants me to leave Berlin he will have to pay me an extra four hundred francs a show.'

Lorett looked at her in dismay and scurried away. He realized that she was adamant and no further persuasion would change her mind. She had made mention of the Max Reinhardt interest in order to strengthen her case.

Lorett conferred with Derval. The show was too far advanced for them to cancel her contract and there would have been no point in taking her to court for breach of contract. Lorett returned to the star.

'Since Monsieur Derval has already invested heavily in the show because of you, he is forced to accept. Please return to Paris at once.'

Sensing her lack of discipline, however, Derval took the precaution of including a clause in her new contract specifying the number of fittings she was expected to attend. But even so, she did not attend, refusing steadfastly to try on her costumes. It was to take a solicitor's letter to persuade her each time. She was highly amused at the lengths to which they went to get her to costume-fittings – particularly since one of the costumes – the one which was to increase her fame considerably – was the girdle of bananas.

Rehearsals began and she spent much time on her appearance. She had not yet begun to accept that the coffee colour of her skin was an essential element of her personality and she spent an hour each day trying to turn herself into a white girl. She had invented a secret ointment for defrizzing her hair. Every morning she rubbed herself all over with a lemon in the hope of whitening her skin, the tone of which became a fashion craze. On the Place de l'Opéra there was a giant moving doll of Josephine in a shop window next to a display for Valaze Water Lily beauty cream. The sign for the exhibit announced: 'You can have a body like Josephine Baker if you use Valaze cream.'

Ever conscious of the effect her unusual complexion had on her audiences, Josephine went to Helena Rubinstein for advice and Rubinstein, who believed that a face could cost as much in upkeep as a Rolls Royce, gave her the full treatment. She blacked Josephine's eyes with kohl, taught her to apply a sticky foundation called Crème Gypsy (which dried to a light ochre), accented her full lips with a dark lipstick to make a vivid contrast with her strong white teeth, and brilliantined her hair.

But although the show was ready to present itself to its audience, and Josephine Baker was confident of success, the first night almost did not take place. At four in the morning, a couple of days before the dress rehearsal, the company was going through the 'globe' scene, which was the highlight of the show.

An immense ball, covered with flowers, was to be lowered slowly from the flies and come to rest, towering perilously above the heads of the orchestra. The ball was designed to open, revealing Josephine, nearly nude, posing on a mirror. After her dance, the ball was to close over her and steel cables draw it slowly up again into the dome of the theatre. This same device with different visual effects is used at the Folies to this day.

At rehearsal she climbed up the little iron staircase to the rafters and the obliging stage-hands helped her squeeze into the ball. They closed the lid over her and the ball's descent was put into operation. She landed with a painful bump, the lid swung open and as the tempo of the music quickened, the brass section took up the beat, and she began dancing on the mirror. The effect was stunning. The cast and stage crew applauded appreciatively. The music stopped and she crouched back inside the ball, the lid closed over her head, and the ball was hoisted, slowly, back into the ceiling. But Josephine Baker then recalls:

> Suddenly my heart skipped a beat. Something was wrong. The ball had begun to rock violently. Although the ropes that controlled one of its sides

continued moving upward, the other ropes hung
slack. As the ball tipped further and further off
centre, the lid began to slide open. How was I
going to keep from falling out? Huddled on the
tilting mirror, which was slippery as ice, I hung
forty-five feet above the orchestra. The musicians
played on obliviously. Too frightened to shout,
all I could do was pray.

Paul Derval takes up the story:

I began to yell at the top of my voice. The girls
stared at me open-mouthed. At last the orchestra
stopped playing, but the stage-hands up in the flies
had still not noticed that anything was amiss. The
ball continued to open. Then a concerted roar
from everyone in the theatre, girls, staff and
orchestra, woke the flymen from their stupor and
it began to dawn on them that something was
wrong. They stopped winding the cables. Pandemonium broke out in the theatre. Everyone began
shouting advice, yelling instructions and running
helplessly up and down the stage. I was at my
wits' end. Bellowing for silence, I dashed up to
the flies. A winch had jammed. What was to be
done now? It was impossible to bring the contrap-
tion down again and we had no ladders long
enough to reach it. I did my best to reassure
Josephine, in my bad English, and told her to hang
on – though what she had to hang on to but a
slippery mirror I can't imagine.

Someone suggested calling the fire department,
but by the time they arrived with a ladder it might
be too late. A stage-hand offered to lower himself
down a rope, gather her up and carry her to safety.
Too dangerous.

Fortunately the winch that controlled the lid still
worked.

'Josephine,' Paul Derval called down from fifteen
feet above her head, 'do you think you can climb
onto the lid? You'll have to move very slowly and

carefully.' She said she would try, but one false move and the delicately balanced ball might overturn. She seized the edge of the lid with one hand, then the other. She finally made it. She stood trembling on the lid. 'I made it,' she breathed. Derval signalled the stage-hands to begin turning the winch. 'Slowly, very slowly,' he commanded.

The ascension was slow; twelve feet, nine feet. The winch, which had been designed to control the lid, was carrying her entire weight. Six feet, three feet, two feet. She stretched out her arms to Derval, who was hanging down from the ceiling, supported at the ankles by the stage-hands, and he hauled her onto the platform. Drenched with sweat, they fell into each other's arms. Her knees shook so badly that she could hardly get down the stairs. In the hall, the applause from the company was ear-splitting.

'Call a doctor, quick,' shouted Derval.

'Don't bother, I'm fine,' Josephine replied.

'It's not for you, Josephine. Two of the dancers have just fainted.'

The ball eventually proved to be a great success. The critics found it ravishing, but not so exciting as the band of sixteen bananas that pointed phallically from her naked waist. This comical device was to be associated with her for the rest of her career.

Enthusiastically received by the press and audiences alike, Josephine Baker had moved from one great success to another. She became firmly entrenched in Parisian life – but not in its society. She did not realize how set, how traditional, French society was. It was as fixed and unchangeable as the French dictionary. She believed that her success at the Folies Bergère was her *passe partout*, but she was to be proved wrong on many embarrassing occasions and not only because of the colour of her skin or her origins, of both of which she became painfully con-scious as time drew on. Despite her great professional success, she could not alter the fact that she was black, half-Jewish – and born on the wrong side of the

Josephine Baker wearing the famous banana costume.

tracks. Although a flamboyant and extrovert personality, the constraints she had to live with hampered her quest for the respectability for which she longed. The Folies, the Opéra and the Comédie Française had long been the time-honoured suppliers of mistresses for French aristocrats, government officials, successful bookmakers and Argentine millionaires, as well as visiting dukes and princes – and Josephine Baker enjoyed her fair share of suitors.

The stage door of the Folies faces onto the rue Saulnier, a dimly lit street where a silent parade of smart cars stood in a neat line. The owners sat in the back of their Rolls Royces waiting for the dancers. Sometimes one of them sent in a bouquet of flowers with an expensive bracelet or anklet tucked between the petals.

It was not only a question of sex; Paris had the best bordellos in the world. But to sleep with a dancer from the Folies Bergère was to realize a dream, to possess the glamorous – the unattainable. 'It hurts me to confess it,' said Albert Camus many years later, 'but I would gladly trade ten conversations with Einstein for one first encounter with a pretty chorus-girl.'

Although Paul Derval had succeeded in capturing the star who was to provide substantial box-office receipts and a new lease of life to the repetitious revues at the Folies, he was to be ever on the alert because of the mercurial character of his star. A true-blue Gemini, born on 3 June, Josephine Baker's twin nature and quicksilver movements became a nightmare. She would seldom be in the theatre by 'the half', the obligatory half-hour prior to the performance, and on occasions would not arrive at all. A rapacious woman by nature, she would accept engagements elsewhere, benefiting from two engagement fees.

On one occasion Josephine's manager telephoned to say that his client was ill and would not be appearing at the Folies that evening. Derval grabbed the telephone and called her apartment. 'Miss Baker left Paris this morning, on doctor's orders,' a dispassionate voice offered.

Derval telephoned her doctor, who confirmed that his patient had contacted him that morning complaining of exhaustion and in need of a rest. He was to send her a medical certificate, but before the doctor could point out that he would need to examine her first, she hung up on him.

Through threats and bribery, Derval managed to ascertain from Josephine's house-keeper that her mistress had left by car that morning with a load of luggage, but could provide no information about her destination. She had, in fact, accepted an engagement in Deauville.

It was naturally a terrible blow to the Folies box-office receipts, which went down and down. Audiences had hardly come to see an understudy. Finally, Derval's telephone rang one morning:

'Hullo! Monsieur Derval? It's me. Josephine.'

'Josephine! Where are you?'

'In the Vendée,' she replied brightly. 'It's lovely here. Beautiful countryside –'

'What are you doing?'

'Shooting. I shot a fox yesterday, a lovely one. I'm going to send the fur to Madame Derval. It's being cured right now. I hope she'll like it . . .'

Derval was hardly in a recipient mood on behalf of his wife. He demanded an explanation. He need hardly have bothered.

'Dear Monsieur Derval, I'm simply dying to see you. I'll be back the day after tomorrow. Let's have dinner together before the show, shall we? I'll meet you at the restaurant opposite, at – say – seven? Must rush now. Goodbye!'

Endeavouring to curb his anger, the director telephoned his lawyers, instructing them to sue her, but he was advised against such action. The show had several months to run; he should turn adversity into advantage. He decided to announce to the press that his star was to return; she had, after all, telephoned to tell him so. Radio broadcasts were made, assuring full houses.

He crossed over the road and waited for her in the restaurant at the appointed hour. By seven-thirty there was no sign of her. He sent someone across to the theatre to see whether she had gone straight to her dressing-room. She had not. He telephoned her apartment. No reply. At eight-thirty, he gave up and left the restaurant. He went back-stage, where the stage director told him the understudy was preparing to go on as they could wait no longer. The curtain was due to rise at nine. The house was full. Photographers and reporters had crowded into the Press Bar, mingling with the usual first-night audiences who looked upon Josephine Baker's return as an occasion.

Paul Derval takes up the story:

> Josephine's first entrance was timed for ten minutes to ten. At a quarter to there was still no sign of her.
>
> I steeled myself to go before the curtain and make the announcement to the house.
>
> Suddenly the stage door bangs, a hat goes flying, a fur coat slides to the floor. Leaving a trail of clothes, shoes and underwear Josephine Baker tears past me along the passage to her dressing-room.
>
> At ten to ten, dynamic as usual and cool as ten cucumbers, Miss Baker made her entrance.
>
> Of course I forgave her. Until the next time. And the next time was never long in coming. Josephine seemed to take delight in cutting things as finely as she possibly could. How many times did my stage director, the show already in full swing, wait at the corner of the street on the look-out for her car? How many times did the orchestra fill in with a reprise to gain time? How many times did the conductor stand, baton poised, at the second when she should have made her entrance, while on stage the girls threw panic-

stricken glances into the wings and the stage
manager yelled up the stairs:

'What the hell is she doing?'

'Dressing!'

'What do you mean – dressing! She doesn't
wear a stitch in this scene!'

However, although lacking in discipline, she
showed compassion when it came to both children
and animals. Dogs were not allowed in the dressing-
rooms, but she always managed to get around the
management.

'I can't leave him. He's my best friend. He'd die
if I left him at home.'

The next night she would arrive with another two
dogs – best friends again. After that, a goat, a rabbit,
two cats, a parrot and a snake – all best friends or
close relations.

The cast threw a party for her twentieth birthday,
deluging her with scent, scarves, bracelets – and
another puppy.

'Poor Monsieur Derval. I could see he was worried
about my dressing-room rug! I smiled and sang and
thanked my friends warmly.' Totally undeterred.

Josephine Baker made a phenomenal success of
her brilliant career; it seemed she could do no wrong.
She opened her own night-clubs in Paris and New
York, but like many great institutions that reach a
peak, unless that zenith is maintained with even
greater perspicacity than it has applied to its rise, a
steady decline becomes inevitable. And so it was
with Josephine Baker and the Folies Bergère itself
at almost the same time. The great tradition of the
Folies had suffered a set-back with the departure of
Louis Lemarchand, and Erté in his wake, together
with the strong competition provided nightly by the
Folies's staunchest rival, the Casino de Paris. Derval,
who was unaware of *La Baker*'s dwindling popularity
when she performed nightly at her night-club in
New York, decided to seek the services of the great
star who had proved such a money-spinner, albeit

a great trial, to him. He paid her a visit in New
York where he dined with her one night after her
cabaret appearance. In the circumstances, none could
have been more pleased to see the entrepreneur than
Josephine Baker herself, but desperate though she
may have been, it did not curb her rapaciousness
when it came to securing better terms for her return
to the Folies Bergère than those proposed by Derval.

The impresario explained that he was planning
an exceptionally lavish production for the autumn,
since 1937 was the year of the *Exposition* and Paris
would be crowded with tourists. He had already
drawn up a preliminary contract offering her a
percentage of the profits together with a handsome
monthly advance. Although more than eager to
accept, she managed to conceal her excitement at
the offer for fear of losing her bargaining power.

Maurice Hermite, who, together with Georges
Charley was to write the new revue *En Super
Folies*, sat around the table at the night-club with
Derval and Josephine for several nights, discussing
the project. He explained that it was to be designed
by Michel Gyarmathy, the brilliant Hungarian costume and set designer (who to this day not only
designs the entire Folies Bergère productions but
produces them as well), who had just started working
for the Folies. Gyarmathy was, as well, to design the
poster which has come to be known as one of the
most evocative designs for the Folies to date. Blazing
with sensuality, freshness and movement, it depicted
the smiling star. Bedecked like an African dancer,
she wore bright red feathers around her ankles,
her waist and on her breasts, which by dint of
Gyarmathy's and the music-hall's magic seemed to
be palm trees which extended into Josephine's hairdo.
It was, in fact, to be a reunion between Gyarmathy
and Josephine, for as a youngster in Budapest in
1927 he had created a poster for her first European
tour.

Hermite explained that the revue was to consist
of fifty tableaux, and Derval implored Josephine that

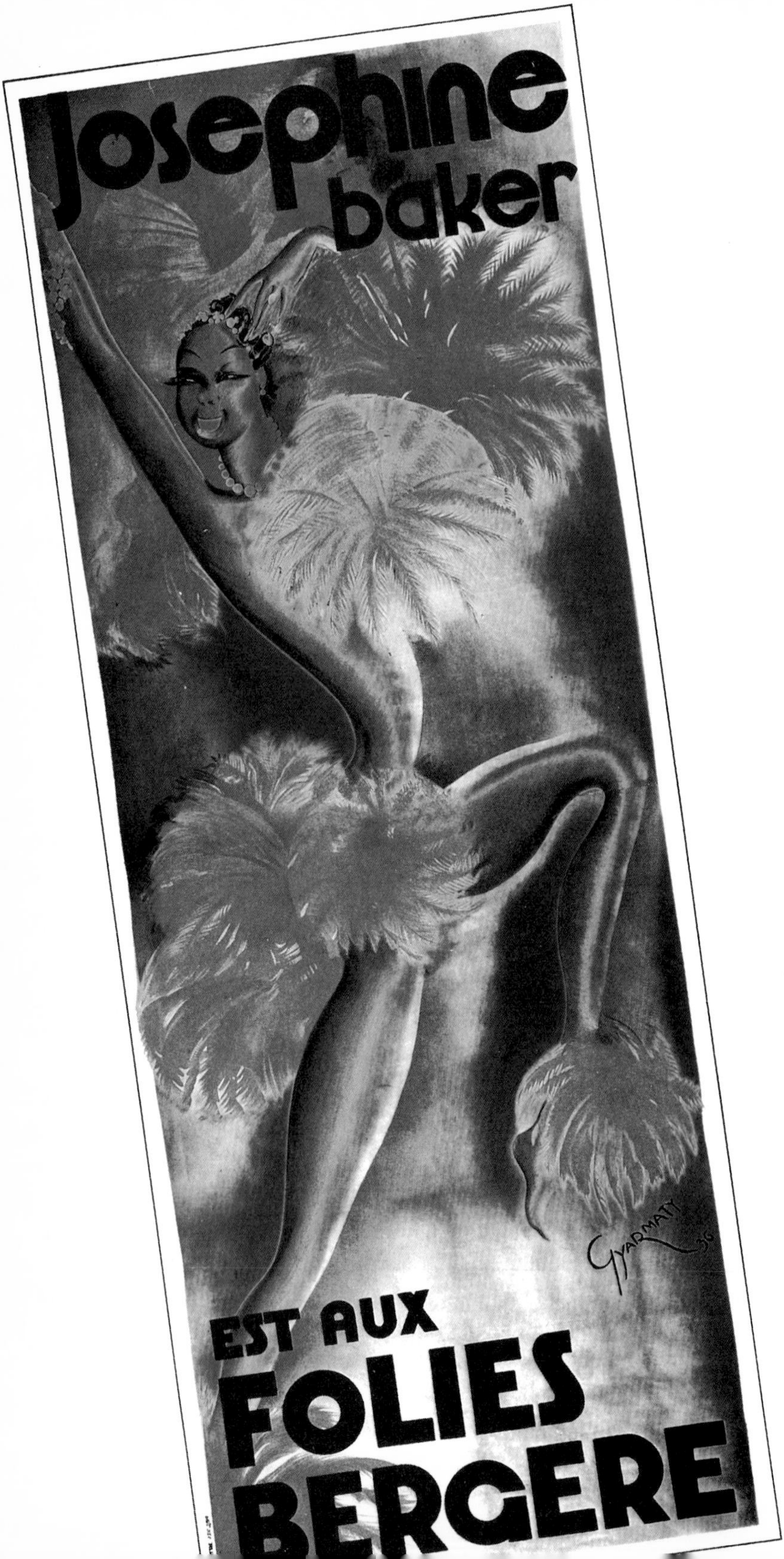

Josephine
baker
GYARMATY 36
EST AUX
FOLIES
BERGERE

she convey to the press her joy at being back in Paris again for her second triumph at the Folies Bergère.

With so much invested and already devised and projected, Josephine knew that she was once again in a strong bargaining position – even though she was desperate for the engagement. 'Varna gave you a leopard. I'm going to surround you with tigers!' Derval announced, and with every promise minimizing his own bargaining power.

'Show me the contract again, monsieur,' *La Baker*, as she had become known to the great French public, asked. She found that the agreement provided that the show would open no later than the first week of October 1936, that she was to be the star and that no other act or performer would receive equal billing. She was to have a say in the design of the poster – which she approved – and no matter how the revue was received she would keep her monthly advance of 42,500 francs, although it was hoped that *En Super Folies* would continue throughout the duration of the *Exposition*.

'Sign here, Josephine,' Derval urged.

She seized her courage with both hands. It was a risk, but she had always taken risks. 'Just a minute, monsieur.' He looked at her with considerable surprise.

'The reason I'm returning to Paris is because of the *Exposition*,' she began hopefully. 'But that's months from now. I'd like you to add a clause stating that if for any reason you decide to terminate *En Super Folies* and stage a new show during the *Exposition*, my contract will apply to that show too.'

The die was cast. 'That's fine with me, Josephine.' And the contract was signed. They both heaved a sigh of relief.

She had always taken a tough line in negotiating contracts, and I found that out at first hand shortly before she made her sensational comeback at the London Palladium and the Bobino in Paris in the early 1970s. I was in Monte Carlo at the time. My

documentary film on the life of Richard Tauber was
nominated for the International Critics Award. I
learnt that one of the organizers of the Monte Carlo
Television Festival, Arys Nissotti, had been the producer of Josephine Baker's films in the twenties and
thirties and I suggested to him that a documentary
film about Josephine Baker might possibly revive
interest in her. He willingly arranged for us to meet
and he brought her along to the Hermitage Hotel
where I was staying. She was slender, lively and
enchanting. The heavy bags beneath her eyes were
half concealed by dark glasses, but that made little
difference to her attractiveness. We arranged for her
to see my film on Richard Tauber and she told me
how much she enjoyed it. She read and approved
my synopsis about the film based on her life and
times. Particular emphasis was put on her display of
sang-froid extraordinaire when she secured secrets for
the Free French in North Africa during World War
Two, winning for her the Resistance medal presented
by General de Gaulle.

We went up to her Roquebrune villa where she
proudly showed me the rooms and bunks where her
'children of many nations' slept. None could forget
her dedication to her twelve adopted children of
different races and religions, her 'Rainbow Tribe' as
they became known, and the Château Millandes
which was to be a monument to human brotherhood
and which was literally sold from under her when
she found herself unable to pay local suppliers. She
and her family were saved miraculously by Prince
Rainier and Princess Grace, who provided them with
this grace and favour villa, where she was to spend
her last days.

She later drove us up to a hotel high on the hill
near the Italian border where we spent a fascinating
afternoon together over tea, with talks about the
proposed documentary. She had immediate warmth
and it seemed as though we had known one another
all our lives; it was one of those spontaneous

encounters that happen so rarely in life. She spoke animatedly in English (she was American, after all) and our combined ideas about the film were in accord with one another's.

I returned to London to arrange the financing and when I got back to Monte Carlo it was time to discuss the details of her contract. We went along to Arys Nissotti's office. She felt it was a good idea for him to act as mediator and explained rather demurely that she left money matters to him. They exchanged a few words in French and from then on he conducted the negotiations. I learned that she would require a new wardrobe of clothes to be designed by either Jacques Faths, Christian Dior or Pierre Balmain. Nissotti then told me the fee she was demanding. It sounded a good deal of money and I asked whether he was quoting in old francs or new. New francs, he assured me. I asked him to convert it into dollars, as it sounded like a figure with too many 'noughts' on the end. He did so and I did a rapid calculation. It worked out at £100,000 sterling.

I tried to explain as tactfully as I could that for a modest television documentary her fee seemed considerable considering the actual costs of film crews, lighting, laboratory processing charges and print costs, but I did not get very far, for the moment we began discussing money she reverted to French, forgetting entirely the brilliant English she had spoken during our previous meetings. My French was not very good – and certainly not good enough for either legal or contractual discussions. I could, however, translate her sentiments; she was in need of the money as she had so many growing children, but when I protested that the film was designed as a documentary, and not a musical 'special', that it could never recoup such an investment, I realized there was no room for manoeuvre. Her fee for three days' work was £100,000 and she would require new clothes from a top French couturier and that was final. I left as graciously as possible.

The next time I saw Miss Baker was at a theatre-in-the-round outside San Francisco in her one-woman show. The house accommodated about seven thousand people but the auditorium, on the night I visited it, held under a thousand patrons; and she played to this meagre, but appreciative, crowd of mixed nations twice-nightly. Her songs seemed to have a message and her presentation lacked the sparkle of the Folies Bergère image we had come to expect. I was greatly excited when a year later she opened at the London Palladium, but this time with a new act, filled with glamour and glitter, feathers and fantasy; her artistry and magic undiminished, she took London by storm.

At the height of her fame and drawing power, she attended one of Mistinguett's performances accompanied by the Rocky Twins, who at the time were the toast of Paris, and Billy Milton recalls that:

> Josephine and the Rocky Twins sat in the box for the first half of the show, and Josephine came back and said to Mistinguett, 'Darling, you were wonderful. It's coming over beautifully.' She gave her a kiss on her two cheeks and took her entourage off. But when the curtain went up on the second half, her box was empty, which was a tremendous insult to Mistinguett.

Apparently when admirers popped into her box during the interval Josephine distributed her own photographs to them with the announcement of her forthcoming Folies Bergère opening, and after seeing Mistinguett, she left the stage door giving autographs to everybody who was waiting for Mistinguett.

Josephine Baker was like a highly polished animal when she performed. She was sensual, electric and vital. She had a beautiful body which you could not take your eyes off, with a little diamond placed at the top of the nether regions which was just sufficient to bring all the elderly diplomats to the theatre; elderly gentlemen with, much to my amusement, slightly rouged cheeks. They wore patent-leather slippers and dinner jackets and absolutely swooned over her.

Erté remembers designing clothes for Josephine Baker, and finding her to be 'marvellous in so many ways. She was so beautiful; so elegant. She had so much charm. Nobody was as good as she was. She was the most sensational music-hall star. We all adored her.'

When she returned to the Folies Bergère in *En Super Folies* in 1936, Josephine Baker's favourite scene presented her gowned in clinging silver lamé, carried onto the stage in a feather-trimmed litter which rested on the back of an enormous jade elephant. She had specified that the beast's trunk point aloft, since Maurice Chevalier had a collection of elephants in his act with raised trunks – he had insisted that dangling trunks brought bad luck. Paul Derval provided the tigers he had promised in New York – ten of them rearing and clawing the air. (One of them managed to claw the trousers of a passing artist, Billy Milton; he had thought for a moment it was one of the chorus-girls until he turned around to examine the source.)

En Super Folies was received enthusiastically by critics and audiences alike – but by none so much as France's most distinguished authoress, who sent a note to Josephine Baker:

Dear Josephine,
In exchange for the garden's worth of flowers you sent me, accept my affectionate thoughts and heartfelt wishes on this ancient sheet of paper which I've treasured for so long that it's yellowed with age. This kind of sentimental writing paper is designed for gentle hearts, children and poets. Which is why I address it to you along with a kiss.
                              Your long-time friend,
                                        Colette

It could be said that Josephine Baker had no rival. Hers was a unique and individual personality which to this day is parodied in many shows, and at the Folies itself – the co-star of the current Folies Bergère show is a tall, slender, dusky entertainer, Lisette Molidor; the show, *Folie je t'adore*, that it succeeded presented another dark star, the delectable Laurence Darpy. But Josephine Baker did feel a sense of rivalry in one performer at least – Barbette, of whom Cocteau was the greatest admirer. 'The two of you are total opposites,' Cocteau told Josephine Baker. 'Barbette hides everything and you show all you've got.'

The well-groomed *La Baker.*

A great favourite at the Folies Bergère and many other venues throughout the world, the beautiful Barbette would leap from the trapeze, walk gracefully to centre stage, snatch off her wig and reveal that she was a man.

The music-hall has always had female impersonators on its bills, but no one went further in the cult of sexual mystification than this young man who transformed himself into a jazz-age Botticelli. And to reward his disturbing, dream-like perfection, the music-halls paid Barbette ten times as much as the average acrobat.

Sir Anton Dolin was a great admirer and close friend of this unique performer:

> I remember the first time I was introduced to Barbette as if it happened yesterday. It was at Tom Douglas's flat in Bruton Street as long ago as September 1925. Tom, who was then the rage of London and acting with Jeanne de Casalis in the play *Fata Morgana*, was giving a party to a few friends and had invited me. I had heard that Barbette was to be one of the guests, and when I met him I found it impossible to believe that this smartly tailored young man, perfectly turned out in every detail, but with not the slightest suggestion of being over-dressed, or too smart, was the same

person I had seen two years before in pink silk tights and a blonde wig swinging and risking his life on a trapeze in Paris. It seemed incredible that this young man, who spoke so well, so intelligently, who discussed books, politics, the arts and life, was indeed the music-hall and circus artist known to thousands.

Barbette was meticulous to a degree about his stage appearance. I have spent hours and hours in his dressing-room at different times watching him make up. His tights were specially woven for him in Paris, and he never wore the same pair twice in an evening. He would whiten the whole of his torso with a thick cream specially prepared for him, and no matter how many times a day he appeared, after every performance he would clean it all off and put it on again fresh for the next show. He never wore the same golden wig twice. As soon as he had finished one performance it would be sent to the *coiffeur* to be dressed for the following day. For the stage, his hands would be whitened, his nails pink-tinted. Off, they were strong and hard, often calloused and broken-skinned, the result of clinging on to the trapeze.

It was an education to me and to the many others who were permitted to see it to watch Barbette transforming himself in front of your eyes from a virile-looking man with muscles of steel into a beautiful soignée woman.

At least a quarter of an hour before he had to go on he would be down on the stage testing the trapeze, strengthening the steel supports of the wire rope, his pink ballet shoes protected by large straw sandals, his hands encased in large chamois gloves. A command here, an order there – he usually got what he wanted done quickly and well – and with the opening bars of his *Schéhérezade* music he would fling sandals and gloves to a waiting dresser, mount the flight of steps, put himself in position at the top, dressed in an exquisite gown

of the most beautiful material and with a towering
head-dress of ostrich feathers, give the order,
'Curtain up!' and Barbette was facing his audience.

Jean Cocteau continues:

> The curtain goes up on a functional *décor* – a
> wire stretched between two supports, a trapeze
> and hanging rings. In the back, a sofa covered
> with a white bearskin. (On the sofa, between the
> wire and the trapeze parts of the act, Barbette
> removes his long evening gown.) A scabrous little
> scene, a real masterpiece of pantomime, summing
> up in parody all the women he has ever studied,
> becoming himself *the* woman – so much so as to
> eclipse the prettiest girls who precede and follow
> him on the programme.
>
> We are in the magic light of the theatre, in this
> trick-factory where truth has no currency, where
> anything natural has no value, where the short are
> made tall and the tall short, where the only things
> that convince us are card tricks and sleights of
> hand of a difficulty unsuspected by the audience.

When Barbette undertook an engagement in
Brussels, Cocteau wrote to Paul Collaer, a Belgian
music critic, alerting him:

> Next week ... you'll see a music-hall act called
> 'Barbette' that has been keeping us enthralled for
> a fortnight. The young American who does this
> wire and trapeze act is a great actor, an angel, and
> he has become the friend of all of us. Go and see
> him, be nice to him as he deserves, and tell every-
> body that he is no mere acrobat in women's clothes,
> nor just a graceful daredevil, but one of the most
> beautiful things in the theatre. Stravinsky, Auric
> poets, painters and I myself have seen no com-
> parable display of artistry on the stage since
> Nijinsky.

In the 1920s Cocteau had shared an enduring
affection for Barbette with a young Irish ballet dancer.

Barbette. Photo by Man Ray, 1926.

A particularly athletic young man, the dancer had already become Diaghilev's favourite. His name was Patrick Kay, but because it was fashionable at the time to be equipped with a Russian name in the ballet, it was changed to Patrikeyev and thereafter to Anton Dolin – Antoine Doline when in France. Dolin, who was forever doing handstands and turning cartwheels in the wings, inspired Cocteau to write a ballet around him and proposed to Diaghilev that the central theme should be Dolin impressing a bevy of bathing beauties of both sexes by his antics on the beach. He called it *Le Train Bleu*, after the Paris-

Riviera express that brought holiday-makers to the Mediterranean. Nijinsky began its choreography, Diaghilev commissioned a score from Milhaud and a *décor* from Henri Laurens, and *Le Train Bleu* became the vehicle that launched Dolin into international ballet history.

Dolin's friendship for Barbette continued through the years. He learned, in the early thirties, that Barbette had had a fall but fortunately it had not ended fatally, although as a result his back was paralysed. He had broken his legs and would never work again. He went to New York where he contracted pneumonia, and on top of this a form of infantile paralysis. Lying in hospital, doubled up with pain, unable to move a limb, he developed a mastoid. He begged the doctors to be allowed to die under the operation, but they were determined to save his life and to restore him to health, particularly one doctor whose son had just died suffering from the same germ as the one that was the cause of Barbette's illness. This doctor tried all sorts of different serums on him until, one day, there was some sort of reaction. His legs slowly began to yield to the treatment, his hands began to move from the wrist, and the fingers, after weeks of torture, could hold a pencil, and after many, many months he left hospital for Texas, where he learnt to walk again without the aid of sticks. It was there that Sir Anton Dolin renewed his acquaintanceship:

> The last time I saw Barbette was a year before he died, in the sixties. I was giving some master classes in Houston and Barbette, who was living in Austin, came over to watch the classes. He still looked as elegant and soigné as he always had, but he was still slightly bitter about not being able to get a visa to return to England. He'd been rather indiscreet when he was topping the bill at the London Palladium many years before. There was no prosecution, thank heaven.
>
> There had been a very pretty little page boy and

Barbette who had the star dressing-room didn't lock the door, which was rather unfortunate, and dear Val Parnell (the theatre's impresario) who wasn't exactly broadminded didn't like the idea. The engagement was finished – and Barbette was never allowed back into London again, which was rather stupid when you think of what goes on nowadays. Anyhow, that upset him and he returned to America. Before his accident, he worked in a circus but that folded, and so he devised a wonderful circus act for a charming young friend of his whom he coached.

Barbette, who was living with his sister in Austin, became despondent. Nobody knew him and there was none of the glamour of Mistinguett, Josephine Baker and the Folies Bergère. He had always surrounded himself with a very cultured entourage but now he was in Austin living out a rather dull life. He sadly took an overdose one night, went to sleep and never woke up.

The golden age of the music-hall seemed to be coming to an end. It was to last until 1934 or 1935 and the only music-hall in Paris to this day to have survived is the Folies Bergère. Since the great female entertainers – Yvette Guilbert, Yvonne Printemps, Mistinguett, Gaby Deslys and Josephine Baker – none were to achieve similar heights at the Folies Bergère. There were, however, two male performers who go down in the annals of the Folies Bergère's history. With the single exception of Maurice Chevalier, the two most popular artists to appear on this stage were Charles Trenet and Fernandel.

Fernandel, who made his début in Paris at the Folies Bergère as Mistinguett's leading man in *Folies en Folie*, was born Fernand Joseph Désirée Contandin, of Provençal stock, in Marseilles, the artist of whom *Life* magazine was to write, 'The face of Fernandel is as unforgettable as the Eiffel Tower. It has helped to make him his country's greatest comic attraction. Britain may have its Alec Guinness, but France still has Fernandel to match against him in any sort of contest of comic talent.'

Fernand, who at the time was 'all teeth', made his début at the age of five in a melodrama at the Théâtre Chave. He attended school during the day, and in the evening, with his father and brothers, he appeared in many of the music-halls of Marseilles, and later entertained at weddings and parties. When his father was mobilized during the First World War, Fernand left school and worked successively in a bank, a soap factory, an importing business, a rug firm and again in a bank. By the time he was seventeen his voice had become 'deep, colourful, flexible, agreeably resonant'.

Fernandel

In December 1922, when the Eldorado Theatre in Nice offered Fernand a contract, the young man quickly gave up his new-found career in banking. Until 1922 he had always used his father's stage name, Marc Sined. In Nice for the first time he appeared as Fernandel, a name given him by Henriette, a bank clerk's sister (whom he later married). Henriette's mother had always called him 'Henriette's Fernand', or 'Fernand d'elle'. The name was propitious; his performance in Nice led to several other engagements.

After completing compulsory military service, Fernandel returned to Marseilles where he worked in a soap factory to support his wife and their first child, Josette. In the evening he accepted music-hall engagements which led him to substitute for a Parisian entertainer at the Paramount Theatre who had failed to please the audience. His performance won him a contract on the Paramount vaudeville circuit and he travelled throughout France and North Africa (later on the Pathé circuit). Everywhere he went audiences responded immediately to his warmth and humour.

The film director Marc Allégret offered him a role in a talking film, *Le Blanc et Le Noir* by Sacha Guitry, which starred Jules Raimu, the great, burly, lovable clown, for which he won the review:

'Fernandel – remember this name; it will become famous!' He went on to appear in some twenty-five films between 1931 and 1933 – and then came his debut in Paris at the Folies Bergère.

Paul Derval had seen his performance in the film *Le Rosier de Mme Husson* (released in Britain as *The Virtuous Isadore*) and, touched by the naiveté of his portrayal of the part and impressed by the considerable notice the film had brought him, Derval contracted him to appear in the Hermite and le Seyeux revue *Folies en Folie* as one of Mistinguett's partners, together with Randall. 'I wanted to exploit his comic gifts, but how?' Derval pondered. 'In a spectacular revue this is not easy. With a pretty woman it is fairly simple. You dress her up in a costume, elaborate or brief as the case may be, give her a dazzling *décor* to set her off, fill the stage with supers and stand her on a staircase.'

But what could he do with a clown like Fernandel? He had very little idea of what to do with him in the show aside from giving him a dance routine with Mistinguett, but he was wasted as a dancer.

Fernandel for his own part did not wish to make his début at the Folies without considerable recognition and therefore insisted on the same treatment as Mistinguett. Having presented Mistinguett from the top of a great staircase surrounded by an immense chorus of boys and girls, Derval decided to repeat the set for Fernandel's entrance. But instead of introducing him on the same set as Mistinguett's, the scenery consisted of a plain backcloth on which was painted a huge but completely bare staircase, with three steps at the bottom on which a crestfallen Fernandel was discovered when the curtain went up, complaining, 'Look at the rotten little staircase they've given me. And yet when Derval signed me up, he said, "Don't worry, you'll get just the same treatment as Mistinguett." And look at it – canvas, that's all it is, and no spangles and no girls or anything!' He went further, though, much to Mistinguett's chagrin: 'Fernandel walked down the staircase parodying my walk. Well, it didn't go down. We cut it out after three days. They simply didn't laugh. Naturally, I didn't care for it much myself, but the main thing was that the audience didn't either.'

However, even though the mimicry was eliminated, Fernandel's success in the sketch proved so great that six months later he went to see Derval, 'grinning his great horsey grin, with a huge sheaf of letters in his hand'. 'Monsieur Derval,' he said, 'do you think you could release me? Look, I've got all these offers.' Derval could hardly refuse, and let him go.

Marcel Pagnol signed him for the part of Saturnin, a country bumpkin in the film *Angèle*, and this led to a string of films in which he scored success after success. Many years later, commenting on Fernandel's nimble skill in playing six roles, a father and five sons in *The Sheep has Five Legs*, the *New York Times* called the farce, 'probably the cleverest and most hilarious French comedy we've seen since the war', and the *New York Herald Tribune* exclaimed, 'Fernandel is a joy throughout! He is one of the most versatile comic actors of the day.'

Born on 18 May 1913 at Narbonne, Charles Trenet, who was to score considerable fame in France as both singer and composer, never felt at ease in music-hall revues and made a habit of walking out of them after only a few days. At the beginning of his career, in 1933, Henri Varna booked him and his partner Johnny Hess for the curtain-raiser at the Palace. After three days Trenet left in anger because it was essentially during his number that latecomers searched for their seats. Having become famous, Charles Trenet was engaged at the Folies Bergère but there too he stayed for only a short while and refused energetically to attend costume fittings and to wear the costumes designed for him.

'He appeared at the top of the stairs in sports clothes with yellow shoes,' Paul Derval complained.

'Of course!' explained the singer, 'Monsieur Derval, yellow shoes go well with the colour of my hair!'

Trenet's triumph at the ABC in 1938 was scored through his revolutionizing the French song. He became an overnight star.

As a composer he did for France what Irving Berlin, Cole Porter, George Gershwin and Rodgers and Hammerstein did for America. Singing his own songs, he once said, 'When I entertain I try to help people forget everyday anxieties for a short while. I want to be happy, and wanting my audience to be likewise, I sing songs of joy and happiness.'

Most of Trenet's songs were up-tempo: fleet-footed, skimming, dancing, wild running melodies such as *'Le grand café'* or *'Pigeon vole'*, the latter a wonderfully gentle, liberal, funny and forgiving song about an unfaithful girl. But some of the songs, like *'La Mer'*, which he composed and with which he is associated are ballads. One of the most moving of Trenet's ballads is *'Douce France'*, which means sweet, or soft France. Affectionate rather than chauvinistic, preferential rather than exclusive, it reminisces about Trenet's childhood and a France that used to be. Beautiful in itself, the song takes on more power when it is realized that it was written during the German occupation, a protest the enemy evidently were too thick-headed to understand. But the French understood, and many were warmed. It is no doubt because of songs such as this that Trenet became a sort of national monument in France.

But in later years one of the reasons for Trenet's comparative obscurity was the fact that he got into a bind with the law. He was charged with a homosexual offence, which produced some disgust in the French who ostracized him. It appeared that the French were not as liberal about these things as the visitor might suppose.

Having become one of the leading figures of his generation, Jean Cocteau championed Charles Trenet. Cocteau, a brilliant poet, novelist, play-

wright, film-maker and artist, designed a poster for
Trenet. It was drawn with an almost unreal soft
touch, showing Trenet with his hat depicted as a
halo, gliding over clouds; he was transported —
floating.

Cocteau recalls that:

> The novelty of Mr Charles Trenet was that he
> popularized superior lyrics which without him
> would never have been sung in the street or been
> on everyone's lips. He imitated no one. He loved
> his songs. He caressed them. From this gracious
> manner a new style was born. One may imagine,
> from the poets Villon to Guillaume Apollinaire,
> what suffering is involved in producing from this
> chrysalis the lightness and gaiety of a song.
> Formerly the clumsy, naïve grace of a song inspired
> poets, in the same way as a rough idea seen on a
> poster has raised Picasso up to great heights. In
> reverse, and at the same time as this painter's fame
> was beginning to inspire the man in the street,
> Charles Trenet was the first to draw his songs
> from the wells of poetry.
>
> Going from comedy to tenderness, he brings
> with him the delicacy with which Rastelli juggled,
> and at the end when, recalled fifty times, he offers
> spectators the last crumple of a large smile and
> swimming blue eyes, I tremble in case this ruddy
> face, this dark shirt, this white tie, this red carnation,
> this dynamism and this orchestra should burst like
> a soap bubble.

Among the other notable artists to have appeared
at the Folies Bergère before the end of this remarkable era were Max Dearly, Jean Sablon and the Dolly
Sisters, but after the great entertainers had come and
gone the audiences packed the house for the spectacle
and the girls alone.

Josephine Baker's 1926–7 début at the Folies was
followed in 1927 by *Un Vent de Folie*, another Louis
Lemarchand revue again starring Josephine Baker

Jean Cocteau's poster
of Charles Trenet.

with a company supported by the high-kicking John Tiller girls dressed in costumes designed by Barbier and Erté. Among the chief sketches in this production were *'L'horloge des fêtes'*, *'Le vol des libellules'*, *'Plantation'* featuring *La Baker*; *'La Galérie de Cléopâtre'*, *'La gondole du Doge'*, *'Sur un lit de roses'*, *'Le monde en prière'*, and *'Sous la tente d'Ali-Baba'*. This was succeeded the following year (1928) by *La Grande Folie*, in which Lemarchand presented sixty tableaux including a Catherine of Russia sequence, and other acts which featured the Dodge Twins. *De la Folie Pure*, with the Alfred Jackson Girls (1929), began with tableaux of the 'Belle of Athens', went on to the 'Belle of Seville', the 'Belle of Moscow', the 'Belle of New York' and the 'Belle of Vienna', and ended with the 'Belle of Paris'.

The Jackson Girls had succeeded the John Tiller

troupe of dancers. The Tillers had become institutions in Britain and France during this period and later throughout the world, the forerunners of the precision high-kicking dancers. Miss Campton, as she was always called, was a vivacious and attractive English girl who had graduated from one of the original John Tiller chorus lines before the First World War and became one of the greatest favourites of Paris for many years; her voluble French with an English accent tickled the Parisians, and for long she held a unique position in revue. She scored a noted success at the Folies Bergère when she appeared with George Grossmith in incredible riding kit, and all Paris flocked to see them as typically British. She became the first Mrs Paul Derval and died in the early thirties.

The impresario C. B. Cochran recalled the delights of Miss Campton:

Miss Campton off the stage and among her comrades was as popular as she was upon it. It used to be said of her, and with reason, that she never did or said an unkind thing. With some English colleagues she went to the Variétés when it was under the direction of the great Samuel, and was the life and soul of the troupe. It was said of her too that for a franc you could make Campton the happiest girl in the world by giving her a few sweets and a cup of tea or chocolate. Prince, then of the Variétés (later the great French movie star 'Rigadin'), taught her to speak French and ultimately married her, but the marriage did not last long. She was then engaged by my old friend, P. L. Flers, the producer of the early revues at the Folies Bergère, and she married Paul Derval. Campton became the darling of Paris, where she had her audiences, and which she was sure of, and hesitated over fresh adventure, without her accent as an asset.

Another ex-Tiller girl was to gain great popularity,

but only for a short time; for the pace was too fast for Hilda May. She was rushed into a hospital for an operation under which she died. Known as the 'Pearl' of the Tiller girls, she went to Paris with one of the John Tiller troupes, which were a feature of all the big French revues. These girls were under strict chaperonage and boarded in a kind of settlement under the supervision of an English clergyman, the Reverend F. A. Cardew.

It was an established tradition of the Tiller girls, and indeed the girls belonging to the other dancing troupes, the Jacksons and the Bluebells, that they were strictly virtuous, but Hilda May had other views, and John Tiller was bowed with sorrow at the escapades of his beautiful 'black sheep'. She left the troupe but was in great demand by the directors of Parisian revues. Her life was short but merry.

In 1930, the Folies Bergère presented *Un Coup de Folie* (Love at First Sight) starring Randall, who had been one of Mistinguett's partners, and who between the two wars was often the top name on the marquee. The dancers of the Ballet Dayelma and the Alfred Jackson Girls were featured together with sixteen nudes. As for all music-hall revues, themes were chosen around which the tableaux were built: 'The Sins of Paris', 'The Extravagant Queen', 'The Folies Bergère at Fifty', an historical retrospective, and 'Naked Paris'.

L'Usine à Folies (The Folies Factory) was presented in 1931, a revue inspired by Maurice Verne's book *Les Usines du Plaisir* (*The Pleasure Factories*, published in 1929). Of the sixty tableaux, with *décors* and costumes by Brunelleschi, Seltenhammer, Wittop, Zig and Shanks, '*Chair et métal*' ('Flesh and Metal') with the Jackson Stars, was the most modernistic. It displayed the women among futuristic wheel works.

Alec Shanks was again one of the designers of the next revue, *Nuits de Folies*, in 1932. This was followed in the same year by *La Revue d'Amour*, which opened on 21 November and starred Florelle,

Dréan and Georgia Graves. It was the first of the
Maurice Hermite and Jean le Seyeux productions,
trying hard to follow in the great Louis Lemarchand
tradition. They failed. Lemarchand had retired from
producing the revues and was succeeded by Hermite
and le Seyeux who in turn were succeeded by the
brilliant young Hungarian, Michel Gyarmathy, in
designing and producing the revues.

The famous Dolly Sisters were great favourites of
the Folies Bergère audiences, as well as of theatre-
goers throughout the world. Daughters of a Budapest
tailor, these twins, Jancsi and Roszicka, grew up on
New York's Lower East Side and left a trail of
broken hearts wherever they went. They rose to
fame by affecting identical costumes, hair-styles and
perfectly matched steps, though they were completely different in character. They Americanized
their names to Jenny (who was the romantic butterfly, reckless, gay and pleasure-seeking) and Rosie
(the cautious, quiet and more stable one). Jenny
reigned over the gambling tables of Deauville and
Monte Carlo, winning and losing sums of unheard-
of proportions. One New Year's Eve in Cannes she
announced that her winnings amounted to four
million francs. Three of these millions she converted
into the finest collection of ear-rings, bracelets and
enormous diamond and emerald rings that Cannes
had ever seen. She went on to win another eleven
million francs.

Rosie shunned the limelight and spent large sums
of her fortune in charity work and on rehabilitating
orphans in her native Hungary. This does not mean
that she did not lead a gay, madcap, exhilarating
existence as well. They both did; and they both had
wanderlust. After rocketing to fame at the Ziegfeld
Follies in New York, they could never stay in one
place for very long. They left for a tour of England
and the Continent and finally became stars at the
Casino de Paris after appearances at the Folies Bergère.

Original poster by Alec
Shanks.

FOLIES BERGERE

L'USINE A FOLIES

ALEC SHANKS
1931

Their first big success in London was in 1919 in *League of Nations*, and by 1925 they had made so much money that Jenny Dolly was able to buy the villa at Fontainebleau under the King of Spain's nose. He had earmarked it for his retirement.

Jenny amassed jewels in preference to husbands – a fifty-one-carat square-cut diamond ring, a priceless emerald necklace, a diamond necklace with a pear-shaped stone dangling from the centre – a collection that has been called the most valuable ever in private hands. Rosie married Mortimer B. Davis, Jr, son of the Canadian tobacco king who had married an actress himself, but Davis had cut Rosie out of his will by a clause that lost her sixty-five million dollars. A divorce reunited the twins again and sent them back to the Moulin Rouge and star billing with Maurice Chevalier.

Mistinguett first saw the Dolly Sisters when they appeared in London, and befriended them. At that time Jenny had become quite successful socially, showing off her jewels as evidence of the fact, while Rosie was less fortunate. Mistinguett once washed and ironed Rosie's only dress in their modest little flat in St Martin's Lane so that she could go to a Press Reception.

In September 1925, Mistinguett began rehearsals for her first show at the Moulin Rouge, *La Revue Mistinguett*, not only as star of the show but as co-producer as well. Earl Leslie, whom she had first seen in London when he appeared on the same bill as the Dolly Sisters, was her leading man, and the Dolly Sisters had also been engaged by Foucret, the director, to appear in the star-studded cast. Apart from their own high-kicking act, the Dolly Sisters had a number with Mistinguett which had been inserted quite late on in rehearsals, called 'The Miss-dollytinguett Sisters'. It was a harmless and amusing scene parodying the supposed rivalries between the stars in the show. The Dolly Sisters had read and liked the script, had learnt the lines and rehearsed

the show for a week, when without warning they
sent word that they would not be appearing in the
show. They had had the sketch translated, and did
not think their part either in it or in the revue in
general worthy of their reputation and talent. They
felt that they had been misled. They had been led
to believe, they claimed, that they were to be the
stars of the show (particularly since they were being
paid a record-breaking three thousand francs a day;
Mistinguett had threatened to walk out unless she
got five thousand!) — and on no account would they
appear as also-rans. They went one further; they sued
the management for 550,000 francs — and the
management, in retaliation, sued them for a similar
amount for breach of contract. The Dolly Sisters
won their case, as well as public sympathy, for they
made over the entire sum to the Actors' Benevolent
Fund. They then went to the Casino de Paris, on
Maurice Chevalier's invitation, to appear in his new
show, where they were received before a magnificent
curtain specially designed by Erté (and which,
nowadays, is framed and hangs in a museum in New
York) by an ecstatic audience.

They had left Mistinguett's show not only four
days before opening night but with an immense bill
for fifty thousand francs for ermine coats which
they had ordered at Mistinguett's expense. They had
also refused to wear the costumes made for the show
in the Moulin Rouge's work-rooms, having insisted
on ordering all their clothes for the show from
another costumier — who also presented Mistinguett
and the Moulin Rouge management with the bill.
It was, perhaps, the first time that anyone had
beaten Mistinguett at her own game. But the
Moulin Rouge's owner, Foucret, who had suffered
so dismally from the financial losses over the whole
affair, had the final word, according to British
designer Alec Shanks:

> The Moulin Rouge had opened in 1889, twenty
> years after the Folies Bergère opened its doors to

the public, and in 1929 I was commissioned to redecorate the Moulin Rouge music-hall as a cinema for Fox Films. The cinema is on the ground floor, whereas the *Bal du Moulin Rouge*, named after the very ancient *Moulin de la Galette* nearby, is underneath.

During the redecorating we stripped off the 1924 'art deco' pearl-like panelling of the famous red windmill-room known as the 'Tic-Tac' from the sound of the revolving sails, and on the bare plaster beneath, I read the following disparaging inscription: '*Mistinguett – la vache qui m'a uriné.*' [Mistinguett – the cow who has pissed all over me.]

It had been written by Foucret as a final comment on the affair.

The Dolly Sisters used to go off on country weekends with Sir Thomas Lipton and Sir Harry Lauder. Sir Thomas always told them that married men made the worst husbands, whereas Sir Harry added, 'But actresses should marry from time to time.' Which the Dolly Sisters had no hesitation in doing. Then off to Deauville and the Casino they would go, to be visited by the King of Spain, gambling for high stakes and winning fantastic fortunes.

The great impresario C. B. Cochran remembered the Dolly Sisters with some affection:

I suppose that I can hardly class the Dolly Sisters among my Parisian friends, friends though they were, and though from the first I predicted that they would take Paris by storm. Two more electric personalities it has never been my fate to meet. They radiated personal magnetism, vibrant energy, or whatever you like to call it, and any revue benefited enormously by their presence on the stage. But I always maintained that Paris was their spiritual home. On the stage and off the Dolly Sisters were unique.

It took me a long time to say whether it was Rosie or Jenny when I met one of them alone,

The Dolly Sisters –
they beat Mistinguett
at her own game.

but I soon got to tell t'other from which when I was with them both. To carry on a conversation with them was amusing. One would commence a sentence, the other would finish it. The following is a typical example of an ordinary conversation with the 'Million Dollar Dollies', as they were called.

'Last Sunday . . .' said Rosie.

'. . . Sir Thomas Lipton said he'd give us a little surprise,' said Jenny.

'He motored us to a little village miles and miles away and . . .' said Rosie.

'. . . when we got there all the village children were waiting for us, and . . .' said Jenny.

'. . . another car came up behind us piled . . .' said Rosie.

'...right up with boxes of candy, and...' said Jenny.

'...Sir Thomas called everybody round him, and...' said Rosie.

'...started to hand out the candy, and...' said Jenny.

'...everybody had a box, and...' said Rosie.

'...it was just lovely. You see, Sir Thomas...' said Jenny.

'...does this every Sunday. When he can't...' said Rosie.

'...go himself, he sends...' said Jenny.

'...somebody else. There was one woman there, with...' said Rosie.

'...a baby in her arms, and...' said Jenny.

'...Sir Thomas looked at the baby and said: "Every Sunday I..."' said Rosie.

'"...see you with a different baby..."' said Jenny.

'"...you must have a very large family to..."' said Rosie.

'"...keep it up all the year round..."' said Jenny.

'...But the woman said: "'It's the same..."' said Rosie.

'"...baby, Sir Thomas," but Sir Thomas said: "I have..."' said Jenny.

'"...my doubts!" Don't you think he...' said Rosie.

'...is a real sport?' said Jenny.

Right here the Dolly Sisters paused simultaneously to draw breath.

'Good...' said Rosie.

'...bye,' said Jenny.

Then tragedy struck, as it had a way of doing with terrific rapidity and terrible force to pleasure-loving, carefree little Jenny, who accepted luck as casually as she had always placed her chips on the green felt gambling tables. Soon after the Dollys retired from the stage, Jenny met and fell in love

with Max Constant, a French flier. Theirs was a
mad, wild love, full of many promises, heated quarrels
and abrupt goodbyes that never lasted. It was during
one of these partings that she met H. Gordon
Selfridge, the owner of London's famed department
store as well as of many, many millions. At the time
of their romance, and as such it was written about
in the American and English press, a close friend of
the Selfridge family announced that Selfridge had
given Jenny ten million dollars and a promise of
marriage. Their projected merger brought Constant
back into Jenny's life. Swayed between domestic
security and the love she had for the flier, Jenny
went with him for one last weekend. Somehow it
did not gel, and as the lovers were motoring back
to Paris in speechless silence their car was involved
in an accident, going at seventy-five miles an hour
near Bordeaux. Jenny nearly lost her life and suffered
such severe cuts to her face and legs that she spent
months in the American Hospital undergoing operation after operation for bone fractures, internal
injuries and facial surgery. Rosie and the forgiving
Selfridge rallied the world's most prominent surgeons
to restore her beauty and they almost succeeded.
But Jenny was broken in spirit. Rosie by this time
had married Irving Netcher, a wealthy Chicago
merchant, and they took Jenny home and married
her to a Chicago attorney, Bernard W. Vinissky.
But hard luck continued to follow the once-gay Jenny
and acute melancholia drove her in 1941 to hang
herself from a shower rod in her apartment.

Rosie became the patroness of a working girls'
club in Chicago where she taught the inmates
the difference between vice and virtue, with the
emphasis of choice on the latter. The dancer and
choreographer Bernard Hall recalls an encounter with
her in old age:

> I originally met the Dolly Sisters through
> Mistinguett in Deauville. They had jewellery given
> them by Pashas, Kings – everyone. Many years

later when I was at the Deauville casino again, I sat beside an old, old lady, who was very beautiful and very slim – and smothered with diamonds. I recognized her as one of the Dolly Sisters, but did not know which one she was, so I asked her.

'I'm the sister who didn't hang herself,' she replied.

I was slightly taken aback at this unexpected form of identification and after gathering my senses, studying her beauty – and the jewels she wore – I said with relief: 'I'm very glad that you didn't!'

'Now, young man,' she said, 'you can put a *mille francs* on for me. I've got a feeling you'll bring me luck.'

I put her stake on for her – and won. She doubled it – and doubled it again, and again. Eventually we went over to the private bar and she asked me what I did for a living. I told her that I was dancing in cabaret at the Casino and she said:

'You're a very silly boy. It's the most stupid thing in the world to do. My sister and I only did it to get to the millionaires.'

And I replied rather weakly, 'I'm not a girl.'

'Then find yourself a rich man who can back everything you do and you'll have no problems. My sister and I never had any problems. We always found ourselves rich men.'

Folies en Folie in 1933 heralded the return of Mistinguett, supported by Fernandel whose sketches and songs were by Albert Willemetz. Fernandel and Randall also had their own 'spots' in the show. This revue was followed by *Femmes en Folie* which presented the new and exciting Bluebell Dancers. Maurice Hermite and Jean le Seyeux presented *Femmes en Folie*, a revue created by the established collaborators of the house; Brunelleschi, Selten, Wittop and the newcomer destined to become 'patron' of the Folies, Michel Gyarmathy.

Mistinguett, Fernandel and Randall in *Folies en Folie*.

En Super Folies in 1936 saw the return of Josephine Baker to the boards of the famous music-hall, followed by *Folies en Fleur*, again with the Bluebell Dancers, and in which Damia presented to the public a repertoire of songs of the special *genre* reminiscent of the great Polaire of the large, gazelle-like eyes, brown skin and mouth made up with violent red, who had triumphed in the early 1900s.

The last revue before the war was *Madame la Folie*, which ran a full year, and in which Jeanne Aubert appeared. It brought with it an end to an era; the end of the golden days of music-hall which had taken place between the two wars.

Miss Bluebell suffered together with many others during the Occupation. In March 1939 she married Marcel Leibovici, the orchestra leader at the Folies Bergère, who was also a promising composer and astute financial adviser. But with the Second World War, her world collapsed as her troupes of girls disbanded. The British girls managed to get out of France. Bluebell herself, expecting her first child, tried to leave via Bordeaux, only to find it was hopeless. She was advised to return to Paris, where her son Patrick was born. Later, when expecting her second child, she was arrested as a British passport holder, and sent to an internment camp at Besançon. The Irish ambassador made representations and a few months later she was released, he having satisfied the Germans that she was born in neutral Dublin. She returned to Paris and her second son, Francis, was born. Her husband was then arrested and put in a concentration camp, from which he escaped. He was half-Jewish, and the penalty for harbouring him would have been death. She took the chance and hid him away in an attic facing the Préfecture de Police for two and a half years, providing food for him on her ration card. She gave birth to her third child, a daughter she named Florence, and fortunately the Germans did not inquire how she achieved the birth with a supposedly missing husband.

'Even at the darkest time I knew that the Germans would never win. Don't ask me how, I always knew,' she says now.

She survived the war with a combination of luck, courage and a refusal to be intimidated. She would talk to the Germans in English, and was not frightened of speaking up to them in an indignant British manner. There were several close brushes. On one occasion, she was stopped on the Boulevard Hauss-mann with a woman she had sheltered. The woman's papers were forged and she was shot without denouncing Bluebell. The only show she staged during the war was for a private club. She was surprised when summoned by a military official and asked to put on a similar show in Berlin. He tempted her with luxury accommodation, good food and plenty of money. Aware that her response was crucial, and an outright refusal could put her in an invidious position, Bluebell thought hard. She finally said to him, 'Look, I have relations fighting in the British Army. How could I possibly put on a show for your soldiers?' The official accepted the reasoning, and she never heard anything further.

There were many, however, who weakened –

some who, nowadays, prefer to forget the incidents. A good few were branded as collaborators. Several were held to ransom, as Miss Bluebell told me:

With wartime, the Folies Bergère closed periodically, mostly for six months at a time. But the management was told by the Occupied Forces, like everybody else in France, that either they remained open or else the Germans would put somebody else in to produce shows for the troops.

After the war, many people in Paris were criticized for entertaining the Germans, Chevalier and Mistinguett being two notable examples, but if they'd refused, the Germans would have taken over the theatres and restaurants and so they had to choose between the lesser of two evils. There were, of course, many that *were* requisitioned – and the proprietors paid the price.

Many entertainers and managements, such as the Folies Bergère's, felt that their own contribution to the war effort was to keep the French flag flying. The ones who stayed at home showed their patriotism by entertaining those left behind. Soldiers on leave needed escapism. They wanted to forget, however briefly, the brutality of the front line; they wanted something to treasure when they returned to the trenches. The fact that German soldiers were present in the auditorium rankled with the performers, but they reminded themselves constantly that they were doing it for France; raising the spirits and the hopes of the French – and not the Germans.

It was in August 1944 that the Germans finally left Paris. Two months later the Folies Bergère reopened, under orders from the French authorities to get life back to normal as quickly as possible.

And that is exactly what it did.

6
From Fantasy to Fact

The revues at the Folies Bergère after the last war and up until the present day continued very much on the lines devised by Louis Lemarchand and perpetuated through the years by Michel Gyarmathy. Long gone was the public appeal, though, for the great stars such as Gaby Deslys, Mistinguett and Josephine Baker. Times had changed. The war had brought with it new styles, new talents and different values. After wartime privation came the longing for a new world with the promise of a new and exciting future. Nostalgia became a thing of the past. The generations of wartime young were growing up. The fifties brought to them the new Dior look in fashion. Jiving and jitter-bugging was the craze. The sixties exploded with Beatlemania, Mary Quant, Carnaby Street and the King's Road and all the world parodied it. With the seventies came recession, bankruptcies and bitterness reminiscent of the late twenties. The beginning of the eighties looked more hopeful, but with fashions in clothing lacking in style, glamour and shape, the wild 'punk' look has become the rage for the young.

But the Folies Bergère refused steadfastly to succumb to any of these changes, preferring to rely instead on its tradition of fast-moving changes of tableaux and fabulous show-girls adorned with feathers and pearls providing its audiences with a timelessness that is unique. The fun factory is as big a draw as it has ever been. Its formula still works supremely well. The highly polished speciality acts

'Les Plumes', Alec Shanks's design for L'Usine à Folies.

Les Plumes

come and go, the sets and costumes are replaced before they become shoddy. The house is full nearly every night.

But in order to maintain these standards the Folies Bergère has had to spend more money on its shows and administration. It is still a vast 'pleasure factory' dedicated to the presentation of grand revue on a sumptuous scale. It has its own work-rooms, where the miles of satins and brocades, the mountains of ostrich plumes and the bushels of sequins which go into each new production are made up; it has its own carpenter's and metal-work shop and laundry, and even possesses a swimming pool sunk into the stage.

On 17 December 1980 the Folies Bergère celebrated the fifty millionth member of its audience to have passed through its doors. This is equivalent to the entire population of France having seen the spectacular shows, but this figure represents audiences from all over the world.

Every evening a staff of over three hundred at the Folies Bergère awaits the arrival of the audience. This includes 80 artists, 20 musicians, 20 technicians, 60 wardrobe staff and machinists, 30 dressers, 15 electricians, 10 props assistants (Assistant Stage Managers), 10 embroiderers and beaders, 20 dressmakers, and front-of-house staff which includes managers, usherettes and box-office staff. In order to create any one of the spectacular revues presented at the Folies Bergère (and because of the tremendous demand, they run for up to four years, although the speciality acts are changed regularly), the preproduction staff on the premises involves 80 dressmakers, 15 milliners, 30 *pailleteuses* who apply the beads to the elaborate costumes, 22 embroiderers, 12 shoemakers, 5 jewellers, 25 assistants who create the feather head-dresses, tails, trains and fans, and numerous carpenters, scenery painters, upholsterers, sculptors, locksmiths, steel-workers and other helpers who work in the region of 125,000 hours to create in excess of 1,200 costumes, 500 pairs of shoes, 300 head-dresses and about 45 sets required for the tableaux.

Given that there are some 45 sets and tableaux, representing a change that requires twenty minutes to assemble and ten minutes to 'strike' for a forty-second scene, the sets are moved with the precision of automatons with expertise and split-second accuracy.

To sequin a costume (all done by hand) more than eleven days' work is put into the garment by two *pailleteuses*, and to make a costume adorned with feathers requires the industry of about four dress-makers involving 200 hours of work. For every performance each artist has about forty costume changes and because the stage is only twenty feet deep, and the dressing-rooms absolutely minute and over-crowded, situated above flights of steep, narrow, winding, iron stairs, the fantastic crinolines are 'flown down' from the 'flies', and the girls climb into them, either moving onto the stage sideways or entering from the top of the perilously steep stair-case, the width of the stage, and when they exit, step out of the creations and scurry back up the dangerous-looking iron treads to repair their make-up and to change wigs and head-dresses.

Statistically, the Folies Bergère's 1,600 seats are sold out every night despite the fact that big names no longer star in the productions. Eleven trade unions are represented. Although Entertainment Tax on straight theatres and cinemas in France is 8 per cent, the Folies Bergère is obliged to pay the French Government 15 per cent of its gross takings. However, because the fabrics and adornments are essentially French, they enjoy reasonable allowances on the purchases of the mile upon mile of cloth, sequins and feathers, as it obviously boosts the French couture trade.

The curtain rises every night of the week except Mondays, their day off, at 8.45 p.m. and falls just before midnight. For this 3¼-hour escape into fantasy the best and most expensive stalls seats cost 250 francs – about £25 at the current rate of exchange. During the interval the star of the show will autograph her latest disc which she has featured in the revue, and on leaving the theatre the tourist may purchase in the foyer 35mm colour slides, in neat packs of five, of the spectacular scenes from the show as a memento of the genius that had been presented during a memorable evening.

Perhaps the perfect woman does not exist, so an illusion of glamour presents to the public the near-perfect woman. On stage at the Folies Bergère the show-girl might take one's breath away with her faultless beauty and dream-like dimensions, but those satin drapes might easily conceal too-narrow hips, that bustle of feathers accentuate or hide an inordinate behind, or exceedingly high heels give a longer line to otherwise fore-shortened legs. The feet must be seen from every seat in the house, otherwise the legs appear too short. The line of the leg must be unbroken. Imperfect hands or arms might be adorned with gloves, jewels or heavily draped sleeves. Costumes are designed to create an illusion; a too-short neck can emerge positively swan-like with expert advice; inadequate busts can be padded – or perhaps injected or operated-on to give them the desired dimension. Enlarged bosoms have never been a disadvantage in spectacular semi-nude extravaganzas of this sort.

Long, false lashes and mascara and eye-liner can enlarge the eye and an inadequate mouth can be made sensuous and inviting with the use of lipstick carefully applied over the lip-line, outlined with the use of eye-brow pencil or brush. A pallid complexion can be disguised with a good foundation and a word in the right direction might persuade the electrician to light them with 'surprise pink' spot-lights. (Theatrical designer Alec Shanks, who created costumes for the Folies Bergère, reminds us that many directors refer to this as 'Rose Mistinguett', the great star's favoured spot. He used to have many requests to bring sheets of 'number thirty-five' to Paris from London after the war.)

Indifferent hair – be it in quality, colour or cut – is generally disguised beneath an array of wigs or exaggerated hairpieces. Because of the speedy changes between sequences, revues such as this generally rely on the multitude of hair changes and head-dresses.

In the 1920s the legendary revue star Mistinguett's favourite costume on stage was a twenty-five-metre-long train made of ostrich feathers, worn with a mighty head-dress of the same quality. One of her head-dresses weighed around seven kilos with its steel frame and feathers. Each feather was elongated three times. Although she was tiny and by no means a great beauty, she made much of her staggeringly beautiful legs, carefully detracting from her obvious physical disadvantages. Enormous publicity surrounding the 1,000,000-dollar insurance of her legs ensured their being the first thing you looked at! 'Miss' was mortally afraid of the murderously steep staircase at the Folies Bergère and kept her eyes firmly closed while making her triumphant descent. The audience never realized that the eye-lid made up was practically identical with the eyes! She obsessively cultivated her exotic appearance until her death in 1956 and even her deathbed – she took twelve days to expire – was stylish as she slowly languished away in a rose silk negligée in rose satin sheets.

It falls upon the expertise of designers, wig-makers and make-up artists, lighting experts, producers and directors – and the craft of the artist herself – to project her good points and to conceal cleverly the indifferent ones in order to create and convey the glory of glamour.

There is no subject, perhaps, on which men can differ more widely than in their ideas of what constitutes beauty in a woman. Artists in different centuries have chosen and immortalized a particular type — the Aphrodites of Greek sculpture, the slender, wistful beauties of Botticelli, the robust nymphs of Rubens. There is no single type of feminine beauty which has not at some time become exalted into an ideal, and each has its own charm and loveliness. Physically, in figure and proportion, in face and feature, these classic beauties may have little in common. What they all have over and above their bodily perfections is some distinction of charm of personality which is as the sun streaming through the window of their beauty.

In the world of the theatre that beauty is not enough, if by beauty one means mere faultlessness of form and feature. Many of the greatest actresses in the world have been plain, some of them even ugly. Yet their charm and genius can so irradiate them that within a few minutes of their entrance they can persuade us that they are among the most beautiful women in the world.

One will find rarely, if ever, in any theatrical entertainment a girl who is chosen for her beauty alone. Even in the lightest entertainment, where the chief duty of many of the women is to be attractive to the eye, one finds that they have some definite talent as well, in acting, singing, or dancing, and some individual charm of their own which makes a chorus not merely a collection of shapely and well-drilled legs, but a band of piquantly different personalities, trained to work as one, but each capable at any moment of coming out of the ranks and holding the audience for a few minutes by her unaided efforts.

C. B. Cochran used this as his yardstick when choosing his 'Young Ladies'. He adopted a very critical standard in selecting girls for a new show:

> When I have had to pick sixteen 'Young Ladies', sometimes as many as five hundred girls, all beautiful in one way or another, all highly trained as the modern chorus-girl has to be, have been seen and heard at auditions before I could get the sixteen

I wanted. When I select a girl for the chorus, I do not merely look at her as a possible part of a mass effect, but as an individual with her own possibilities, still perhaps latent, but capable, if she has the will to work hard and take the trouble, of being developed along her own lines until she can leave the chorus and take on more important parts.

In spectacular revue, apart from the artists who have parts to play or special turns to present, there are usually two types of girl; the more *petite*, or dainty 'Young lady' of the dancing chorus, full of vitality, energy and high spirits, and highly trained in all forms of dancing, modern and classic, as well as in singing and acting; and the 'show' girls, usually of a more languorous and classic type, who must, of course, be able to dance and sing and act as well, but whose work calls less for the whirlwind of modern dance steps than for

Lemarchand and Derval together with artistic director Pierre Fréjol and the brilliant costumier Max Weldy at a final dress rehearsal.

graceful posing and beautiful carriage to display elaborate costumes.

Florenz Ziegfeld, however, adopted a different approach. The founder of the famous Ziegfeld Follies in 1907, Ziegfeld had moulded his pattern for revues on the Folies Bergère's formula together with his own almost invulnerable sense of showmanship. First married to the European beauty Anna Held, and then to Billie Burke, among his great discoveries were Mae Murray, Marilyn Miller, Ina Claire, Lillian Lorraine, whose rare beauty was endlessly extolled in the press, Dolores, perhaps one of the most famous show-girls of all time, of the proud, patrician posture and silky blonde hair, and many star artists who appeared in his shows including Irene Dunne, Fanny Brice, Paulette Goddard, Ruth Etting and Helen Morgan.

'A Pretty Girl is Like a Melody' was composed by Irving Berlin for the 1919 Ziegfeld Follies and became the theme song of Florenz Ziegfeld's sensational spectacles. Ziegfeld stated that 'In choosing the girls for my shows the first thing I look for is beauty. The girls must attract men. You cannot define the quality. In one word, I would say it is promise; a promise of romance and excitement – all the things a man dreams about when he thinks of the word, *girl*. She must have a haunting quality, as the Irving Berlin lyric informs us: "A pretty girl is like a melody that haunts you night and day". Some plain women have it, only when they have it, they're not plain any more.'

Throughout the twenty-five or so years of Ziegfeld's successes, until his death in 1932, he had auditioned some 15,000 girls a year. His ingredients for enchantment were: bust 36; waist 26; hips 38. The accent for perfection of figure was on the hips – they should always be two inches larger than the bust. He professed that bare legs were never as enticing as legs sheathed in the finest silk and chiffon, and tights were more seductive than nakedness. It was the art of concealment rather than of disclosure.

To be labelled a Ziegfeld Girl was the American girl's dream. Although their average salary was $75 a week, they wore ermines, sables, mink and diamonds. If anyone gave a party for them, they took for granted the emeralds or at least the thousand-dollar bills tucked into vanity cases as their due.

Ziegfeld was their finishing school, but it was not only on stage that he was a hard taskmaster. He demanded that they be well-groomed on all occasions – in the streets, hotels, restaurants or wherever they were seen by the public. He insisted upon gloves, hats, high heels and stockings at all times. They were to conduct themselves as 'ladies'. They were immediately identifiable as a 'Ziegfeld Girl'. One good suit, expensive and well-cut, was far more important than several cheap ones. A single evening dress, simply fashioned of fine material, was preferable to several changes of ill-fitting evening wear of cheaper material. Too much rouge, mascara or lipstick off stage was forbidden. And woe betide the girl who appeared at a rehearsal untidily or overly dressed. No girl would risk losing her position as a member of the famous Ziegfeld Follies.

Beauty of hair in the revue performer counts for a great deal. Nowadays, with the advent of modern beauty consultancy there need be no such thing as dull or ugly hair. Even where nature has not been too generous, hair can be treated and adjusted to suit the particular style of the wearer and bring out her best points. It does not mean that it should be subjected to ruinous and unnatural chemical bleaches and dyes, but that its natural beauty should be encouraged and that it should be so dressed as to accentuate the fact that it is, indeed, the 'crowning glory'.

Many a woman with comparatively undistinguished features has played havoc with beautiful and expressive eyes. Despite lack of actual beauty,

amazingly expressive eyes can convert a woman into
a most attractive person. Eyebrows are important
too, but if the secret of personality has been achieved
the artist could go through life without them and
no one would ever notice.

A shapely figure, well-proportioned to its stature
and type are of utmost importance. A woman can
be four feet tall or six feet tall and still have a beautiful
figure appropriate to her build. A six-foot woman
should not expect or try to have the childish figure
of a four-foot woman, and vice versa. The six-footer
should be proud of it and make every shorter woman
wish she were taller!

When selecting for the stage, regularity of feature
is of comparatively less importance, since miracles
can be performed with lighting and make-up where
a feature needs to be emphasized or reduced. Anyone
who can combine all the other good points and have
perfect features as well has more than a fair share of
good fortune.

The indefinable but unmistakable qualities of
charm and personality which can replace actual
beauty, or transcend it, are a compound of wit,
intelligence, sex, personal warmth. The virtues in
women which appeal to men even without beauty
in addition, or long after beauty has faded – loyalty,
good humour, sympathy, courage, and so on – are
inextricably bound up with them. That is the beauty
that shines from within.

The girls are, as well, disciplined not only by the
management but by the leading lady of the show,
as Mistinguett explains in her autobiography:

> If my chorus put a foot wrong on the opening
> night there was trouble. I chose the girls myself.
> And I can tell you it was by no means easy to
> find the right ones, neither too tall, nor too short,
> nor too fat, nor too plain – nor too pretty ...
> [as Mistinguett herself was neither tall nor a great
> beauty by any manner of means, she was all too
> conscious of competition on stage]. I interviewed

them by the score. 'Take your clothes off,' I would say. I would study the girl from all angles. 'No, you won't do for a nude. Leave your address with Mr Leslie here. You may be engaged as a show-girl.' I might undress a hundred in order to find ten.

On the first night it was I who dressed them. I had to keep an eye on them. 'Haven't you any soap at home? Go on, quick march to the pump.' I made short work of any who showed themselves rebellious to cleanliness. I myself could not breathe all day if I did not have my bath night and morning, and any girl who appeared more than once with grubby nails and greasy hair could find herself another job.

After the hundredth performance I had a show parade. Every pair of slippers worn in the show was laid out on the stage for my inspection. It is the shoe that makes the foot and the foot that makes the leg. The leg is one of the most important elements in Grand Revue and the public must always have their money's worth.

Having achieved these prerequisite qualities for her appearance, the artist is then seen by the public only on the stage, and in order for audiences to be attracted to the box-office to pay its admission fee, the need of advertising is paramount. In order to entice the public to the delights of these fascinating women to be seen at the great houses such as the Folies Bergère, poster artists were commissioned by the management and the stars themselves. Aside from Toulouse-Lautrec, the finest poster artist was the Frenchman Jules Chéret (1836–1932). His work adorned the streets of the French capital with examples of his exuberant style. He was a prolific poster artist and was to produce more than a hundred posters for the Folies Bergère alone.

'Life is enough as it is,' said Chéret. 'I want to turn the streets into an open-air museum which everyone can enjoy for nothing.' Chéret's posters were also popular because of their enormous *joie de vivre*. Georges Meunier followed in Chéret's footsteps when he began designing posters in about 1881, observing what had by then become a virtual rule: 'Always women and always laughter.'

But perhaps it was Paul Derval's philosophy that really summed up glamour and the success of the revue formula: *'Il faut donner à rêver et à rire.'* ('You must give them something to dream about and something to laugh at.') No doubt that is why Josephine Baker once described the Folies Bergère as being 'like Ziegfeld with a heart'.

Certain music-halls, notably the Folies Bergère before World War One, staged the sketches at the beginning of the evening. And then gradually, as the lavish revue established a formula of its own, these more dramatic sections of the entertainment shortened and disappeared, to be replaced only by two or three very short sketches embraced within the framework of the show itself and played by members of the company assisting one or more of its comic stars.

Spectacle as the prime ingredient came after the First World War. The post-war boom promoted the lavish spending on clothes, personal and domestic decorations, and public entertainments. If the designer was one of the vital creative forces, the costumier was one of the principal technicians. At the start of the great designer Erté's career, the most significant theatrical costume designer was Madame Rasimi. Max Weldy was her greatest competitor and certainly more prolific on an international scale. The role played by Weldy in revue is indicated by Paul Derval: 'The artists are a façade, a beautiful façade, but behind the *décors* is a little unknown world ... concerned with curtains and costumes. The fabrics required for a revue measure some 500 kilometres – the distance from Paris to Lyons; 17 kilometres of ribbon are needed to execute a special curtain. There are two workshops for costumes, one occupied with repairs and the other making new dresses.'

In charge of the unseen world at the Folies Bergère was Max Weldy.

An article in *Paris Soir* on 18 December 1928 describes how

> Max Weldy, from his office and *ateliers* next door to the stage door of the Folies Bergère in the rue Saulnier, controls the studios which furnish the entire world with revue, ballets, operettas and musical comedies. Two or three hundred people work here every day.... I opened the despatch ledger, one revue is in the Cape, others at Calcutta, Bombay, Shanghai, Hong Kong, England, at Oslo, etc. Current commissions include a revue costing one hundred thousand dollars for the USA. Costumes, *décors*, curtains are exported by Weldy to the Winter Garden, to Ziegfeld, to the Apollo Theatre, New York; also to the Admirals-Palatz in Berlin, the Olympia in Barcelona, the Queen Victoria, Madrid; the Maypon at Buenos Aires, without counting C. B. Cochran's London revues. For Paris, Weldy mounts the revues at the Folies Bergère every year. That means a million and a half each year.

Erté himself recalls that it was through Max Weldy that he first began to work for the Folies Bergère: 'I was living in Monte Carlo at the time and I received a letter from him asking whether I would care to pay him a visit in Paris. We met, and he recommended me. I designed for the Folies Bergère from about 1918 to 1930 when Louis Lemarchand, the author and producer at the Folies, retired.'

Erté's is a fascinating success story. Celebrating his ninetieth birthday on 23 November 1982, he admits to never having suffered a major disappointment in his entire career. Born into a naval family in Russia, his only desire was to be a painter, but he had to travel to Paris at an early age to find an outlet for his talents:

My desire to be independent and to be a painter is what prompted me to go to Paris. My family had been in the Russian navy for two hundred years. Every male member of the family had been an Admiral; my father, my grandfather and my great-grandfather. Of course, my father wanted me to carry on in the family tradition, but I told him that the only thing I wanted to do was paint. I hated everything military. I didn't go to art-school in Russia, however. Painting came to me naturally. I painted in oils in a very classical way – landscapes, portraits and still-life.

When I completed my schooling – with flying colours – my father said, 'I want to give you a present. What would you like?'

'A passport,' I replied.

Of course, he was disappointed about my not choosing the navy as a career, but he said, 'I promised to give you what you wanted, and I have to do it.' I was eighteen at the time, and it took almost a year for the passport to come through. While I was waiting for this invaluable document, I started designing dresses, and finally left for Paris at the age of nineteen, without any support from my family. I had fallen in love with Paris in 1900 when my mother took me over for the Great *Exposition* when I was eight years old, and I remembered vividly Loïe Fuller doing her famous Dance of Fire. She created such an impression on me that I knew from that moment on that Paris was the only place for me.

When I returned to Paris, on my own, in 1912, I only had one meal a week with meat. By the end of the year I managed to find a job with a second-rate dress-maker by the name of Caroline. But she fired me at the end of the first month.

'Do what you want with your career,' she advised me. 'But never try to design. You will never be a good designer.'

Anyhow, I asked her if I could take some of

Erté at his drawing board.

the designs I had done, and she said, 'They are all in the waste-paper basket. You can empty it.' So I parcelled them up – and left.

At that time Paul Poiret was the top French couturier. I went to his salon and left my portfolio. The next day I received a telegram from him: 'Come and see me as soon as possible.' When I went along to see him, he said, 'What I have seen of your work is very interesting. You can start tomorrow.' That was 1913. I worked with him for a year and a half until he was forced to close down because of the war.

I started out on my own and submitted designs to *Harpers Bazaar* and they asked me to continue designing their covers. And then *Vogue* commissioned me to do some covers for them and William Randolph Hearst got jealous and put me under a ten-year exclusive contract for magazine covers for *Harpers Bazaar*.

This led to contract after contract, success after success throughout his ninety years, during which time he has been decorated by the French government and achieved world-wide fame. Although his real name is Romain de Tirtoff, he chose instead to use only his initials, 'R.T.' – pronounced *Er Té*, in French – 'because I did not want to offend my father by bringing the honourable family name and its naval history into ridicule or disrepute.'

During the ten years in which Erté was under contract to *Harpers Bazaar*, he also designed for the theatre, not only for the Folies Bergère in Paris, but for the George White Scandals and the Ziegfeld Follies in New York. He worked from Paris where all the clothes for New York and Paris were made by Max Weldy under Erté's supervision, and shipped to New York without the need of Erté having to travel to the USA.

With the advent of war, Erté explained, Max Weldy left Paris for America in 1938: 'Max Weldy lives in Florida, and looks fabulous. He worked for years and years for the Ringling Brothers Circus making costumes, and now he rents them out. He has a wonderful business which is thriving more than ever now in the eighties.'

The producer and author of the shows, Louis Lemarchand, was really the soul of the Folies Bergère, Erté says, and during his reign the shows reached their zenith. When he left the Folies in the early 1930s, they gradually became dreary and banal.

Erté contributed two scenes for his first commission for the Folies – a huge showpiece based on Venice in the eighteenth century, and for a ballet, *Fonds de la Mer*, a group of witty costumes for octopus, lobster, goldfish, rayfish, etc. This was the beginning of an amicable association with the house.

He recalls that 'in that period you had such wonderful fabrics which you don't get any more. I remember there was a velvet you could draw through a ring on the finger, and it draped beautifully. But nowadays the fabrics all seem to contain man-made fibres and this makes them too hard. You can't get the shape you want.'

Aside from Mistinguett, Erté admits that there was only one other star throughout his long and illustrious career with whom he had a disagreement and that incident, too, involved fabrics:

> The star in question was Lilian Gish. I designed the costumes for *La Bohème* for MGM in Hollywood, and of course the part of the heroine that Miss Gish played was that of a poor girl, so I made the costume in wools and cottons. She came to the fitting and took one look at the costume, and without trying it on, said, 'Oh, I can't wear that.' And then, caressing her skin, she added, 'My skin is so sensitive. It is as sensitive as the part I am playing. I can play the role only in silk.' I said, 'I'm sorry. I won't make it in silk. Go somewhere else for your costume.'
>
> She was furious.
>
> However, there is nothing more difficult than

creating costumes for so-called naked dancers. Generally speaking, I was always guided by two principles. The first was to find one detail (hairstyle, jewellery or some other accessory) which was sufficiently interesting or striking to suggest the idea for a costume. The second was to build a costume by extending the lines of the naked body into decorative arabesques. Of course, those days you had more to dress on the nude – they wear far less these days, in the eighties.

But I never had any trouble at the Folies Bergère in all the years I worked there. It was marvellous to work at the Folies Bergère. Of course, the stage had no depth, but once you accepted that, you used certain tricks and devices which never showed. But one thing I didn't like was the fact that far too many costumes and sets were made and not used, and I don't like *gaspillage* – waste. They weren't kept for the next production because it was a year later, and it was a new show with a new script.

On the other hand, there were certain economies. For instance, the tableaux and costumes of Aladdin I first designed for the New York production in the George White Scandals then came to the Folies Bergère in 1927 in *Un Vent de Folies*. In fact, many of the scenes I designed for the George White Scandals between 1923 and 1929 came to the Folies Bergère.

When I asked Erté whether, in the creating of costumes, he ever cut, sewed, embroidered or beaded any of his work, he laughed:

'No! I can't sew on a button!'

As Erté explained, his association with the Folies Bergère lasted until Louis Lemarchand retired to his yacht in the South of France in the early 1930s. 'Louis Lemarchand had been identified with the Folies Bergère's more brilliant period. After he left, the Folies gradually became an institution for foreign tourists and provincials and ended up as a Musée

Grévin of the music-hall, the Paris equivalent of the famous Madame Tussaud's in London.'

Many artists feel that an institution will decline after their own departure and contribution to it has ended. History has, however, proved that the Folies Bergère continued in its popular tradition, with box-office receipts to prove it.

Erté readily admits that much of his rapid international fame was because of Weldy's influence. Aside from the costumes and *décors* Weldy made in his studios for the Folies Bergère, he also executed copies ordered by theatres throughout the world.

Erté was one of the greatest designers to have created outstanding costumes and sets for the Folies Bergère in the twenties, and these designs are among his finest work. For the 1921 revue his costumes and *décor* for the *Conte Hindou* tableau represented a ravishing sequence of colour and form, endlessly inventive of and evocative of the India of times past, exquisite in the tiniest details. Some of the designs, with their patterned fabrics and curious side movement, are reminiscent of the drawings of the Viennese artists Klibt and Schiele, although there is no evidence that Erté knew their work at the time. Erté's influence and remarkable genius remains in evidence on the stage of the Folies Bergère to this day.

Georges Barbier, a well-known illustrator and designer even before Erté's day and who designed costumes and *décors* at the Folies Bergère for some of the same productions as Erté's, composed the following description for the catalogues of Erté's exhibitions which took place in Paris:

I appreciate him above all when on the stage of the music-hall he brings out of the earth a network of diamonds throbbing on nude bodies, when he unfurls curtains embroidered with fantastic birds, or when again he raises curtains woven with ostrich feathers and heavy with fur, or harems afire, or on Eastern cities built of snow, of nacre

or metal. It is no easy task to wrench the blasé spectator from his seat in the stalls or to carry him away on the magic carpet to a world of splendour to the accompaniment of stormy music that rises to the head like a strong beverage. The velvet curtain raises slowly, one might even say reluctantly, on the large golden staircase down which descend beautiful snowy women. Their bodies, almost immaterial, are so perfect that all carnal desire is absent before these virginal forms, covered with the pollen of cosmetics, so fragile beneath their towering crowns, and head-dresses and accompanied by a cortège of winding sheeny robes resembling dragons held in leash.

However, many other distinguished designers succeeded in adorning the shows and the show-girls, including Alec Shanks, the British designer who, through Max Weldy, worked with Erté for many years and whose great contribution to the look of the Folies Bergère continued to fill the house:

> Between 1930 and 1931 the whole look, the format of the Folies Bergère began to change. The Colonial Exhibition in Paris in 1930 altered the whole outlook of music-hall spectacles, and, even possibly, of Parisian life, and to Louis Lemarchand, author of the revue, it seemed time to take a new look – and to *give* a new look to the venerable Folies Bergère.
>
> Lemarchand conceived the idea of calling the new revue *L'Usine à Folies* (Folies Factory). Luckily the title contained thirteen letters and the word 'Folies'.
>
> As a comparative newcomer to the Paris world of design, I was picked by Lemarchand to interpret the new formula in a number of 'key' tableaux and, more important, to design the giant poster, which created a furore and a small scandal. For the début of one whom the author Maurice Verne referred to as *'Shanks, le chaste anglais'*, it wasn't bad!

'La Princesse', an Erté design for the 1927 *Aladin* sequence.

An oriental costume designed by Erté for *Conte Hindou*, 1921.

Every revue at the Folies was the product of
the combined efforts of individual artists, who
were responsible for different scenes; and a pretty
cosmopolitan group we were, the majority not
French at all.

Our numbers included José de Zamora (Spanish); Erté, who was Russian; Brunelleschi, an
Italian; an Englishman named Willoughby who
had provided an occasional costume; Freddy
Wittop, a young Dutchman who has since made
a very successful career in American musicals;
Count Czettel, and (of course) Michel Gyarmathy
– both Hungarian; and from Sweden came the
inventive and very talented young Paul Seltenhammer, whose career, I understand, was cut short
during the 1939–45 war. This designer in '29/'30
introduced a really Freudian element of eroticism
in complete contrast to the glacial caryatid-like
figures of the Erté of 1924.

Alec Shanks went to work in Paris in 1928 partly
through general curiosity for what was taking place
in the great French capital, and partly ambition. He
felt, too, that the time had come for him to make
a move from his job at the Theatre Royal, Birmingham:

> I had been assistant to the quite eminent resident
> scenic artist there, W. R. Young. Already in his
> seventies, he needed all the help he could get in
> the very strenuous physical work involved in
> producing the vast amount of scenery required
> for the annual pantomimes. In those days, the
> principal theatres in all the main provincial cities
> produced their own spectacular Christmas shows,
> and all scenery, costumes and properties were
> made entirely on the premises, a process that oc-
> cupied staff for the greater part of the year.
> The scenic artist made elaborate coloured scale-
> models of the scenery, and made drawings for the
> props. In the case of the Theatre Royal, the

L'USINE À FOLIES
La Musique

ALEC
SHANKS

costumes had been designed by Dolly Tree in London, and were made up in the theatre wardrobe. One year she persuaded Philip Rodway to allow Max Weldy to supply some of the more exotic and complicated costumes, including some for Dorothy Ward as 'principal boy'.

It struck me that the dress-designer had an easier and more glamorous job – as well as a better-paid one – than the scene-painter, working alone in a vast, chilly paint-room high above the level of the 'flies' in a darkened theatre.

There were, in fact, very few actual scene-*designers*. Such names as Claude Lovat Fraser, Aubrey Hammond and Ernst Stern come to mind. Famous Royal Acadamicians like de Loutherbourg and Clarkson Stanfield painted scenery at Drury Lane or His Majesty's in the Haymarket.

Dear old Mr Young, who had grown up with Joe Harker in the great tradition of scene-painting, was a dignified, white-haired gentleman, with a face like portraits of Philip IV of Spain, with a beautiful waxed white moustache, a hand-tied white cravat, immaculate dark suit and a fresh buttonhole each day.

I said to him one day, 'There would be no chance for me in London; coming up from a provincial theatre to the very competitive paint-rooms of the Harkers, or Alec Johnstone, and I would never become known as a designer. But what if I worked in Paris for a while, and came back with experience behind me, and a reputation?'

The dear chap sadly agreed, and then more cheerfully added, 'One thing – you have never seen bad work in *this* theatre.'

Philip Rodway readily gave me a letter of introduction to Max Weldy, and fully expected to see me back again to paint a few more acres of daffodils and/or heather for next season.

Alec Shanks

But although Birmingham did not see Alec Shanks back again, the West End of London was to receive him with open arms after his huge successes in Paris at the Folies Bergère, Les Ambassadeurs, Le Paramount and the Théâtre du Châtelet. He was to design productions for the Hippodrome, the Prince of Wales, the London Palladium, the Coliseum and many other theatres including the Saville and the Adelphi.

Though his parents were Scots, they lived near Birmingham, where Alec Shanks went to King Edward VI School and it was there that he found his *métier*, as he says:

At school you have to be good at something, and as I was appallingly inefficient at games, I made up for it by painting vivid posters advertising the sporting activities of the 'hearties'. They made a splendid show against the blackened walls of the school's Gothic corridor, and I was much in demand. Eventually an indulgent headmaster allotted me a room under the eaves, and permission to found an Arts and Crafts Society. This gave me a new status, and I was asked to design the annual school play. Instead of the Greek play given up to the war, it was to be *Twelfth Night* with Raymond Huntley as Sir Toby. 'The Shoe-string' *décor* was much acclaimed.

The next year's play was *The Merchant of Venice* with Godfrey Winn as Antonio. We disagreed over my choice of colour for his costume, leading him to refer to me in his autobiography as 'a good-looking red-head with a vitriolic tongue'.

But all this time I got a great deal of help from the Birmingham Repertory Theatre. Sir Barry Jackson and Paul Shelving [the brilliant scenic artist and costume designer], put the paint-room at my disposal, and I learnt much, and definitely made up my mind to work in the theatre.

When he got to Paris, Alec Shanks was to be impressed with the various 'stage' tricks and devices employed at the Folies Bergère, and to meet and work with the 'king-pins' of the Folies; the author/producer of the shows, Louis Lemarchand; the show's costume-maker, Max Weldy; and later, Michel Gyarmathy, who was to succeed Paul Derval in the years to come, but who at this time was one of the contract designers of the spectacular shows:

> Louis Lemarchand was tall, well set-up, grey-haired and moustachioed. He projected the perfect image of the '*bon viveur*', the French woman's ideal – '*un Bel Homme*'. Immaculately turned out, his appearance alone showed how good life had been to him (since, of course, the author's rights on eleven Folies Bergère revues had rolled in, buying for him his Paris 'Hôtel Particulier' and his yacht at Antibes).

> His predilection for such esoteric adventures as the (then fashionable) nocturnal gatherings in the Bois de Boulogne, known as 'partouzes', is reported to have led to difficulties with the '*police des Moeurs*', from which not only did he extricate himself, but emerged, later the same year, with '*Les Palmes Académiques*', awarded for his services to (of all things) Education – to which his button-hole thereafter bore permanent testimony.

> When I first met Max Weldy in Spring 1928 he struck me as the neatest, and, I suppose, 'smartest' little man I had ever encountered.

> Short, slim, in his perfectly tailored double-breasted brown suit, shiny dark hair brushed back, and alert, *very* French, brown eyes. It was the charm of his smile – at its most innocent when telling the most outrageous fibs – that had won him the business of all the world's producers, and, equally important, their affection.

Among the many ingenious devices used repeatedly over the many years at the Folies Bergère, two tricks stand out in Alec Shanks's mind:

> The first is the one known as '*Le Plan Incliné*',

Paul Derval as seen by Shanks.

Louis Lemarchand by Shanks.

where the effect is of a scene viewed from above (with, say, supper-table or ornate grand piano, and people standing or seated around), generally framed three-dimensionally, to imitate a painting. The effect is achieved by three or more vertical 'ground-rows' or cut-outs concealing narrow rostra on which the 'figurants' are posed. The flat piece representing the central table (or piano) is inclined very slightly out of the vertical, and various ornaments, candelabra are fixed in it. The people on the 'far' side of the table are, in fact, only about two feet further back than those in front, but around four or more feet *higher*. The trick depended on mastering draftsmanship and 'forced' perspective, used also by the great Italian painters. These basically static set-pieces encouraged the Parisian sneer that the Folies Bergère had become a 'Madame Tussaud's'.

Max Weldy by Shanks.

An example of '*Le Plan Incliné*' illusion.

The other stock effect, Shanks recalls, 'was that of a large and transparent (or two-way) mirror suspended above the stage at an angle of 45 degrees. By the alteration of lighting, this enabled one to see

the action taking place at stage-level reflected in such a way as to appear on the backcloth. It must be stressed that this was only *perfectly* effective from certain parts of the house.'

Michel Gyarmathy admits that the mirror device is no longer practical because the mirror takes up too much valuable space in this cramped, very old theatre. Although the tricks are much favoured by Gyarmathy, and are included in the shows to this day, they were largely the brain-child of Lemarchand. No other theatre or show does them as well as the Folies Bergère.

Alec Shanks used the mirror trick, which he first saw at the Folies in 1929, in shows at the Blackpool Opera House, but it never worked well there as the auditorium was too wide and the balcony too high.

Mention of the costs of the revues is as irrelevant today as it was then. The figures put out are what the public relations people think the public will stand. The cost to the Folies Bergère of a costume or a set bears no relation to what an individual would pay for it. Shanks recalls that many entire sets were 'scrapped' before seeing the light of day, as well as about one *half* of the scenery built for the tableaux actually used.

As for what the designers were paid, it was less than they would have received for their normal work as illustrators or poster-artists. Shanks's case was not typical, since he received a retainer from Max Weldy, plus a 'bonus' from Derval. His poster for *L'Usine à Folies* in 1931 brought him in the equivalent of £30, enough to live on for a month in those days!

The Derval–Lemarchand association ended in the early thirties when Lemarchand retired. This was followed by an interim period of a few short years when the musical director from the Casino de Paris, Maurice Hermite, and Jean le Seyeux, devised the Folies Bergère shows between them, but their attempts to emulate Lemarchand were far off the mark and business began to dwindle until Mistinguett and Josephine Baker were enticed back for a season. Max Weldy was still in control of the execution of the sets, curtains and costumes under Derval's administration, but when he departed for America with the advent of *Anschluss*, Gyarmathy became resident designer and together with Jeanne Sairnal, the head of the workrooms from the early days, they mounted show after show. After the death of the first Madame Derval (the dancer, Miss Campton) and Derval's re-marriage, Gyarmathy inherited complete control as Artistic Director and designer, first under Paul Derval himself and there-after under his widow after Paul had died. Costumes were then made under Madame Derval's supervision and this became the routine at the Folies Bergère until the death of Madame Derval herself in the early seventies.

The ownership of the Folies Bergère fell into the hands of one of its former show-girls, Hélène Martini, who presented her first four-year running revue in 1974 (*J'aime à la Folie*); a woman who today is not only one of the richest in France, but as 'Queen of the Night' reigns over Parisian night-life as one of the most influential figures of the world where we sit in the dark and weave such wonderful dreams.

7
Everybody on Stage!

Aside from the months of planning for the future
spectacular, the elaborate shows presented at the
Folies Bergère take at least ten months to mount. In
addition to the complex electrical and mechanical
effects, the cost of presenting the revues up until the
1970s amounted to half a million pounds a show;
but the cost of the new show that opened at the
beginning of 1982 rose to double that figure. The
investment used to be realized and a profit made
within its four-year run, but the current show will
have to continue for five years before it can provide
any reasonable return.

The post-war productions followed a set formula.
The three revues in 1958, 1961 and 1964 each ran
for three years, but there is little to add to them
as they lacked the distinctive content of the great
individualistic pre-war shows. *Folies en Fêtes* (Folies
in Celebration), which opened in 1964, for instance,
was, as usual, lavish, and Paul Derval even advertised
the cost of mounting the revue on the poster – 350
million (old) francs. This supreme publicity stunt,
showing the conversion of all these millions into
feathers and costume jewellery, is rather exceptional,
but was often used between the two world wars
when the managements of the theatres regularly
announced the astronomical cost of their revues, as
well as the receipts and attendance records, in the
daily press.

For the 1974 revue, *J'aime à la Folie* (I Love to
Distraction), Erté was commissioned to design a

FOLIES BERGÈRE

Folies en Fêtes

Production
PAUL DERVAL
Grandissime spectacle de
MICHEL GYARMATHY
qui a couté
350 MILLIONS A.F.

poster for the Folies Bergère consisting of a woman draped in ostrich feathers on a blue background. In 1970 Roland Petit had asked Erté to design some costumes for Zizi Jeanmaire's appearance at the Casino de Paris (the last production to take place at that theatre before it closed). This marked the beginning of a new career for Erté, and he is currently planning to design a new production for the husband and wife team when Petit presents Zizi Jeanmaire in a sparkling musical on the life of Mistinguett which is to open at the Châtelet in Paris in 1984 – the year Erté celebrates his ninety-second birthday!

Michel Gyarmathy is the Folies Bergère's artistic director. He also has the mammoth task of designing all the sets and costumes, contracting the artists, choosing the composers and lyricists (he also composes some of the music himself) and selecting a suitable choreographer. A Bohemian-type bachelor, the moustachioed, balding Gyarmathy is not as tall in physical stature as he is in vivid imagination. A man in his seventies, he has surprising energy for one who has developed the silhouette of an Alfred Hitchcock. In the preparation of the show, he ascends the stairs to his *atelier* high above the theatre – at midnight, after the evening's performance – where he works through the night until seven in the morning and then goes home to bed for three hours. When he was working on one revue, he did not go home for almost a month. He shaved and dressed in one of the dressing-rooms, and kept going on sandwiches and a few snatched hours' sleep in an armchair. When he *does* get home to his sumptuous house in the rue Chazelles not far from the fashionable Avenue Haussmann, his creature comforts await him. Here, in his spacious Louis XV furnished drawing-room he is attended by a valet who moves about the elegant edifice as quietly and sedately as his master. No evidence here of the owner's profession. Not a single theatrical clue is given to Gyarmathy's background or craft. The 'very French' household could be that

Michel Gyarmathy

of an aristocrat.

Back at the theatre, his penchant for discipline could, perhaps, be illustrated by one of the theatre's back-stage rules. Some of the artists are quite well known socially, but once they step through the stage door, they are regimented into the Folies Bergère's tradition for discipline. Should one of the girls so much as mislay an ear-ring, she will turn the theatre upside down in order to find it, lest she receive a black mark in the morning. For three black marks, she will receive a warning letter from the management. For five such letters – dismissal.

Although Gyarmathy has pride in his work, he has no vanity. He has not kept a single original design of the exquisite costumes and sets he has created for the Folies, preferring to tear them up once the work on them has been completed. A most practical man, he makes the original model for each set of, say, twenty-four costumes himself, painstakingly sewing each seam and embroidering each bodice. Although the overall effect of his costumes is stunning, his clothes have great simplicity in their design and execution. He relies on the addition of feathers and jewels for embellishment. He feels that British musical and revue costumes are 'too busy; cluttered with shiny sequins and beads sewn onto unsuitable fabrics'.

As if to prove his point, the costumes for the finest tableau in the new production, *Folies de Paris*, which is scheduled to run until 1987, are evocations of his own country, with the Hungarian tableau '*Au Pays des Czardas*' showing exquisite national costumes in a period Hungarian setting. The love story culminates in a wedding ceremony. The finale of this sequence is the most inventive of the show. Above the proscenium arch and on the walls of the sides of the circle, high up to the ceiling, appear stained-glass windows illuminated by arc lights. The theatre appears to be transformed into a Gothic cathedral as the bells ring out and the choir's voices fill the air. Gyarmathy is rightly proud of the stupendous reception from a rapturous audience.

This same device was used when Josephine Baker last appeared at the Folies Bergère. Josephine, playing Mary Queen of Scots, was led up the stairs to the executioner, and at the moment the axe fell and a prop head rolled down the staircase, the orchestra rose into a crescendo with the choir raising their voices to 'Ave Maria', at which point the stained-glass windows appeared, transforming the stage and theatre's interior into a cathedral.

Donn Arden, author and artistic director of the Lido in Paris as well as many other international shows including the largest of them all, Las Vegas's MGM Hotel (in partnership with Rene Fraday – a combination of some thirty years' standing), is filled with admiration for Gyarmathy's achievement: 'Gyarmathy does a fantastic job considering the space he has to work in. Besides, it's a very old theatre.

Rare examples of Gyarmathy's sketches.

All of us in the American theatre know who Michel Gyarmathy is and admire him tremendously. Paul Derval was the money-man, but behind it all was Gyarmathy.'

And a tribute from Miss Bluebell: 'Those effects are a speciality of the Folies Bergère. Nobody does it as well as they do, thanks to Michel Gyarmathy.'

He is a disciplinarian, but there is hardly anyone who can boast his theatrical achievement that is not a task-master himself. On my own visits to the Folies Bergère, I found him hard at work in his office back-stage an hour before the start of the show every night. Once he was satisfied that the curtain had risen on time, he moved through the pass-door to the front of house, where he kept an eye on the smooth running of the show and the discipline of the artists. He kept touch, too, with the front-of-house staff and lent a sympathetic ear to their problems. At the end of the performance, shortly before midnight, I again found him in his office. On several occasions when we waited on the pavement outside the stage door in the rue Saulnier for the taxi that had been ordered for him, husbands and boyfriends waiting for their charges greeted him loyally; '*Bonsoir*, Monsieur Michel,' and as the artists left the theatre, he received an equally reverent, '*Bonne nuit*, Monsieur Michel,' accompanied by affectionate kisses on the cheek.

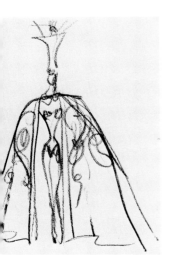

On one occasion when he asked me to dine with him after the show, at *Le Jardin du Louvre*, one of the most fashionable restaurants in Paris, I observed how charmingly he was received by the proprietors with warmth and friendliness and treated with deserved respect. As friends and acquaintances of his passed our table, they paused to pay their own respects to him. He chain-smoked throughout the evening, as he does during the day. He does not drink. Vichy water, not wine, was his choice; yet he is a connoisseur of wine – he went through the list and chose the right one for the meal that had

254 The Folies Bergère

been ordered for me. He talked about his work at the Folies Bergère where he began in 1933 when he arrived from Hungary. He had always been passionately interested in the theatre and after graduating in the Fine Arts, he left Budapest to try his luck in Paris. He had taken one or two designs to show Paul Derval. They were rejected but, determined to join the team of designers at the Folies, he did some further work on them, re-submitted them and this time his work was accepted. He consolidated his position with the Folies Bergère throughout the next fifty years, relying on his particular genius for perspective. This came as the result of spending his lean years as a student when the only theatre seat he could afford was in the gallery. From that view-point he learnt to give extra depth to his sets by raising the up-stage levels in such a way as to obtain, at times, a vertical arrangement. This device has proved particularly effective on such a tiny stage where space is so limited and effects and staging so vital.

As Gyarmathy explains:

My sole aim is to make a spectacular show on a tiny stage which is only twenty feet deep. This is not easy because the show lasts for three and a half hours and consists of forty different tableaux. We have a hundred and fifty artists in the company and almost as many technicians and a tremendous physical and technical effort is required of everyone for the coordination of the show, because there is a different tableau every three minutes, requiring new scenery and new costumes. But in spite of the immense problems we face, I am always confident that with the experience we have in this kind of show it will be a success when it finally opens.

And it always is. He does, fortunately, have four years to prepare a new show, and five years for the next, the length of the run of the current new show, *Folies de Paris*.

Once the stars have been signed and the opening date set, Gyarmathy's first task is the choice of subjects for the tableaux around which the show will revolve – not forgetting that the first meaning of tableau is 'picture'. From the sheaves of notes Gyarmathy keeps in his *atelier* above the theatre, he chooses twenty or thirty of his ideas in consultation with Madame Martini, the proprietress of the Folies Bergère, but as she admires his taste and trusts his judgement, there is no conflict between them. They both know that the ideas should appeal to all tastes of the public who pay to see the show. 'Always a cocktail; something sweet, something sour – something strong, something effervescent.' The first choice is usually directed towards the women in the audience because in most households it is the woman who decides where she and her partner will spend the evening. Headings for the tableaux might read something like 'Fashion through the Ages', 'Perfumes from Paris', or simply, 'Lace', 'Furs', or 'Frills'. Then, if the men are to be permitted to gaze longingly on the ranks of the semi-nude lovelies, their wives or girlfriends could hardly feel indifferent to the charms of a few virile-looking dancers or musclemen, so a place must be found for these within the structure of the show. Masculine tastes are pandered to with the inclusion of tableaux glamorizing the race-track, the roulette wheel, the 'live' chess game, or anything of a sporting nature that lends itself to colour and movement. Add a few scenes that can be sumptuously dressed – 'Châteaux of the Czars', 'Waltzes of Old Vienna', 'Beau Brummel at Bath' – for her, and a few undressed ones – 'Venus Arising', 'The Judgement of Paris' – for him, and all that remains is the collection of crowd-pullers, the more sensational tableaux for the masses. These follow a fairly constant pattern, with recurring Balinese temples, oriental forests, Russian Cossack festivals, pagan dances and an occasional Daphnis and Chloe pastorale, according to the finance available for special effects.

Once these visual highlights, which determine the broad outlines of the revue, have been settled, Gyarmathy works on the book and the design, and the selection of costume-makers. Some costumiers are better at lavish effects, others excel with the simple and fashionable; some score with period costumes, others with fantasy or novelty. In the old days it was the same with the scenic designers; this one would be successful with exteriors, that one specialized in eighteenth-century ballrooms; one was a master of the set piece, another found his genius among stage machinery and revolves. Each one of them was furnished with details of the scenes in the revue affecting him and asked to produce his sketches by a certain date, but nowadays the entire task of design for both *décors* and costumes falls on one man alone – Michel Gyarmathy, who is, as well, the show's artistic director.

Gyarmathy is not only a designer and a draughtsman, but a musician too. He works out his numbers on the piano. The classical Russian composers and the Hungarian ones too, such as Emmerich Kalman, have had a great influence on him and have done much to develop his visual skills. Some of the music will be semi-classical 'evergreen' material selected to tie in with the tableaux he has in mind. Some will comprise contemporary hits that he hopes will last the run of the revue. He also commissions a handful of contemporary composers and lyricists who undertake the responsibility of the rest of the show's musical output, which is considerable. A large proportion of the music is original, and for this there are auditions, conferences, try-outs, in the hope that one of the sixty-odd songs in the production will take the public's fancy, capture its imagination and become a hit. Much depends on the stars who have been signed and the numbers they themselves like. If a single song from a revue takes off, everyone is well pleased. Two is fantastic. More would be a miracle. The music is then scored and arranged by the show's conductor.

Once the production has reached this stage, the remainder of the company is contracted – featured performers, dancers, speciality acts, and, of course the show-girls and the chorus – which means more auditions.

Gyarmathy and the choreographer sit in the stalls. The stage is bare except for a rehearsal piano and pianist and unshaded 'working lights'. One by one the applicants are called from the wings, where they are waiting, to the centre of the stage where they are asked to give an example of their work in singing and dancing. Most of them, who have come in response to advertisements in the theatrical trade papers, or who have heard about the auditions 'on the grape-vine', are prepared, with 'set' rehearsal pieces, and hand the pianist their sheet music. Many of them are, perhaps not unnaturally, nervous, and the producer tries to put each applicant at ease with a word or two first; he might ask about her experience – is she straight out of ballet-school? Which shows has she appeared in? The choreographer might ask which other choreographers she has worked for; in this way he can gauge her style and technique even before she starts her first dance step, as there are different styles demanded by each different choreographer. But before the duo begins to hear how she sings or how she dances they already have a mental documentation on one or two points.

The first is how she walks and how she holds herself as she crosses those few yards into the bright light. To achieve a natural, unselfconscious walk across the stage is as difficult to master as coming down a steep flight of stairs on stage. Does she scutter like a frightened rabbit, or hold herself humpily, or has she the natural ease and poise which come partly from training but is often inborn and a useful first sign of whether the artist has any stage talent at all? Potential revue artists would be wise to cultivate a good carriage and graceful, free-and-easy walk, for this is more important than many women realize, and far more important than perfectly proportioned features.

The producer and choreographer notice too how the artist stands in repose and how she holds her hands. There are women with beautifully shaped hands who detract from their beauty by hanging them clumsily, making restless, ungraceful use of them. Not every woman may be blessed with beautifully shaped hands, but she can do wonders by watching how she uses them: large hands, for instance, should not be cluttered with rings on each finger – this simply attracts attention and comment to the hands. From the producer's point of view, hands and feet are of the utmost importance. Attractive and talented artists who perform splendidly with their voices and their brains, sometimes have no conception of the importance of carrying the process through to their hands and feet.

Auditions at the Folies are not, of course, confined to the ladies and gentlemen of the chorus, and not everyone, no matter how good they are, happens to be chosen. They might not easily fit into the preconceived pattern of the new revue, as Billy Milton, the British entertainer, recalls:

> This wonderful internationally known pleasure-palace brings back to me a thwarted desire. I loved Paris so much when I was working over there, particularly since I was having such a success partnering the famous ex-Folies Bergère star, Mistinguett, at the Casino de Paris. I asked my agent, Albert Turvelle, whether he could possibly arrange a private audition for me at the Folies Bergère, without anybody knowing. Nothing could have given me more pleasure than to secure a contract for the new Folies Bergère show, which was practically every other artist's dream as well. Fortunately my wish was granted and I arrived for the audition, extremely nervous, and was

LES BELLES DE PARIS

amazed to find that the stage of the Folies Bergère
had so little depth and, of course, it was clear of
any scenery for the audition.

So I sang in French, danced, and played the
piano. I was thanked and I waited for days and
days for news of the result. Not a word. I was
very crestfallen when, eventually, nothing came
of it. I had thought that my name, Milton, which
was the same name as an established French comic
called Milton, who had appeared at the Folies
Bergère several times, might possibly prove to be
an asset and sway their decision in my favour, but
no. The scheme hadn't worked. Naturally I didn't
mention this to Mistinguett because it would have
caused a great deal of trouble.

The show has been cast. Contracts are signed –
some of them for the run of the show. But although
the artists have signed their Equity Agreements, the
documents are hardly worth the paper they are
written on. A girl could go ill or find the long run
tedious after a time and seek pastures new. It is not
worth the management suing for breach of contract.
It is time-consuming and costly. There are many
more artists where the defectors come from (90 per
cent of the theatrical profession is out of work), and
it is up to the ballet-mistress to rehearse the replace-
ments, or for the understudies, or 'swings' as they
are called, to take over under the supervision of the
'captain' of the troupe.

Before Gyarmathy took over the sole responsibility for the *mise-en-scène* as well as the design of
all the *décors* and costumes for the show, the designs
for the revue had to be approved by the artistic
director long before rehearsals had begun (and sometimes they had to be changed four or five times
before the designer's ideas coincided with or
expressed those of the artistic director). Together
with the *chef machiniste*, who has always been present
at all the early stages, the designer went off to choose
the materials for each costume. The *chef machiniste*
was the only one who knew what the other thirty
or so designers were up to and which sets of lines
(for hanging back-cloths, etc.) were available.

Satins, silks, velvets, lamés, metallic weaves and
decorative laces are all minutely scrutinized, separ-
ately and together, always in artificial light, as colours
change drastically under the 'spots'. Often specialist
dyers have to be called in to make sure that the many
shades in ensemble tableaux harmonize; that the sets
and curtains do not clash with the tones of the
costumes.

Gyarmathy makes the final selection of materials.
He pins each sample to the relevant costume design
so that he can make sure his *décors* will either
complement or contrast suitably with the performers

who appear in front of them. He then produces a *maquette*, a scale model of each set, complete with entrance, exits, staircase, revolves, movable 'flats' and curtains for transformation scenes, etc. Once he is satisfied, he sends scale plans of each element and every component in all the sets to the *chef machiniste*, so that the necessary machinery can be constructed, and flats, chassis, podiums and structural units built, fire-proofed and sent back to the studio for painting.

After the final choice of sets has been made for the new revue, the designs go to the master carpenter and the workshops take over. With the book written, the music chosen and scored, the company and speciality acts booked and the designs approved, the preliminary work is finished. It will have taken two or three months. Next comes the choreography and the rehearsal period which will continue for a further eight weeks. Rehearsals take place on stage, in the foyer, in the 'hall' and also in the basements, with time taken off for costume-fittings, wig-fittings, shoes, boots and props. Gradually, the revue takes shape; with chairs and chalk-marks on the bare boards to indicate the sets, the dancers, show-girls, chorus boys and walk-ons go through their routines, during which time the costumes and sets will arrive at completion. As is the case with any theatre (except those that are 'dark' – and there are far too many in such a state in these days of recession, unfortunately), this is made more difficult by the fact that nobody can set foot on the stage until the very last minute – there will be a few days at the most between the closing of whatever is currently running and the premier of the new show. For the spectacular revue, this brings design problems that are unknown to the director of straight plays or even musicals. Plays require three sets at most, musicals seldom more than six or eight. For a revue of this kind, forty complicated sets have to be surveyed, measured, built to precise specifications, dismantled and numbered ready for re-assembly without a single chance to check that they accurately fit the stage.

And then there is the question of Unions. There is hardly anyone back-stage, or on stage, whether they be carpenters, electricians, scene-shifters, machinists, artists or stage-management who do not belong to one or other of the dozen Unions. There is always an imminent strike over something or other. Negotiations for better and higher salaries and conditions are constant and it is for this reason that the current show costs twice as much to mount as the previous one. A million pounds to mount a show nowadays in a theatre the size of the Folies Bergère, which seats only 1,600 people, is a considerable amount. It is therefore not surprising that the best seats cost £25 each.

At the first rehearsal, the show-girls and the chorus are divided into groups according to size and type. Each is then allotted the costumes most suitable for her looks,.and the costumier, the wig-maker and the boot-maker are called in to take measurements. The choice of the right costume for the right girl is a very delicate job requiring a great deal of experience and a specialist's eye to know exactly how to display each girl's good points – and, above all, to hide the bad ones.

Once rehearsals are in full swing, a routine establishes itself: dancers in the morning from 10.30 to 12.30; show-girls from 1.00 to 3.00 p.m.; the two troupes together from 3.00 until 5.00 – after which selected members of the cast are sent to the costumier for fittings. When a tableau has been finalized and the movements keyed in with the choreography, the music is sent to the arranger for scoring. The orchestra starts rehearsing eight or ten days before the last performance of the existing show.

Then the headaches start: major alterations to costumes, dances which for reasons of space have to be re-thought, orchestrations which have to be re-scored, sets that require extensive amendment because an eye-line from one side of the circle penetrates the wings, or there is not enough room for twelve girls to enter at once from the opposite side in a particular tableau – all of which consumes time, time, time. And this is one of the commodities with which the producer cannot afford to be lavish. The place is a hive of activity. A streak of light in the corridor signals a seamstress dashing by with a spangled dress; hairdressers hurry along carrying fabulous wigs...

At last, the final performance of the outgoing show arrives. Traditionally, to enliven the sadness of the occasion, the artists gag outrageously on stage – and no one complains. The girls do not go back to their dressing-rooms to change; they switch costumes in the wings and throw the discards into huge hampers which are taken away by the cleaners. Later, along with the dismantled sets, they will be hired out or sold to touring companies (costumes and scenery from the Folies have been known to turn

Costume fittings.

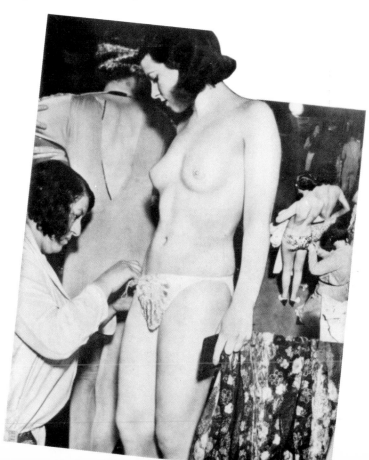

up, years later, in places as far flung as Alexandria, Hong Kong, Buenos Aires and even Blackpool and Atlantic City). The footwear will be put into stock or used for rehearsal work.

Two of the Folies Bergère's productions found their way to the West End of London. In 1946 Paul Derval wrote to Alec Shanks, who had designed several Folies Bergère productions, proposing a sale of the current revue, at the end of its run, but instead of selling only the scenery, wardrobe and properties, as he had to Shanks in 1939, he wanted to include the entire *mise-en-scène*, supervised by himself. Shanks approached the eminent impresario Val Parnell, who numbered among his theatres the London Palladium, but Parnell sneezed at the condition – that Derval should be involved. Bernard Delfont, however, went ahead.

The other distinguished British theatre producer, Robert Nesbitt, whose name is synonymous with some of the most lavish productions to be seen in Britain (and, as well, in Las Vegas, where he produced the first spectacular show at the Dunes), from the London Palladium and the Prince of Wales Theatre to the Blackpool Shows, and back to London's Talk of the Town spectacular shows, takes up the story:

> Bernard Delfont had a deal with Derval to present two or three Folies Bergère shows in London. I returned to London from America at Delfont's request, to do shows at the London Palladium, which I did for the next two or three years. He then felt that I was the right man to do a Folies Bergère show at the Prince of Wales. The Folies Bergère shows had been imported in their entirety before this, but we decided to remount a Folies Bergère show of our own because it seemed that the ideas were the same. I said, however, that we couldn't call it the Folies Bergère, for obvious reasons.
>
> Michel Gyarmathy came over to London to

'Economical Splendour', an Alec Shanks design from the Folies Bergère show at the Prince of Wales Theatre, London.

The Folies Bergère –
London style.

discuss the project. We met on several occasions and discussed what we proposed to do, or what we would *like* to do, based on Derval's plans. However, when Gyarmathy got back to Paris, everything seemed to go wrong, and they withdrew from the proposals.

Undeterred, however, the British proceeded with their own plans, and Robert Nesbitt produced a show of his own, with the exception of one Folies Bergère scene. Entitled *Plaisirs de Paris*, it proved to be a great success.

The irony of the *quid pro quo* was that when in London Gyarmathy saw the work of Billy Petch, Nesbitt's choreographer, he contracted him to do two shows at the Folies Bergère. 'Pinched him from me,' Nesbitt laughs.

Bernard Delfont tells how the Folies Bergère came to open in London, from his own point of view. It gives us an insight into the technicalities and the problems involved in staging a show in London's West End, particularly when confronted with the power of theatre owners of the calibre of the late Val Parnell, who controlled, among many other theatres, the London Palladium, the London Hippodrome (later the Talk of the Town) and the Prince of Wales Theatre:

> It must have been about 1950 when I thought of doing the Folies Bergère in this country, so I went over to Paris a few times to see Paul Derval and Gyarmathy, originator of the marvellous scenic effects which worked supremely well in Paris, but had to be done differently here for technical reasons.
>
> After months and months of negotiating, I signed a contract to do the Folies Bergère in London and when I got back to England, I discussed with Val Parnell the possibility of bringing it to the London Hippodrome.
>
> We decided to open the Folies Bergère show

at the Birmingham Hippodrome because we thought it was the right place for a try-out. Of course, the Watch Committee there were very anxious about any nudity; the girls had to stand perfectly still and if they moved, you were for it! There was enormous publicity in the press about the opening of the show, and on the first night the theatre was packed. It was a very, very good show indeed even though I hadn't put in all the costumes and scenery I wanted for the West End production. There was a train scene, for instance. Nowadays a show like that would cost a million pounds to stage. However, at the end of the performance I was congratulated by the Watch Committee who said it was presented with great taste and that they were relieved that the girls didn't move!

Val Parnell came up to see the show two days later and much to my horror he said, 'I'm sorry. It's not good enough for the West End.'

Naturally, I was shattered and didn't know what to do because he was the lessee of the London Hippodrome Theatre which we had earmarked for the show. At that time my own theatre, the Saville, was the only one I controlled; I decided to do a bit of propaganda, and I let word get around that I was going to do the show at the Saville. Of course I knew that I couldn't because the stage could never have taken all that scenery, but I hoped that Val Parnell wouldn't realize all that. Word got around publicly that the Folies Bergère was going to open in London at the Saville Theatre and when Val Parnell heard this he thought that he'd been wrong after all and got me up to his office.

I said, 'Val, the show you saw in Birmingham was only part of the show I have planned for the West End, and I promise you it will be fantastic.' That was how I managed to get the London Hippodrome. We ran there for about four years

with different Folies Bergère shows. Then Val had
problems in finding shows for the Prince of Wales
Theatre; it seemed he was able to find shows for
the Hippodrome far more easily and asked me to
switch the Folies Bergère to the Prince of Wales
to make way for other incoming shows.

The Folies Bergère shows in London had very
lovely scenes, all done by Gyarmathy. He came
over and spent several months here to do them.
After the first two shows we put stars in them.
For instance, we had Frankie Howerd and Wini-
fred Atwell, then we had Benny Hill and Tommy
Cooper in one show, and Norman Wisdom in
another.

Then, as Robert Nesbitt says, Paul Derval
wanted more money and made the terms too
difficult to carry on so I said, 'We'll just do French
revues,' so we changed the title to *Plaisirs de Paris*
and it worked just as well for a number of years.

But in Paris, while the old sets are dismantled and
the new scenery is delivered for the new Folies
Bergère show, the stage is left free and the incoming
company assembles in the auditorium for the alloca-
tion and fitting of costumes. For two days and nights
the theatre is the scene of chaos. The artists become
irritable and exhausted, standing for hours on end
surrounded by gesticulating costumiers and fitters
pinning up hems and taking in tucks – for every
single costume has to be tried on, inspected, checked
against the design, and probably altered. The costumes themselves look awful at this stage because
there is no proper lighting and the cast wear
rehearsal tights and leotards under them to keep
warm. Tempers fray, temperaments explode! The
producer tears his hair out and screams at everyone;
a costumier collapses into a fit of tears.

But at last it is all done and everyone is sent home
– to return on the third day for the first band call,
when all the musical numbers are rehearsed with
the orchestra. They look confused. Is this the music

they have been rehearsing to for weeks? The tempos
are different. They can barely count the bars when
the strings sweep into magical melody. But excitement mounts as the production swells into life. On
the fourth day, the first half of the show is run
through on stage with the sets in place – though the
cast are still in rehearsal costume because the
costumier has not delivered the alterations yet. The
day after that, the second half is rehearsed. During
these two run-throughs, the electricians familiarize
themselves with the show. Each has been provided
with a detailed lighting plan charting the colours
and intensity together with the cues for each tableau,
but there are many subtleties to add. The chief electrician sits beside the director, jotting down his
instructions for each entry and exit. Much will
depend on the accuracy with which he passes them
on – especially in the case of the spotlight operators
posted in isolation at each wing of the circle and
gallery. A spot which 'opens' too soon, to reveal the
shifting of scenery or to massacre a blackout sketch,
can kill the momentum of the revue stone dead.

Only on the seventh day can Gyarmathy finally
run through the entire revue from beginning to end
– on stage, with costumes, with scenery, with music
... and with luck. That is when he starts the most
trying part of his own work. In the three or four
dress rehearsals which remain before the opening,
which are nerve-racking for everyone, but particularly for him, 'he has to think of everything,
correct everything, bring everything up to scratch
in the tiniest detail'. Specifically, he must summon
the full potential of his own nervous energy to
galvanize and electrify the whole company in order
to give the revue the pace on which its success will
depend. He is the captain of the ship and every order
he gives will be carried out to a word.

After that, he has only to sit back and keep his
fingers crossed. Once the curtain goes up on the first
night, it is up to the others.

The late Josephine Baker recalled:

> The atmosphere back-stage was wonderfully alive and busy, very different from New York and the Champs Elysées. The army of chorus girls was English and they lived like schoolgirls, with an Anglican clergyman who settled their disputes. Unlike American dancers, who had identical long necks, similar proportions and the same weights and heights, as if they were factory made, the English girls were individuals. Monsieur Derval liked variety. 'I offer something for every taste,' he boasted. The show-girls, who paraded around the stage in a series of dazzling costumes, one more revealing than the next, also came in various shapes and sizes, including a voluptuous redhead and a slinky brunette. The redhead showed me a picture of her baby one night. It was for him that she was working.

A Folies Bergère choreographer describes the atmosphere during these last few days before the opening as very chaotic: 'There are many problems that have not been solved. Many problems that can't be solved until the last minute and you wonder how it's going to take place or come about, but it all does seem to work out, somehow. You take each problem as it comes – problems like where do the costumes go. People think you just put them in the dressing-room. But that isn't possible because the dressing-rooms are so tiny, so you just hoist them up into the ceiling; there are many costume changes to be made back-stage, fast costume changes.'

There is a room set aside back-stage, where shelf upon shelf is piled high with the artists' head-dresses, feathers three-feet high, and plumed bustles which are hooked onto the backs of the costumes before the artists move onto the stage for each routine. These are removed, and replaced in the store-room, when the artist leaves the stage, and then rushes up the narrow winding stairs for the next costume change while perhaps a speciality act fills in for her change and the striking and re-setting of scenery behind one of the tabs takes place.

An American choreographer coming to France for the first time found many problems working with French dancers:

A French dancer is not at all like an American dancer – although they have two arms, two legs and a head, but the way that they use them is totally different. I think the basic reason for this is because Americans have a basic negroid heritage in music and dance. The French dancer has a classical background. For example, an American dancer may do a step with a certain amount of physical energy while on the other hand the French dancer may take exactly the same movement and interpret it with a more classical, sophisticated approach. It is something I cannot communicate to them in words because of the language barrier so I must do it with actions, because, as we all know, actions speak louder than words – well, certainly as far as the dance is concerned.

The maximum amount of dancers you will find on stage at the Folies Bergère at any given time would be approximately twenty-four. There are many other dancers here. They are what you call 'swing' dancers. They know everybody's part and when somebody has a day off they can step in and do that part at a moment's notice. So altogether in the show there are perhaps thirty to thirty-five dancers.

The nude lead dancer in the show, Michèle France, was probably one of the most sensuous women I have ever seen. She was absolutely ravishing and on stage she was incredible to watch. She had a lovely quality when she danced. She was not what you may call a great technical dancer, but at the same time she was almost better than a technical dancer because something else came through that was very, very special. She had a warmth and magnetism about her that drew you to her, and, of course, that is what every artist would love to be able to do; to have a public look at only them even though there may be thirty or forty other artists on stage at the same time.

Although show-girls and dancers at the Folies aspire to stardom, there are nudes whose only ambition is to remain nudes. Before coming to the Folies Bergère in the old days they might possibly have posed for artists in Montparnasse or perhaps Montmartre. Nowadays, they emanate from ballet school, become 'covered' show dancers and then audition for the nude roles. Whilst they work at the Folies in the evenings, during the daytime some of them pose for picture postcards, artists, or for 'light' – or slightly 'blue' – films or home-video tape markets.

Being a nude is a job like any other even if it is done without much ambition.

There is a considerable difference between the salary paid to a dancer and a leading artist. The leading artists at the Folies Bergère are paid less than in other countries because as each show runs for four or five years they are guaranteed regular work.

A leading artist from Germany recounts that:

> All the kids of the show, they sign for four, five years, because this show will run for as long as that, but I only signed for two years because I think that's enough for me! Many of the girls and the boys have been at the Folies Bergère for fifteen, sixteen, seventeen years; for them it's like going into an office to work, each night. But that's not the way I like to work. I love my profession and I want to do more and more and not just be sure of the salary I would receive every month.
>
> I think Michel Gyarmathy, the show's designer and artistic director, is a very nice person but I think a lot of the people here are afraid of him because he has a rather short temper. But that's

because not everyone here at the Folies Bergère is professional and he expects them to be perfect on stage. He doesn't understand that some people simply aren't perfect on stage, and you can't blame them for it. First of all, many of the dancers are paid rather poorly, and life in Paris is very, very expensive. You just can't live on tuppence a day. Appearing in beautiful costumes on stage and becoming a little famous isn't enough. You need to make money.

Another leading artist has been with the Folies Bergère for ten years.

I started as a nude model but Michel Gyarmathy saw the pleasure I took in my work and gave me a few words to say, and then I was a double for the leading artist. I have really climbed the ladder of the Folies Bergère. They call me *l'enfant de la maison.* I have eighteen changes of costume during the show. This is very difficult because the dressing-room is so small.

One of the leading singers expresses her fear that the show will not be ready in time, 'because there's still so much work and so many changes and additions to be made. Even today I have been given a new song and the première will be very soon; but you know, everyone is nervous and excited, so I hope I will get it right!' And a leading dancer decribes how her husband and daughter often come to the theatre to watch rehearsals.

> I think my daughter would like to become a big star because she likes the costumes, *décor* and make-up very much. But in fact she doesn't understand how much work goes into becoming a big star. I met my husband on the stage of the Folies Bergère; he was a singer and comedian. Therefore he understands my job very well and advises me, and in fact he is never jealous when somebody offers me flowers.

And flowers will be sent by the truck load to the many artists on the opening night of the new revue at the Folies Bergère.

Without the support of the staff of over three hundred, the curtain at the Folies Bergère could not rise. Behind the façade of the painted backcloths, the bustling army apply their craft; seventy stage hands, fifteen electricians, as many property men, a crew of scene painters, some twenty dressers and a battalion of cleaners. The activities of these helpers are combined and controlled from the stage director's switchboard on stage left – the nerve centre of the Folies Bergère like any other theatre. The stage director, who runs the show with the authority of a ship's captain, is in control of all activity that takes place behind the curtain. He is anchored to his post, from

Working the flies.

where he sends out orders to every part of the building by means of five telephones, six loudspeakers
– tannoys connected to every dressing-room, wardrobe department, etc. – and direct telephone links
with the director's office and the front of house.
Liaison is complete. He gives the signal for the curtain
to rise – and fall – the set changes and the lighting
cues and starts the orchestra by remote control – by
the press of a button. Yet none of this bustle, noise
and sometimes panic is generated to the audience.
An error of thirty seconds can disrupt the entire
show, which has been mounted with split-second
precision.

When the 'live' orchestra takes a break during the
show, recorded music is cued-in for the speciality
acts who 'front' for the hectic scene-changes that take
place on the other side of the 'scrim' behind them.

The electric switchboard generates the some 5,500

lights in use every night at the Folies Bergère by means of no less than 72 switches.

Aside from the fully employed staff of the theatre – all members of one trade union or another – a vast number of tradesmen and craftsmen form the backbone of the presentation as major contributors to the look of the show: painters, wig-makers, boot-makers, creators of stage jewellery, feathered head-dresses and the like. The budget of £500,000 for each show provides work not only for those directly involved with the revue, but for the local shop-keepers as well, who rely on the trade that emanates from the flow of audiences to the show.

In the area surrounding the Folies Bergère, the cafés and restaurants specialize in ethnic dishes for foreigners, with an emphasis on Tunisian, Algerian and North African menus. One is hard put to find a genuine French restaurant.

The curtain rises at 8.45 p.m. precisely and between 8.00 p.m. and then, the Métro (station 'Cadet') bustles with a considerable volume of the 1,600 audience who flock to the theatre, and again before midnight to take them back home.

Extra police are on duty each night to direct the endless stream of cars and taxis that line up to deposit their passengers outside the doors, and the charabancs and coaches consisting of parties of forty and fifty tourists at a time park around the corner in the rue de Trévise. The theatre's stage door is in the narrow one-way rue Saulnier, which runs down the side of the theatre.

Inside the theatre the hubbub of activity begins at 7.00 p.m. and finishes shortly before 2.00 a.m. Save for the stage-doorman and the caretakers, the theatre is deserted; by 7.30 p.m. the staff are at their various posts. Dressers lay out the costumes in the artists' dressing-rooms in readiness for the evening's per-formance; electricians check their lights and switches; the three stage crews divide themselves between the first bridge and second, and the third busies itself on

A Paris street scene, 1977, advertising the latest Folies Bergère show.

the stage below in readiness to move the sets. The property men check and lay out their innumerable props and the wardrobe mistresses check the countless feathered head-dresses and skirts in the 'feather room' back-stage.

Front of house, the usherettes put on their uniforms, the firemen, police and ambulancemen scatter themselves about the theatre. At 8.00 p.m. the doors are thrown open and the audience admitted.

The fireman's stool on the side of the stage, in the wings, is the most sought-after seat in the house. From this vantage point, the fireman has a perfect view of everything that goes on both on stage and off, but although it is not available to the general public, the management often allows VIPs the seat for either the first or second half of the show.

The Folies Bergère has probably seen more crowned heads and important personages than any other theatre in existence. Edward VII, Leopold II, Gustav V of Sweden, the King of Greece, Alphonso XIII, Edward VIII then Prince of Wales, the Princes of Arabia, Anthony Eden, General Eisenhower and many theatricals including Charlie Chaplin and practically every other well-known film star.

The general public either book seats through agencies, hotel concièrges or buy them direct at the box office. Although complimentary seats are available at the management's discretion, the foils, excuses and reasons conjured up to secure them are legion, as witnessed by Paul Derval:

> There are a certain number of people who seem to consider it a point of honour never to pay for a theatre seat, and they will go to all lengths to achieve this end.
>
> 'Can I have two complimentary tickets?' said one gentleman. 'I met your mother in 1889. I've come here tonight in memory of her.'
>
> Then there was the man who greeted me with open arms one evening.
>
> 'My dear sir,' he beamed as he pumped my

hand, 'it's good to see you again! I don't know if you remember, but two years ago at Coulommiers I dented your rear mudguard. I hope you'll give me a couple of seats for old times' sake.'

Then there was the gatecrasher who turned up at the *promenoir* entrance and said authoritatively, indicating a man standing directly behind him:

'This gentleman is with me!'

The bewildered doorman stood aside to let them pass.

Another time a complete stranger came to the box-office to ask for seats he said I had left in his name. I told him it was the first I had heard of it and he seemed genuinely pained.

'Monsieur Derval must have forgotten,' he said with a puzzled frown. 'He definitely promised them to me this morning.'

'Really? Monsieur Derval in person?'

'In person.'

'Well, that's most odd. I am Monsieur Derval. Of course, it might have been my father...'

'That's right,' he said emphatically. 'Monsieur Derval senior it was.'

Derval's father had been dead for over thirty years.

A country priest once wrote to the producer asking his advice. He wanted some one-act plays suitable for the children's amateur theatricals in his parish. Another time a nun wrote asking a favour. Letters arrive at the theatre with requests for lectures on various subjects connected with the theatre. One such was a lecture on Nudity in Grand Revue.

Visitors come to the Folies Bergère from all corners of the world, as far-flung as Papua, Tibet, Korea, Mongolia and the Arctic Circle. When I visited the theatre recently, a party of Japanese occupied some fifty seats around me – and every one of them fell fast asleep during the show. They had flown into Paris that very day, and so eager were they to see the Folies Bergère revue that they made it their first port of call, even before unpacking. Neither the

The Folies Bergère, 1982.

spectacular show with fantastic nudes nor a large orchestra blaring away at them could wrest them from their somnambulence.

The first five rows of the stalls consist of the most comfortable leather armchairs in the house. These rows are the deep armchairs, each with a little cushioned neck-rest. They have their regular visitors, and one of them once wrote asking if he could buy his usual second-row seat outright; he had retired and felt sure that to slumber in that same chair at home would evoke some of the happiest of memories.

On entering the foyer of the Folies Bergère one is aware of money flowing at every turn, but not all of it finds its way into the coffers of the box-office. The programmes are bought by practically everybody who comes to the theatre as more-than-worthy souvenirs of an exciting night out in Paris. Next, the doorman who collects the agency's ticket slip takes it to the box-office, returns with it, stamped – and awaits his tip. Then comes the usherette who leads you down the aisle to your seat – and blocks your way until she has pocketed your tip – but this is an accepted practice in all French theatres, and not confined to the Folies Bergère.

The gifts on sale in the foyer include paintings, jewellery, souvenirs, sweets and cigarettes, books, colour slides of the spectacular tableaux, postcards of scenes from the show. Here, too, telephone calls can be made, and correspondence written – and posted after the purchase of postage stamps at the counter. It is a veritable way of life.

A doctor is attached to the Folies Bergère – probably the only man in his profession who does not need to ask his patients to undress – and he is never short of work as the young ladies in the cast panic at the merest sneeze for fear of being 'off'. But for the most part, sprains, bruises, bumps, minor cuts and pulled tendons are his major calls.

Aside from hats and umbrellas, some rather unusual items have been left with the cloakroom attendant, including a baby whose parents had forgotten him. At about two o'clock one morning a distracted young mother tore into the theatre; she had been so carried away by the show that she had gone off to dinner with friends and had clean forgotten her child.

The first night of the new revue is upon us. Backstage, the artists, as on any other night, go through various emotions of nerves mixed with excitement together with panic and fear of forgetting routines, lyrics, costume changes – and the final running order. The atmosphere is admirably conveyed by Colette in her *Music-Hall Sidelights*:

> A small third-floor dressing-room, little more than a cramped closet with a single window open on a narrow side-street. An over-heated radiator dries up the air, and every time the door opens the funnel of the spiral staircase belches up, like a chimney-stack, all the heat from the lower floors, saturated with the human odour of some sixty performers and the even more potent stench of a

One of the Folies
Bergère dressing
rooms.

certain little place, situated near by.

Five girls are packed in here, with five rush-
seated stools jammed between the make-up table
and the recess in which are hung, hidden and
protected by a greyish curtain, their costumes for
the revue. Here they live every night from seven-
thirty till twenty minutes after midnight and,
twice a week, for matinées, from half past one till
six. Anita is the first to come in, rather out of
breath, but with cool cheeks and moist lips. She

shrinks back and exclaims: 'Lord above! It's not possible to stay in here, it turns you up!'

She soon becomes accustomed to it, coughs a little, then doesn't give it another thought, since she only just has time to undress and make up. Her frock and underslip are removed quicker than a pair of gloves and can be hung up anywhere. But there comes a moment when she curbs her haste and her face assumes a serious expression. Anita cautiously extracts two long pins from her hat, and carefully sticks them back through the same holes. Then, under the four turned-up corners of an outspread newspaper, she religiously protects that garish yet mingy edifice that contrives to look like a combination of a Red Indian head-dress, a Phrygian cap and a dressed salad. For everyone knows that grease-powder, flying in clouds from shaken puffs, spells death to velvet and feathers.

Because she is fair-haired and young, a rather skinny girl with huge blue eyes, she fulfils exactly all the requirements we expect of a 'little English dancer'. She speaks some French, with all the vigour of a young duckling, and to articulate these few words of our language she expends a useless energy which brings a flush to her cheeks and makes her eyes sparkle.

When she emerges from the dressing-room she shares with her companions next to mine, and walks down towards the stage, ready made-up and in costume, I can't distinguish her from the other girls, for she strives, as is most fitting, to be just an impersonal and attractive little English dancer in a Revue! When the first girl comes out followed by the second, and the third, then the others up to the ninth, they all greet me, as they pass, with the same happy smile, a similar nod of the head that sets their pinkish-blonde false curls bobbing in the same way. The nine faces are painted with identical make-up, cleverly tinted with mauve around the eyes, while the lids are burdened, on each of their lashes, with such a heavy touch of mascara, that it is impossible to distinguish the true colour of the pupil.

But when they leave, at ten past midnight, having hastily wiped their cheeks with the corner of a towel and re-powdered them chalky white, their eyes still barbarously enlarged, or when they come to rehearse in the afternoon, punctually at one o'clock, I immediately recognize little Gloria, a genuine blonde, with two puffs of frizzy hair tied round the temples with a strip of black velvet inside her hideous hat like a bird nesting in an old basket. Her upper lip protrudes a little from two pointed canines, and this makes her look, in repose, as if she were sucking a white sugared almond.

The call-bell is the only sound to break the silence. On my way down I pass stage-hands, half-stripped and mute. Girls of the Andalusian ballet cross the foyer in full costume, without any greeting other than a ferocious glance at the great mirror. Brague, suffering agonies under the black cloth of his short waistcoat and skin-tight Spanish trousers, whistles out of sheer vanity to show that he's 'not going to snuff out like the others!' An enormously fat boy, round as a barrel in his inn-keeper's clothes, looks about to suffocate and terrifies me: supposing he were to die on the stage!

Somehow or other, the mysterious forces of discipline and musical rhythm, together with an arrogant and childish desire to appear handsome, to appear strong, all combine to lead us on. To be truthful, we perform exactly as we always do! The prostrated public, invisible in the darkened auditorium, notices nothing that it should not, the short breaths that parch our lungs, the perspiration that soaks us and stains our silk costumes, the moustaches of sweat and drying powder that so tactlessly gives me a virile upper lip. Nor must it notice the exhausted expression on its favourite comic's face, the wild glint in his eyes as though he were ready to bite. Above all none must guess at the nervous repulsion that makes me shrink back at touching and feeling only damp hands, arms, cheeks or necks! Damp sleeves, glued hair, sticky tumblers, handkerchiefs like sponges – everything is moist or ringing wet, myself included.

And the great Mistinguett recalls:

> The first night arrives, agonizing and intolerable like all first nights. The producer, thinking of his invested thousands, is prowling around back-stage with a face as long as your arm, wishing everyone 'good luck' with a heartiness which does nothing to disguise his depression and which leaves the miserable actors more down in the mouth than ever. The 'fun factory' is in a state of gloom. Everybody wishes profoundly he were somewhere else.
>
> Eight o'clock. Time to make-up. Time to dress. time to stop worrying – if you can.

We move through time; we are transported from the great epochs of Colette and Mistinguett to our own day.

Eight-forty. The 'five minutes' call summons the company to the stage. The Cyril Ornadel lyrics for a London Palladium revue perfectly sum up the next phase of the process of getting on stage:

> Overture and beginners, please!
> Overture and beginners, please!
>
> We're ready dressed, with make-up on our faces
> We've had the cue from the call-boy to hurry to
>   our places
> The time has come for putting on our smiles now
> We've butterflies inside us – we'd like to run a
>   mile now
> But made up, and dressed up, we're ready to give
>   our all –
> In answer to the call-boy's call –

Everybody on stage, longs to be in the limelight
Everybody on stage, longs to be in the headlines

When you've got a tiny spot of greasepaint in your
   veins
Then the overture has the same allure as champagne.

Everybody on stage, longs to be in the limelight
Longs to be in the headlines, on the front page
And your hope never dies, when the call-boy cries:
'Everybody on stage!'

We've got the lights lit and the scene set and all
   the singers and the dancers we can get
We've got the music, the make-up, the costumes,
   the props −
But without one person, the whole thing stops . . .

The stage is bare; space is needed for the opening
routine − twenty-four dancers need room to move.
They line up for their plumed head-dresses, which
are handed to them by the wardrobe mistress in the
'feather room' on the side of the stage. The flute,
the violin are heard testing a note, a cadence. Another
instrument joins in. The hubbub of the audience
drowns any other discordant note.

Eight-forty-five. *Trois Coups!* Three thumps of the
staff on the stage, the traditional signal in France to
the audience that the performance is about to begin.
The orchestra strikes up. The lights are lowered in
the auditorium and the spell is cast as the curtain
rises.

We are comfortably seated, prepared to enjoy the
new 1980s revue. The theatre is ablaze with colourful
activity. The stage fills with glamorous, glorious
girls, whirling and twirling. The music swells as the
vampish *vedettes* are lowered from the ceiling on
glass elevators, looking lovely, wearing nearly nothing, as they loom above the lively orchestra. They
sing of the spectacle that will razzle and bedazzle for
the hours to come. They vanish as if by the same

magic that transports us from that moment on. Illusion is all.

Contrasts between period costume and modern modes are evident as the sequences change from scene to scene – every performer immaculately dressed – or immaculately undressed. Artists in vast crinolines but with bare bosoms perform side by side on the narrow stage; the fresh, colourful displays change with astonishing speed. A Josephine Baker ethnic routine is performed, reminiscent of the great star, perhaps an unconscious tribute to her memorable appearances at the Folies Bergère. Another rapid scene-change and the disco-type strobe-lighting production number that takes place reminds us that we are in the modern, supersonic present day. Speciality acts appear as 'front cloth' fillers while scene changes take place back-stage. Audience participation plays

A current Folies Bergère scene.

an integral part of the revue when the *grande vedette* invites members of the audience up onto the stage. They make fools of themselves; but who cares? It is fun. It is the Folies. It is tradition. Then, the stage and artists are transformed yet again, this time in pink and silver glitter, to dazzle the audience even more. The girls in their high-feathered head-dresses descend from the steep staircase that reaches from the back of the narrow stage to within feet of the footlights. Will they topple over? We hope not! The next routine is presented in Carmen Miranda vein, headed by a virile male singer. This is followed by a Twenties sequence in black and white with flickering lights. Next, bathing belles, dancing naked to Thirties music reminiscent of an early silent musical. A South American 'El Cumbanchero' routine in brilliant red with semi-nude dancers swirling colourful Spanish trains now takes the stage. The live orchestra accompanies the production numbers, but recorded music is played for the speciality acts – even the musicians need a break.

During the intermission the audience pass the time in the turquoise decorated foyer where the *grande vedette* of the revue autographs her latest disc as featured in the first half of the show. Without the stage, the dancers, the music supporting her and the colourful lamps lighting her, she seems smaller – duller. She has destroyed the illusion so carefully created.

The second half consists of a gigantic waterfall on stage with gallons of water cascading down as a background for a nude adagio act. This is followed by an act on roller-skates performed on a ten-foot-diameter skating rink. More emphasis on ethnic aspects – 'Summertime' routine; into a Yiddish sequence (the only tableau in the show *sans* nudes), followed by a tableau depicting The Last Supper. There is something for every nationality. A superb Spanish routine in black-and-white costumes and set is followed by an even more erotic number – and then back to a period piece to enable the audience to catch its breath again, to sit back and relax from the speed and sparkle of the tableaux.

The finale presents itself in turquoise and white – the staircase bursts back into life with show-girls; glass elevators descend from the ceiling above the heads of the audience, spilling over with elaborately feathered nudes who are lowered through the dome of the house. Thunderous applause almost brings the place down with the threat of sending the be-feathered nudes toppling from their perches.

But can it all last? What is the future of the Folies Bergère? Of shows such as this? The Casino de Paris, the only other music-hall in Paris, closed because of the recession and other financial difficulties. In London, the long-surviving Talk of the Town, the only night-spot in Britain to present shows comparable with the great Parisian spectacles, closed in the middle of 1982 for the same reasons, having greatly succeeded under Robert Nesbitt's brilliant direction for over twenty years.

And, 'Whatever happened to chorus-girls?' laments Eric Shorter, the incisive critic and journalist, whose contributions to Britain's *Daily Telegraph* make avid and informative reading. He tells us what – and where to find them. Outside of Paris, Las Vegas, Buenos Aires and perhaps somewhere else as far afield, there is only one other place, and that is far away – in the Far East:

> The chorus-girls are still stepping out in certain places. In cabaret and revue they crop up from time to time. And in a show like *Pal Joey* they give the evening a special zest. But, by and large, the chorus-girl has been losing her status in roughly the same degree as the nations of the West.
>
> They have gone, as it were, into a joint decline: and though it may sound frivolous to bracket the world's economies, ideologies, religions and racial conflicts with the art of girl dancers, their loss of status seems to match the general loss of esteem

for what used to seem so estimable – Western values, Western philosophy, the Western quality of life.

Chorus-girls used to be very much part of that quality. No one would try to pin a philosophy to them, unless it were hedonism. But they surely earned their place in aesthetics, since their only purpose was to spread a little pleasure and good cheer, as well as feminine elegance. 'Nothing but splendour and feminine gender.'

Why do they have to be spoken of in the past tense? Because they are so seldom on our stages. In our musical comedies, yes. In the Busby Berkeley films from Hollywood, yes. And here and there in revue. But it isn't any longer safe to count on a chorus line as one used to. Indeed the show from New York which calls itself *A Chorus Line* does not exhibit the charms which we would look for in a chorus, even though the girls line up throughout the show across the stage.

It is not the kind of chorus line I hanker after because it acknowledges that a chorus line is something from the past; and besides Michael Bennett's show is frankly Freudian. We hear of the girls' individual dreams and fancies, their anxieties to get the part, to make themselves into stars. Whereas what I want most from a chorus line is movement, drill, the female form and plenty of dance – not just psychology.

If, however, the West has turned its back on dancing girls parading in the European tradition (they have gone more often than not literally underground) the East is pressing on in its Asian way and raising Westerners' spirits whenever they get out there. For the Eastern girls not only seem to dance better. They also have (for the European visitor, anyhow) more pronounced personalities.

Indeed they have made such a hit lately with Western visitors, anxious to resume the kind of pleasant, harmless ogling which musical comedies of a certain nostalgic kind encouraged, that although the traditional American musical thrives in the Orient it doesn't seem to give half the kicks obtainable from the latest fad to hit the capital of the Philippines. This is the hotel floor show, with lunch or dinner, on the skyscraper's top floor; and it flaunts ethnic dancing or rhythmic haute couture. It is all the rage of Manila.

At the Hilton or Silihis you can count on a display of dancing to revive your finest memories of show-girls, and because they blend so much native choreography and costume into their numbers, the exhilaration and verve of their movement give the untutored visitor an unexpected pleasure. How often, if he isn't in the world of fashion, can he count on its presentation being so vivaciously theatrical?

Instead of taking a lift to the upper reaches of these smartish hotels (which charge about £10 for a meal and a view not only over Manila Bay but also of *les girls*) he might, if naive, head more immediately for the Manila version of *A Chorus Line*, billed as 'adapted' from Michael Bennett's Broadway show. But he might be (as I was) disappointed. For the capital of the Philippines is disconcertingly sophisticated in sexual matters. *A Chorus Line* in Manila was an all-male show.

But the fashion and/or ethnic dance show is purely feminine in charm, and a reminder that if the chorus-girl has gone underground in the West, she has re-surfaced in the East with becoming confidence, precision and good taste.

Nothing crudely erotic is ever implied (never mind what we spectators infer) so that you wonder almost piously how striptease ever caught the popular fancy when clothes and dance traditions can be displayed so attractively.

Is it the dress or the girl? The spectator is bound to wonder what it is that seems – in its quite seemly way – so beguiling as a bevy of Filipino girls comes and goes in a series of quick-change numbers, synchronized with a pre-recorded variety of rock or ethnic music. For there's an undulation in their movement and an hauteur in their manner and a power behind their smiles which stirs nostalgia in anyone who remembers when chorus-girls and their art were taken seriously.

Mind you, there's an extra novelty at midday as blinds are drawn in the top-floor restaurant to shut out the sun while half-a-dozen leggy girls dance in sarongs or celebrate the imminent renaissance of the mini while sporting candles or bongo drums or both. They are Australians whose fashion show called 'Jungle Fever' was directed by Tanya Powell, a dancer who runs a jazz ballet school and modelling agency.

Were there any buyers about? Sometimes (I was told). Mostly, though, this is a branch of musical theatre rather than a fashion show. The conjunction of couture and a chorus line discovers, to my mind, a new form of entertainment which, though it echoes cabaret or musical mannequins, dignifies the kind of floor show on which diners or lunchers traditionally turn their backs.

No one can eat while Filipino girls are on. Especially not when they are summarizing different dances from the Orient, twirling knives in the air or stepping between two thick, long bamboo rods.

Before the girls went on in Sammy Tiongson's show at the top of the Manila Hilton, they each said a silent prayer and crossed themselves before a sort of topless Buddha on a plinth at the entrance to the restaurant. Their prayers in the succeeding show were obviously answered, to judge by the applause. Were they also answering mine for a restoration to her former eminence of the chorus-girl?

8
The Queen of the Night

Although the Folies Bergère is the sole surviving music-hall in Paris, and one of the greatest tourist attractions in France, it does, however, have rivals in terms of other spectacular shows vying for the lucrative tourist trade. Naturally enough they compete too for available artists. But the Folies Bergère's competitors are theatre-restaurants which present cabarets and not traditional theatres with revues such as their own. Their only equivalent, a theatre to present non-stop music-hall revues, was the Casino de Paris.

When on 11 December 1917, Léon Volterra, the former small-time vendor of programmes at the Olympia, opened his newly refurbished Casino de Paris, the modern music-hall was born. Saint-Granier, an actor and author of revues and comedies, remarked that 'the extravagant revue was a response to a public which demanded movement, the fast pace which it finds in life, and is thus swept up in the tempo of our shows'. In a world that was being invaded by the automobile, radio, cocktails and jazz, the music-hall was king. The remaining establishments produced extravagant shows: the Dufrenne-Varna group in Paris, little by little, acquired the Mayol, the Palace, the Casino de Paris and the Empire. The Moulin Rouge and the Folies Bergère were other houses where big shows were still presented.

'How pleasant it was, in 1900, on a summer night, to take a walk on the Champs Elysées,' remarked

Folies de Paris

Jacques-Charles. 'There one could find many of the leading summer *café-concerts*.' Walking up the Champs Elysées there was first the Ambassadeurs, on the left immediately after the Place de la Concorde; l'Horloge then came up, situated next to where you will find the Ledoyen Restaurant today; and then, further up, as you would come closer to the Arc de Triomphe, there was the Alcazar d'Eté (the summer Alcazar). This was opened in 1861 by the owner of the Alcazar d'Hiver (the winter Alcazar) and was very popular. The Alcazar d'Eté offered ballet, pantomimes, operettas and sketches. The orchestra consisted of seventy musicians and was conducted by Litolff and Barbier. The Alcazar d'Eté gradually made the transition from *café-concert* to music-hall, a style which triumphed definitively in 1898 and culminated in the showing of revues. It remained in operation until it was demolished in 1930.

Vying with each other in ingenuity, luxury and grandeur, these music-halls offered revues in which dozens of tableaux followed each other, and hundreds of costumes sparkled. Roland Petit was the last director of the Casino de Paris's shows, in which he had starred his wife Zizi Jeanmaire.

The world famous Crazy Horse Saloon in the fashionable Avenue Georges V, which first opened on 19 May 1951, is also threatened with extinction because of the recession. It presents small-scale revues on a tiny stage about fourteen feet wide with a proscenium arch no higher than seven feet. In pre-war Berlin cabaret style, with one of the stars of the house, Bertha von Paraboum, fitted with boots and helmet, a swastika in place of a pair of pants – a classical, trashy, titillating figure but one which at the Crazy Horse Saloon may well attain the sublime – they cram onto this tiny stage half-a-dozen artists in various stages of nudity, relying for the most part on enlarged, naked buttocks and clever 'flicker-ing' lighting effects as a substitute for expensively

The Folies
Bergère
programme 1982.

designed and executed sets and costumes.

The spectacular show at the Alcazar de Paris (not to be confused with the Alcazar d'Eté or Alcazar d'Hiver) across the river on the Left Bank on rue Mazarine specializes in burlesque, satire and female impersonation in outrageous vein. Here, too, the shows are twice-nightly, finishing at about four in the morning, and the sets, costumes and lighting effects in this compact restaurant are stunningly inventive. The members of the cast and waiters are encouraged to mix freely with the customers, adding a rather friendly, if bizarre, note to the evening – for the artists remain in costume and heavily made-up for the stage and it is difficult to distinguish the real female artists from the males in 'drag'.

The origins of the Alcazar de Paris lie in Henri Varna and his partner Oscar Dufrenne, who was murdered one night in the theatre. It was run in the 1920s as a music-hall revue similar to the Casino de Paris. Gaby Deslys and many Spanish stars, including the singer Raquel Meller, appeared there. Another star to appear there was Polaire, a comedienne who was a sensation in Paris in the early 1900s. She had a repertoire of songs of the special *genre* which, later, Damia, Fréhel and Yvonne George triumphed in. For several years Polaire was advertised as having the smallest waist in the world: '*Quarante centimètres de tour de taille*' was the perpetual advertisement. When, in the nature of things, this was no longer true, she was at once *démodée*. For several years the Alcazar attracted audiences who longed for the *Belle Epoque* type of entertainment. These were modern style *café-concert* programmes where the survivors of the *café-concerts* golden age reappeared. The greatest success was a revue entitled *Viens Poupoule* (C'mon, my Pet), also one of Mayol's biggest successes. It was a spectacular show based on a 1900s formula without great stage effects, but with a good deal of *frou-frou*. A chronicler of the *Petit Bleu* described it as, 'a charming, joyous, sometimes moving revue in which we find the former headliners still youthful'. At the end of the sixties, all Paris rushed to the Alcazar de Paris. There, Marc Doelnitz and Jean-Marie Rivière, two old hands from the nights of Saint-Germain des Prés, presented a new kind of spectacle in which the main ingredients consisted of playbacks which evoked the stars of the music-hall; travesties, sometimes tragic, sometimes burlesque, and sumptuous tableaux including a French can-can, a terrific re-enactment of the Moulin Rouge at the time of La Goulue. 'Drag artists do not pretend to be beautiful,' the programme notes boast of the current show. 'On the contrary, they are really ugly – and really funny too.' It is no longer a revue. It is high-class American-style music-hall. Fréhel, a seventy-eight-year-old drag artist, sets the audience abuzz with song. The trapeze artist performs dangerous acrobatics above the heads of the audience (and their dinner-plates!).

Although hardly a threat to the Folies Bergère's tourist trade, two other *dîner-spectacle* shows which rate highly in the Paris night-life calendar are the Paradis Latin and the long-established La Nouvelle Eve. Alec Shanks, who directed the revues at the Nouvelle Eve throughout the 1950s, recalls that during the final dress rehearsal in the small hours, a male Spanish dancer vigorously stamped his feet right through the stage! The opening, next night, was attended by an illustrious audience which included the Duke and Duchess of Windsor. At this intimate cabaret show, visitors dance on a glass floor with plinth lights (the one through which the poor Spanish dancer almost descended). The Paradis Latin, unlike the Nouvelle Eve, does not seem to have found its level. Although it tries very hard to be, it is neither funny nor French. A visit to this night-club can be included in the price of a package tour. Square tables, jammed together in long rows, are over-crowded with a capacity of some six hundred. A four-piece band with players dressed in white tuxedos

introduces the waiters to the audience; they jump
on stage, singing, clapping hands, setting the mood
and the tone of the show. A charming Wizard of
Oz sequence with the performers dressed in rather
inventive costumes and masks mingling with the
audience is followed by act upon act playing to music
with acoustics that one does not find easy on the
ear. It proves, however, to be a pleasant enough
evening. A third, small night-club, Madame Arthur's
specializes in female impersonation, or *revue de
travestis*; outrageous transvestites who pass admirably
for the most beautiful women in Paris. Coccinelle
was, perhaps, their most famous star, a young male
performer who passed for a Brigitte Bardot on the
beaches of the South of France wearing the briefest
of bikinis, revealing the most voluptuous breasts.

However, the two major spectacular revues in
Paris are undoubtedly the Lido and the Moulin
Rouge, the Folies Bergère's greatest rivals in the
tourist stakes. But unlike the Folies Bergère, which
is essentially a theatre, both the Lido and the Moulin
Rouge present outstanding shows which include
dancing, cabaret, dinner and champagne. The cabaret
performances take place twice nightly at ten o'clock
with a second show starting shortly after midnight,
playing to capacity houses of some 2,000 at each sitting. Coach-loads of tourists from all over the world,
nowadays predominantly Japanese, fill the streets
outside and audiences wait in queues three deep to
enjoy these magnificent shows – the sort of queues
generally seen only outside Wimbledon or a football
match.

In 1929, in the heart of the Champs Elysées, in
an enormous subterranean room, an establishment
comprising a swimming pool, a Turkish bath and a
cabaret opened its doors to the public. Thus was the
Lido born. The Folies Bergère, prompt to score,
produced a replica, with a pool on stage and, with
the device of a mirror set at an angle, the audience
were invited to witness an 'Under-Water Wedding'.

Taking over in 1945, a group headed by Joseph and Louis Clerico transformed the Lido, with the aid of the decorator Henri Rigal, into a sumptuous Venetian banquet-hall, the glittering palace of luxurious revues. The management was put in the hands of Pierre Louis-Guérin, and the Lido, under the authorship and artistic direction of Donn Arden and Rene Fraday (who are still in partnership at the Lido and at the MGM Hotel in Las Vegas), rapidly became the most celebrated cabaret in the world. The glamour of the exceptional Bluebell dancers under the organization of Miss Bluebell, the richness and colour of their costumes, the exacting standards of their immaculate appearance, their exceptional good taste and quality together with the rapid, yet graceful, tempo of their stage movements has reached unparalleled heights.

In 1977 the Lido moved premises to the cabaret restaurant Normandie, presenting its new show in the same neighbourhood of the Champs Elysées, nearby. This establishment, conceived and beautifully decorated by the architects Peynet, Bartoccini and Veccia, is the largest and also the most luxurious night-club in Europe, if not the world.

Before the show starts, the spectators leave the dance floor, which is elevated to stage-height. The chandeliers in the restaurant disappear into the ceiling, and within seconds the restaurant has been transformed into a theatre with an apron stage. The new Lido premises encompass a network of movable platforms, ice rink, swimming pool, elevators, comparable to nowhere. With its gigantic machinery, the Lido revue has become a show as if in fabulous technicolour. The entertainment bursts into life with the stage flanked with enormous mirrors and chandeliers in a 'Still of the Night' sequence which makes MGM musicals look like end-of-the-pier shows. Nudes with diamond-studded head-dresses and breath-taking feathers (Gyarmathy at the Folies Bergère complains that they use too many feathers)

and satin drapes cascading from arms held high adorn the stage; and suddenly sixty or more Bluebell dancers embrace the scene. They are accompanied by twenty-four Kelly Boys (minimum height six foot; so-named Kelly after Miss Bluebell's real name, Margaret Kelly). A Russian sequence follows in the Borodin tradition of great fantasy and charm; the audience is so overawed by all this magic that it is almost incapable of immediate response in applause. Suddenly an ice rink appears on stage and there is a 'New York' sequence, performed to 'West Side Story' orchestrations. The ice rink disappears and an African sequence follows complete with a pair of live baby elephants. Then, a magnificent waterfall with nude bathing beauties – all in the first half of the show leaving the audience spell-bound.

On a recent visit to the Lido I found Miss Bluebell back-stage. She is there every night to ensure the smooth running of her famous troupe's contribution to the show. 'And to make sure the boys aren't wearing eyelashes,' she says. Donn Arden, the American co-author and artistic director of the show had been present the previous night.

'Did you see that Kelly Boy's big arse?' he said to Miss Bluebell. 'How the hell did *he* get into the show?'

'Which one?' she asked. How could she have possibly missed *any* imperfection in her company? Both she and Arden are meticulous in their production and observation.

'Charles,' he said to me, 'when you see the show tonight, you watch out for this boy, and tell Miss Bluebell which one it is. He's in the back somewhere.'

The day after I'd seen the show, Donn Arden asked me anxiously:

'Did you see the boy with the big arse?'

'I wasn't looking at boys' bums,' I laughed. 'I was too captivated by the entire show to notice anything like that!'

Nowadays, under the directorship of Roland

Léonar, the Moulin Rouge opens its show with thirty-six Dorris dancers flanked by eight statuesque nude models and four nude dancers; a far cry from the exposition of the can-can for which the famous music-hall was renowned. The Brazilian female lead singer Watusi is the *grande vedette* of the show, which emphasizes the current multi-racial vogue in Paris. The stage is filled with red and white befeathered beauties of incredible sparkle and *tout d'un coup* there are seventy of them singing and performing to the 'Invitation to the Dance' routine. The production numbers have a live orchestra, but the artists mime to backing tracks. Speciality acts, jugglers, nude adagios and animal acts fill-in while sets are changed back-stage and the chorus put on even more stunning costumes and feathers. But possibly the highlight of the 1982 show is the dolphin act. A section of the stage descends into the bowels of the earth to re-appear with a huge water tank containing a live dolphin. This act involves the amusing dolphin who plays games with his trainer by removing first her bra and then her loin-cloth, leaving her in a glittering G-string. She dives into the tank to retrieve her scanty costume from the saucy dolphin, and there is an under-water ballet between them as he swims about with a catch-me-if-you-can grin on his face.

But despite these would-be competitors, the Folies Bergère still maintains its pre-eminence.

After the death of Paul Derval's widow in the early 1970s (she had succeeded her husband in the financial wizardry and costume organization of the shows at the Folies Bergère), Hélène Martini bought the Folies Bergére and presented her first revue in 1974 under the artistic direction of Michel Gyarmathy. Madame Martini's aim was to provide an even more sumptuous, sparkling and dazzling revue than ever before. In order to maintain the tradition of the theatre, she relied on Michel Gyarmathy's irreplaceable experience for the *mise-en-scène*, the *décors* and the costume design. In order to retain the lively pace of the revue, she employed the talents of the youthful Jean Moussy to choreograph the new show and a team of composers and lyricists headed by Pierre Porte for the musical content of *Folie je t'adore*.

Hélène Martini's late husband had owned several night-clubs in Montmarte and the Champs-Elysées, as well as the famous Russian restaurant-cabaret Schéhérazade in Paris. He had also bought the Moulin Rouge and asked Erté to decorate it and to design all the sets and costumes for the first production which was to be put on there under the title 'Champagne Cocktail'. In those first days, Hélène Martini and her husband worked very closely together. Soon afterwards they bought a cinema and converted it into the Narcissus, a cabaret-theatre. They also acquired the night-club Les Folies Pigalle. Erté again designed the sets and costumes.

Monsieur Martini died unexpectedly in 1960. His generosity had been boundless; whenever he heard that one of his employees was in difficulties, he would help him or her without being asked to do so. His position in the theatrical world had been extremely powerful. He had directed eight cabarets and two theatres (Les Bouffes Parisiennes and the Comédie de Paris); shortly before his death he was negotiating for the acquisition of the Olympia. But his widow wisely secured the Folies Bergère instead.

Hélène Martini's is a fairy-tale story; a fascinating development from rags to riches; from a chorus-girl at the Folies Bergère – to its present owner.

Her father, Monsieur de Creyssac, was a Frenchman from Normandy who was studying geology. He travelled to Poland in the 1920s to further his studies and there fell in love and married a beautiful young Russian girl. Their daughter, Hélène, was educated in Poland. They lived on the Russian border, and it was not long before Hélène lost both parents through Russian and German invasions and ended up in a Prussian concentration camp. She was released in 1945 and travelled to Normandy where she reconstructed ordnance survey maps of bomb damage in the area.

After the war, she moved to Paris, where she auditioned for the Folies Bergère and became one of their top models. She was the ideal show-girl, tall and elegant, the possessor of a lovely figure, large, pale blue eyes and brown hair. One evening, Nachat Martini, the Lebanese-born owner of a string of night-clubs in Paris, visited the Folies Bergère, admired the statuesque beauty of Mlle Hélène de Creyssac, forged a meeting with her – and they soon married. He had realized all too soon that a young woman of such intelligence, intuition and knowledge of theatre and design would be the perfect partner in business. He was to be proved more than right.

Martini was kind, generous and a much-loved, fat, jolly man in his fifties. The Martinis always spent the weekend at their château outside Paris, with Tuesdays to Fridays being spent in Paris at their luxury apartment situated above their night-club, Les Folies Pigalle. Their Lebanese cook travelled with them, preparing Martini's traditional favourites at both establishments. It was their regular habit to travel in to Paris each Saturday night to visit Le Drap d'Or, one of their restaurant-cabarets (which was renamed Raspoutin when Hélène bought it in 1965). Here, Madame Martini's friend, confidant and designer, Erté, takes up the story:

> After dinner at their château one night, Monsieur Martini told Hélène that he didn't feel well, and she said, 'Then let's stay here tonight, and not go out.'
>
> 'No, no,' he said. 'I feel well enough to go to Le Drap d'Or.'
>
> And so they got into the car, with the cook who sat on the back seat. When they got into the local village, the car stalled. They had engine trouble. Monsieur Martini got out, lifted the bonnet of the car, and realized that they needed

a mechanic. Just as he was about to set out in search of one, he fell to the ground.

He'd had a brain haemorrhage from which he did not recover.

Erté and Hélène Martini – *diner à deux*.

His wife suddenly found herself in sole charge of his vast nocturnal empire, but fortunately she had been trained for the role. None could be a greater admirer of Hélène Martini for the success she has made of the colossal undertaking, than Erté:

She had *everything* in her favour. Quite aside from her intelligence, experience and perspicacity, she has fantastic intuition and energy.

To describe her more fully, all would agree that she is quiet and distinguished looking. She is very elegant; her clothes are made by a fashionable young Norwegian designer in Paris, Per Spoke. She looks after all her business interests, and never leaves a stone unturned. She is always fresh; never gets tired. She knows exactly how many patrons are in the house – and exactly *who* is there; and how much money has been taken at the box-office.

Having designed the interior of her château, I am now working on the interior of her flat in the Place Pigalle. The château, which is not very large, is very different from the flat. For the château I chose a Victorian theme for the living-room with lovely old antlers and ivory, some of which I bought in London. The walls are encrusted in patterns of shells. Her bedroom is round, and looks somewhat like an enchanted tent inside. I decorated it in pale blue satin — to match her fantastic blue eyes — and white lace. The furniture is also Victorian. Instead of buttons on the up-holstered chairs, I chose little rosettes in pale blue and white satin. It all sounds terribly grand, but it is not, really. She keeps only a small staff.

I am designing the interior of her flat differently from the château. The furniture is period, mostly Louis XV or XVI. The library is Empire, and the bedroom is in the spirit of Napoleon III, in champagne colour. The hall is blue, and the living-room and *bureau* are yellow and mahogany.

Many people thought that Monsieur Martini's 'empire of the night' might collapse after his death. They were greatly surprised when his wife took over all his affairs. It required great courage and strength of character to protect her interests from the predators who try to dominate the cabaret world.

They had no children, and it seems unlikely that Hélène Martini will remarry. She is an astonishing woman by all accounts. She appears to be the perfect society lady, yet she strikes people as shy at times. Beautiful and elegant, she is the epitome of Slavic charm, with a tall, slim figure. The combination of her sharp eye for detail and her demanding standards are remarkable. She is known as 'The Queen of the Night' — yet she is seldom seen by day or by night as she divides her time between the Folies Bergère, her night-clubs, restaurant-cabarets, her flat in the Place Pigalle and her château outside Paris.

Hélène Martini, of Franco-Russian extraction, is a woman of the theatre by training and a show-woman by experience and instinct. She combines the qualities calculated to continue the objective of the Folies Bergère – to be and to remain the most famous music-hall in the world.

It is no wonder that Erté exclaims enthusiastically: 'She should be the President of France!'

Michel Gyamarthy and Hélène Martini during final rehearsals for the 1982 revue, *Folies de Paris*, with a star of the show, Lisette Malidor, centre.

Bibliography

Victor Arwas, *Belle Epoque – Posters and Graphics* (Academy Editions, London, 1978)

Josephine Baker & Jo Bouillon, *Josephine* (W. H. Allen, London, 1978)

La Belle Epoque – Fifteen Euphoric Years of European History (William Morrow, New York, 1977)

Charles Castle, *La Belle Otero: The Last Great Courtesan* (Michael Joseph, London, 1981)

Charles Castle, *Noël* (Sir Noël Coward) (W. H. Allen, London, 1972)

Charles Chaplin, *My Autobiography* (The Bodley Head, London, 1964)

Maurice Chevalier, *With Love* (Cassell, London, 1960)

Mayol & Julien Clerc, *Le Music Hall Français* (Olivier Orban, Paris, 1978)

Charles B. Cochran, *Showman Looks On* (Dent, London, 1945)

Colette, *Les Vrilles de la Vigne*, from *La Vie Parisienne* (1908)

Colette, *Music-Hall Sidelights*, translated by Anne-Marie Callimachi (Secker & Warburg, London, 1957)

Colette, *My Apprenticeships*, translated by Helen Beauclerk (Secker & Warburg, London, 1978)

Jacques Damase, *Les Folies du Music-Hall* (Anthony Blond, London, 1962)

Paul Derval, *The Folies Bergère*, translated by Lucienne Hill (Methuen, London, 1955)

Anton Dolin, *Ballet go Round* (Michael Joseph, London, 1938)

Erté, *Erté – Things I Remember* (Peter Owen, London, 1975)

Marjorie Farnsworth, *The Ziegfeld Follies* (Peter Davies, London, 1956)

Michael Freedland, *Maurice Chevalier* (Weidenfeld & Nicolson, London, 1981)

Arthur Gold & Robert Fizdale, *Misia – The Life of Misia Sert* (Macmillan, London, 1980)

Lynn Haney, *Naked at the Feast* (Josephine Baker) (Robson Books, London, 1981)

Dominique Jando, *Histoire Mondiale du Music Hall* (Jean-Pierre Delarge, Paris, 1979)

Tamara Karsavina, *Theatre Street* (Heinemann, London, 1930)

Peter Leslie, *A Hard Act to Follow – A Music Hall Review* (Paddington Press, London, 1978)

Guy de Maupassant, *Bel-Ami*, translated by Marjorie Laurie (T. Werner Laurie)

Agnes de Mille, *Dance to the Piper* (Hamish Hamilton, London, 1951)

Mistinguett, *Mistinguett*, translated by Lucienne Hill (Elek Books, London, 1954)

Jean Prasteau, *Casino de Paris* (Editions Denoël, Paris, 1975)

Michèle Sarde, *Colette*, translated by Richard Miller (Michael Joseph, London, 1981)

Marlies Scholtens, *Gay Paree in Posters* (V.O.C., Amsterdam, 1980)

Charles Spencer, *Erté* (Studio Vista, London, 1970)

Francis Steegmuller, *Cocteau – A Biography* (Macmillan, London)

Alain Weill, *100 Years of Posters of the Folies Bergère and Music Halls of Paris* (Hart-Davis, MacGibbon, London, 1977)

Philip Zeigler, *Diana Cooper* (Hamish Hamilton, London, 1981)

Index